# OBJECT DATABASES

## *AN INTRODUCTION*

Barry Eaglestone and Mick Ridley

**McGRAW–HILL BOOK COMPANY**
**London** • New York • St Louis • San Francisco • Auckland • Bogota
Caracas • Lisbon • Madrid • Mexico • Milan • Montreal
New Delhi • Panama • Paris • San Juan • Sao Paulo
Singapore • Sydney • Tokyo • Toronto

Published by
McGRAW–HILL Book Company Europe
Shoppenhanger Road, Maidenhead, Berkshire, SL6 2QL, England
Telephone 01628 502500
Fax 01628 770224

**British Library Cataloguing in Publication Data**
The CIP data of this title in available form the British Library, UK


**Library of Congress Cataloging–in–Publication Data**
The CIP data of this title in available form the Library of Congress, Washington DC, USA

Typeset by Barry Eaglestone and Mick Ridley
Printed and bound in Great Britain by the University Press, Cambridge

# OBJECT DATABASES

# CONTENTS

# PREFACE

These are interesting times for those involved with database technology. A new generation of databases, Object Databases, is emerging which addresses many of the weaknesses of Relational Databases by providing object–oriented features. In particular, this allows databases to be used for a wider range of applications, including, for example, those which require multimedia, such as images, video and sound. In addition, the population of potential database users is enormously increased by the emergence of global communications through the Internet and World Wide Web.

Until now it has not been possible to present Object Database Technology in a cohesive form. Rather, it has been necessary to review the research and development towards it. However, with the recent emergence of de facto standards this is no longer the case. This book therefore presents a cohesive description of Object Database Technology, using the de facto standards for Object Databases, proposed by the Object Data Management Group (ODMG), and the proposed standard for object–oriented systems design, the Unified Modeling Language (UML).

The book is intended to be suitable for an undergraduate course. Accordingly, it should not be necessary for students to have undertaken prior courses on relational database technology or object–oriented design, although some background knowledge of these areas may be helpful. The book should also be useful to anyone considering buying or using an object database and will hopefully aid them in selecting an object database product. We have tried to present the material in an accessible way, avoiding excessive use of mathematical notions and including realistic and familiar examples.

Much of the book is tutorial in style—many of the issues, such as the database languages, are presented through a progressive series of examples. This material is reinforced by exercises at the end of each chapter. Where possible readers are encouraged to implement examples and their solutions to exercises using an ODMG–compliant Object Database Management System, if available.

The content is organised to answer the following questions:

- What is the database approach and what is an object database? (ch 1 & 2)
- How is an object database constructed? (ch 3 & 4)
- How do you make use of an object database? (ch 5, 6, & 7)
- How do you design and maintain an object database? (ch 8 & 9)
- What might the future hold? (ch 10)

When we completed this book, in early 1997, we used the most up to date information we had on a number of standards, especially ODMG, UML and SQL3. Since this is a very dynamic area, changes in standards are still underway and later usage may differ from the versions available to us. A number of sources for up to date information are suggested below.

There are a number of newsgroups that may provide information on object databases and other object technologies. These include:

- `comp.databases.object`
- `comp.databases.theory`
- `comp.databases`
- `comp.object`

The following Web sites should also be useful starting points for more, and up to date, information:

- `http://www.odmg.org`—Web site of the Object Database Management Group, this includes links to the member Object Database system suppliers.
- `http://www.omg.org`—Web site of the Object Management Group.
- `http://www.rational.com`—Web site of the Rational Software Corporation, which includes extensive documentation on the Unified Modelling Language.
- `http://www.jcc.com/sql_stnd.html`—The SQL Standards homepage.
- `http://speckle.ncsl.nist.gov/~ftp/`—A starting point for the SQL drafts available.
- `http://www.staff.comp.brad.ac.uk/~mick/odb/`—We will maintain a Web page for the book at this address.

# 1

# THE DATABASE APPROACH

Computer programs are used to assist people and machines to carry out many of the activities that enable organisations of all types to operate effectively. To do this, these application programs will usually have to access stored information about the organisation and the environment within which it must operate. For example, a program which produces pay slips for a commercial organisation must access information about the employees working for the company, pay scales, pension schemes, and the taxation rules within which the company must operate.

Information about an organisation and its environment is usually represented within computers as data, which is stored as data files on storage devices, such as disks and CD-ROM. A database management system (DBMS) is a particular type of computer program which is used by application programs to manage and provide access to the stored data. The collection of data managed by a DBMS is called a database, and the database and DBMS, together with the applications programs that use the database, are collectively called a database system.

DBMSs are commonplace on all types of computer, ranging from large mainframes to small personal computers. Most up-to-date DBMSs are of a type called relational DBMSs (RDBMS). RDBMSs are powerful and often easy to operate, and have been used successfully in many types of organisation, e.g., in business, manufacturing, and services industries, education, government, and scientific research (see [Eaglestone 91] for a comprehensive explanation of relational database technology). However, there are also many applications for which RDBMSs provide a poor solution. In particular, RDBMSs are poor at representing information about things with complex structure and where modifications to data involve complex operations. For example, a RDBMS is not an appropriate tool for representing information about electronic circuits in a system for designing VLSI chips. This is because the circuits can have complex structures; they can be composed of many interlinked components each of which may also have a complex structure. Also, modification to the data representing an electronic circuit is complex because it is necessary to compute the electrical effects of the component modification on the circuit as a whole.

A new generation of database technology, called Object Database Technology, is now emerging which can overcome many of the limitations of relational database technology. Object database management systems (ODBMSs) are based on a particular type of computer programming language, called object–oriented programming languages. Examples of such languages are C++, Smalltalk, and Java. The combination of object-oriented programming capabilities and conventional DBMS facilities provided by object database technology has produced a powerful environment for representing and making use of information about an organisation. The advantage of object database technology over relational database technology is that it can represent both complex information structures as data, and also complex processes associated with the information represented.

This book provides a practical explanation of object database technology. This preliminary chapter provides an understanding of the set of ideas, called the database approach, which is the basis for database technology.

## 1.1 THE ORGANISATION

A database system exists to provide an organisation with the information necessary for it to carry out its activities. An organisation is a very general term which refers to "any organised body or system or society" [Concise Oxford Dictionary], and the database approach is applicable to organisations in general. Database systems are used in all walks of life, including manufacturing industry, businesses, service industries, education, government, and scientific research. In this section this diversity of application is illustrated by a set of example database systems.

In the early days of database technology, i.e., the 1960s and early-1970s, the installation of a database system represented a major investment for large organisations, and accordingly the scope and importance of the database system to the organisation had to be significant. A database was therefore seen as a tool for large scale computer applications of large organisations, such as big businesses and government departments. The aim was often to create a single collection of data relevant to the operation of the organisation, which the different application programs could then share. A database of this type is called a corporate database and is illustrated in Example 1.1.

---

### EXAMPLE 1.1

*Bruddersfield Bikes is a large manufacturing company organised to produce and sell its products at a profit. A DBMS is used by the company to store data which represents information concerned with running the business. For example, the data represents information about employees, sales and purchase orders, manufacturing processes, and products held in stock. The database applications include: financial control, management planning, inventory management, production management, research and design of products, and sales order processing.*

---

The costs of the hardware and software needed to implement a database system are now relatively small, as is the cost of computer network facilities needed to allow one computer to access databases stored on other computers. Consequentially, DBMSs are now used by all sizes and types of organisation, not just the large ones, and are often used to build database systems for individual applications. Example 1.2 illustrates a very small scale database system, which is now feasible because of the availability of database software as a standard feature of low cost personal computers.

---

### EXAMPLE 1.2

*The Eaglestone family household is an example of a small organisation. The family is a society that is organised at least sufficiently to ensure that the members are housed, fed, and clothed. The family uses a DBMS on a personal computer in order to assist in managing the family's finances. The database system is used to represent information about financial commitments, such as mortgage payments, insurance premiums, taxation dues, and investments. The* database applications include generating the financial statements which assist in tasks such as buying a new car, or filling in tax returns.

Often, many databases are connected by computer networks to provide wider access to the data. There are a number of ways in which a set of interconnected databases can be organised (see Section 10.6, Multidatabases). Example 1.3 illustrates one form of distributed database system, called a multidatabase system.

## EXAMPLE 1.3

*A national museum is organised for the maintenance and study of collections of historically interesting artefacts, such as stone age axes, and fossil collections. The museum uses a number of DBMSs, each of which stores data to represent details of artefact collections held by a particular department in the museum. The databases hold textual descriptions and also images of individual artefacts. Database applications are used for museum administrative activities, such as accession, preservation, dating and loan of the artefacts, and also to support historical research, by allowing academics to access the information represented. Network facilities within the museum (a local area network) make it possible to access the data held in any department from any of the museum's computers. The museum's network is also connected to an international computer network, which allows researchers outside of the museum, possibly in other countries, to study its contents by remotely accessing the museum's databases.*

Databases have traditionally been used to represent information as conventional data, i.e., numbers and text. However, modern database technology now supports the representation of many different forms of information, such as sounds and images, as well as text and numbers. Examples 1.3 and 1.4 illustrate this capability; both store images as well as numbers and text. Example 1.4, the final example database application, also illustrates the use of a database system as an embedded component of a machine.

## EXAMPLE 1.4

*A component of a ship's navigation system is organised to help ensure that the ship gets from one place to another without mishap. This system uses a DBMS to store data which represents information about the ship's surroundings. This information is input from the ship's radar system, and is used by applications programs which control other components of the ship's navigation system. For example, one of the database applications is a vessel identification system, which analyses the radar images, and identifies the ships and other vessels detected on the radar.*

The above four example organisations are each very different in terms of how they are organised and what they do, but have important similarities when analysed from a database perspective. These similarities are explained in the following sections.

## AN ORGANISATION'S INFORMATION SYSTEM

One way of viewing an organisation is as a system of activities. The activities take place within the organisation in order for it to fulfil its function. Each of the above example database applications (Examples 1.1 to 1.4) can be analysed in this way. For example, Bruddersfield Bikes (Example 1.1) must design products, buy materials, manufacture products, sell and deliver the products, and collect and bank the remittances. It must perform these activities in order to achieve its objective of selling products at a profit.

The activities of an organisation do not operate at random or in isolation. They must be coordinated by a flow of information within the organisation and between the organisation and the outside world. Bruddersfield Bikes (Example 1.1), for example, produces products on the basis of information concerning sales orders placed by customers, sales forecast, manufacturing capacity, and the available stocks of raw materials.

There is therefore an underlying system of information activities concerned with maintaining the flow of information necessary for an organisation to function. This underlying system is called the organisation's information system, and is concerned with capturing, storing, and transmitting the required information. The information system of Bruddersfield Bikes (Example 1.1), for example, includes financial control, management planning, inventory management, production management, research and design of products, and sales order processing. This provides the information necessary to manage activities such as purchasing raw materials, and manufacturing, pricing, storing, and selling products.

## FORMAL AND INFORMAL INFORMATION FLOW

Information flow within an organisation can be formal or informal. Formal information flow is a consequence of predetermined procedures for recording and communicating information. For example, when the museum (Example 1.3) acquires a new artefact, the accession procedures require that details of the artefact are recorded by filling in special forms and filing them. These forms are used in subsequent museum procedures in which the dating and preservation of the artefact takes place. At Bruddersfield Bikes (Example 1.1) a salesperson will record orders placed by customers on special order forms which will be filed and processed so as to ensure that the ordered products are produced, delivered, and paid for. Automated systems (such as the navigation subsystem (Example 1.4)) rely exclusively on formal information flow, since all information is automatically captured, stored, and used by the computer programs. Formal procedures for communicating information are essential in large organisations, such as big businesses, where the work of many people must be managed and coordinated.

In addition to the information that flows formally as a consequence of an organisation's procedures, other information flows informally, for example, as a consequence of observing other activities taking place or by word of mouth. Informal information flow becomes more important in small organisations involving just a few people. For instance, the Eaglestone family (Example 1.2) will rely almost exclusively on informal information flow between members (it is unusual for a family to operate within a set of rigidly prescribed procedures). However, the family also benefits from the formal information flow from other organisations, such as bank statements, tax demands, bills, and receipts.

## DATA AND INFORMATION

The formal flow of information can take place only if the information can be expressed and communicated in some tangible form. However, information is an abstract commodity; you cannot touch information, but can gain information by touching something. Database technology is concerned with one particular form of information representation within a computer system, i.e., as data. Data consists of symbols written on some recording medium, such as paper, magnetic disk, or CD-ROM, to represent facts, concepts, or instructions in a formal manner so that they can be interpreted or processed by humans or machines. Information is the meaning that the human observer assigns to the data by means of the known conventions used in the representation.

---

*EXAMPLE 1.5*

*The museum (Example 1.3) may represent the date on which an artefact was acquired by entering the symbols 010895 onto the appropriate field of a form. This number is data and is intended to convey the meaning "the first day of August in the year 1995". However, this information is correctly conveyed only if the observer knows the convention used. An American, for example, may misinterpret the data as meaning "the eighth day of the first month in the year 1995" by assuming a different convention for representing a date.*

---

In practice, computers will have a single internal representation for a particular type of data, but produce multiple representations in print or displays to conform to the conventions understood by different users. For example, data storage systems will typically include a date datatype which will allow you to enter dates in a number of formats such as 1st Aug 1995 or 1/8/95 (assuming a European convention). The dates will be stored in an internal format hidden from the user and it will be possible to query or alter this information with an understanding of what a date means.

In general, the numbers and text on an organisation's records are its data, and the information is the meaning assigned to those numbers and text.

## AN ORGANISATION'S DATABASE

Information represented as data is retained within an organisation for as long as the information is of potential use. For example, the museum (Example 1.3) will retain data describing a particular historical artefact at least for as long as the museum owns that artefact. Bruddersfield Bikes (Example 1.1) will retain details of an order placed by a customer at least until the order has been delivered and the remittance has been paid. The total collection of data stored within an organisation at any particular time is referred to as the organisation's database. This data may be stored in various forms, including both paper records and magnetic disks. However, the term database usually refers only to the information recorded as data and stored on computer storage devices.

## 1.2 THE DATABASE APPROACH TO INFORMATION SYSTEMS

An organisation's database is often stored as a collection of data files, usually stored on magnetic disk, and the application programs which access the database are often written to do this by directly reading and writing the records stored in these files. Alternatively, a database management system (DBMS) may be used to store, maintain, and access the database. This section analyses the limitations of implementing a database as a set of files. It then explains the database approach and how database technology can provide a superior way of implementing a database.

### FILE–ORIENTED SYSTEMS AND THEIR LIMITATIONS

The traditional (pre-database technology) approach is to design computer programs to support specific information activities, and to design data files which provide the application programs with the data they need, and in a convenient form. In such systems the database exists as a collection of files. This approach is centred on the application, rather than the data that must be processed.

---

*EXAMPLE 1.6*

*A file-oriented sales order processing system at Bruddersfield Bikes (Example 1.1) would typically include the programs and files shown in Figure 1.1.*

---

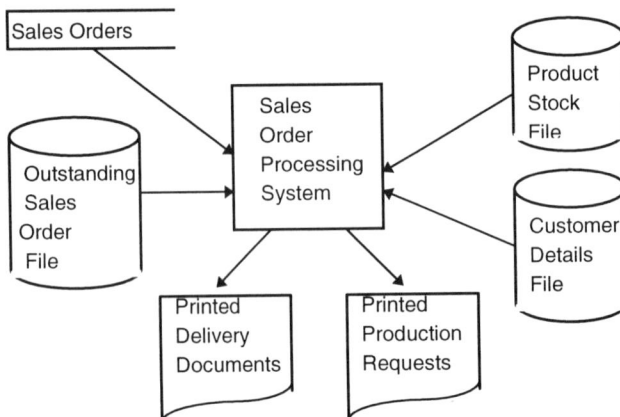

Figure 1.1 An example file oriented computer system

Here we have files in which are recorded details of customers, products, and outstanding sales orders. The sales order processing system is a program (or possibly a set of programs) which inputs data detailing new sales orders, checks that the new data is valid, and updates the appropriate files. It also produces the documents needed to ensure that the ordered products are produced and delivered.

Example 1.6 illustrates a number of characteristics which are typical of file–oriented systems.

1)  Each file represents a particular thing, or entity, which we are interested in. The three files in the Example form a part of the organisation's database and each represents entities of a particular type, i.e., customers, products, and sales orders. Each record of a file represents an occurrence of an entity. For example, records in the customer details file represent the customers of the organisation. The fields of the records represent facts about the entities. For instance, a record in the customer details file will record the customer's name, address, credit rating, etc. These are the attributes of a customer.

2)  Relationships are represented by duplicating data. The relationships between the entities represented in the files are represented by storing the same values in more than one record. For example, a sales order is related to the customer who placed that order, and so the value of the customer's identification number is stored in both the sales order file record that represents the order and  the customer details file record that represents the customer.

3)  Applications share data. Many applications may require access to the same information, and so may share the same data. For example, the Production Control system and the Inventory Control systems will also require access to data stored in the Product Stock file.

The above characteristics are a consequence of the function of the data, i.e., the representation of information about the entities relevant to the organisation. It is therefore necessary to use the data structures available to model the entities, their properties, and relationships between them.

A weakness of the file–oriented approach is that whereas files are structures for storing data such that it can be accessed efficiently, different programs may have different data access requirements. There are therefore two additional characteristics of file–oriented systems:

4) Data files are organised for the convenience of specific programs.
5) Programs must have built into them knowledge of how files are organised, the ways in which records can be accessed, and the meaning of the data.

These characteristics have two undesirable consequences:

1) File–oriented computer systems are likely to be unstable. This is because their design is based on the ways tasks are performed, rather than the structure of the information used in performing those tasks. Ways of doing things can and do change frequently within organisations. New systems must be developed and existing systems must be modified to accommodate these changes. However, changes to a file–oriented computer system can be expensive, because the data collected for applications may not be in an appropriate form for the new or altered applications. Data may therefore have to be duplicated and reorganised, or some compromise reorganisation of existing files may be necessary, so that the files can be accessed by both old and new applications. Modification to the structure of existing files will also require modifications to the existing programs that access them. Consequentially, neither the investment in collecting data nor in developing programs is preserved.
2) Management of data can be difficult. Data may be distributed across a number of files to be accessed by different application programs, and the duplicated data may be stored in different forms for the different programs. This makes it difficult to ensure that the data is consistent, up-to-date, correct, and secure.

## THE DATABASE APPROACH

The database approach to computerising information activities is to treat the organisation's data, i.e., its database, as a resource which is shared by all relevant application programs. The data is made shareable by structuring it in such a way that it has the same structure as the information that it represents. Application programs can then be programmed to access the logical structures of the information that is processed, rather than the structure of the files that are used to store the data that represents it. This means that programs which require access to the same information can access the same parts of the database.

A general objective of the database approach is therefore:

> A database should be a natural representation of information as data, with few imposed restrictions, capable of use by all relevant applications (including the ones not thought of yet) without duplication.

In general, information may be thought of as being about interrelated entities. For example, the manufacturer (Example 1.1) will record information about customers, products, and employees, some of whom are salespersons. These are interrelated; for example, products are related to the customers who place the orders for them and the salespersons through whom the orders are taken. The database approach is therefore to store information as data in such a way that the data is structured to represent the entities (there will be collections of data to represent each salesperson, each product, and each customer) which are linked in some way to represent the relationships (the data for a product will be linked to the data that represents the customers who have ordered it).

The database approach is therefore centred on the data, rather than on the processes applied to the data (see Figure 1.2).

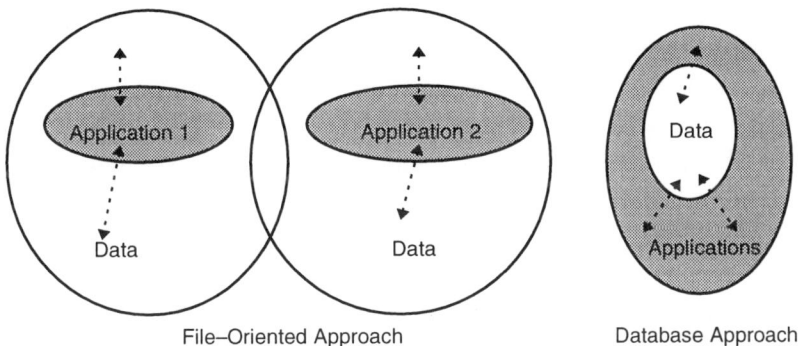

File–Oriented Approach       Database Approach

Figure 1.2 File oriented vs database approach

The extent to which a database and the programs that use it are maintained as independent resources depends on the nature of the organisation that the database is designed to serve. Where a database is designed to solve a very specific problem, as is the case in the navigation system (Example 1.4), the database and the programs which use it are very closely connected. In such cases the database is embedded within the system and is only accessible by operating the system. Alternatively, the database may be designed to store data for a wide range of applications (as is the case for the manufacturing organisation (Example 1.1)). In such cases, the database exists as a resource in its own right, and is managed and administered by a specialist group or person, called the **database administrator** (DBA).

## THE DATABASE MANAGEMENT SYSTEM

A database management system enables an organisation to implement the database approach. It does this by supporting descriptions of data, both in terms of how it is physically stored and in terms of the logical structure of the data. The physical structure of the data is to do with how the data is represented on storage devices such as disks, i.e., the file structures and the methods used to access data. The logical structure of the data is to do with how it appears to the users of the database. The logical structure of the data determines the ways in which the data values are combined and interlinked, and the ways in which they can be accessed and modified. The advantage of this separation between logical and physical structures is that the user of a DBMS can define logical data structures which are the same as the structures of the information represented, but also define physical data structures which implement the logical structures in such a way that the data can be used efficiently. In this way, a DBMS makes possible a natural representation of data by shielding the user from the physical data structures. The user sees only the data which is structured in a way that models the structure of the information it represents, and not the ways in which it is stored (see Figure 1.3).

The descriptions of the data structures are called **schemas**. The database has two parts: the database **intension**, which is the set of schemas which define the structure of the database, and the database **extension**, which is the data values themselves, contained in the database.

Real World Objects       Logical View of Data

Customer Data

Salesperson Data

User/ Application

Sales Order Data

DBMS

Physical Storage of Data

101110     11

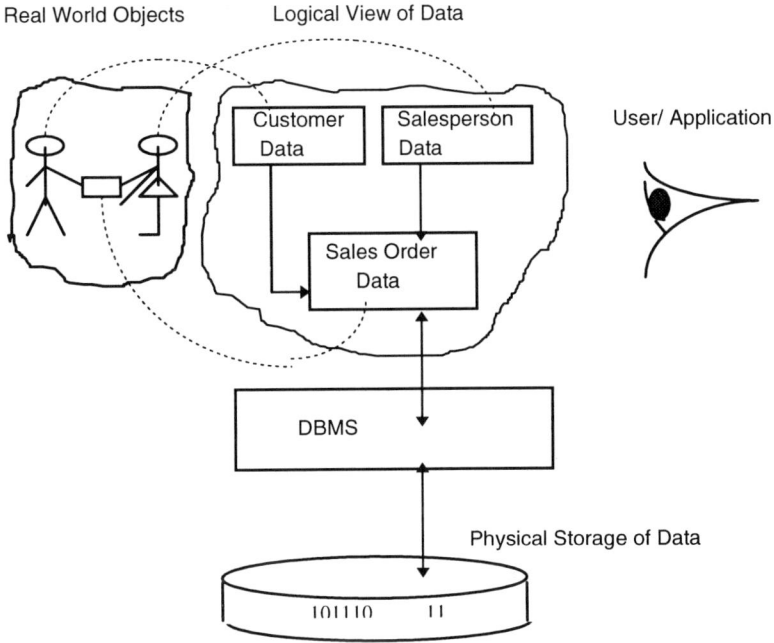

Figure 1.3 The DBMS and the world

Schemas are conventionally organised into three levels (see Figure 1.4): the internal, logical, and external levels. The internal model describes how data is physically represented, the logical model describes the logical structure of the database and the external models describe logical data structures which have been defined for specific applications.

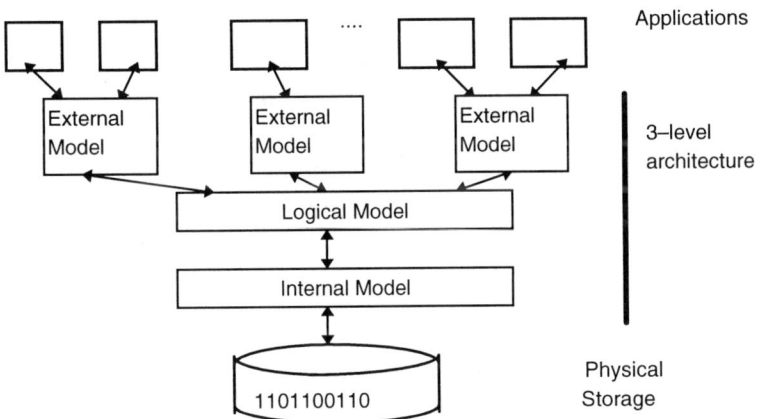

Applications

External Model

External Model

External Model

3–level architecture

Logical Model

Internal Model

1101100110

Physical Storage

Figure 1.4 The 3-level database architecture

The feature by which the logical view of the database is made independent of the way the data is actually stored is called **data independence**, and is the source of many of the benefits gained from using database technology. Data independence provides the following advantages:

1) The database may be tuned without it affecting the users. For instance, in order to make a database system run faster, hashing algorithms may be changed, new indexes may be introduced, or methods of linking related records may be altered. None of these changes will affect the logical structure of the data, and so the only effect on the user will be a change in the speed and size of the database system.

2) The database may evolve without upsetting existing applications. The database may be changed to represent information about new entity types, relationships, and attributes. However, this will not affect an existing user, providing those entities, attributes, and relationships which are relevant to his or her application are still represented.

3) Data may be shared by applications, including future ones. Since the users of the data are only concerned with its logical properties, there is no need to re-organise data for a new application.

4) Greater productivity is possible. In general it is easier and faster to create applications programs in a database environment than it is in a conventional file–oriented environment. Programs are simpler because there is no need to include details of how data is physically stored; and a database system typically includes tools which automatically generate applications programs from descriptions of what they must do, rather than how they must do it.

In addition to the above advantages which stem specifically from data independence, there are other advantages which are a consequence of maintaining data as a separate and integrated resource.

5) Greater security and integrity control are possible. When the database approach is applied, the data is treated as a central resource which must be managed. This management is done by the DBA. The responsibilities of the DBA are the design, maintenance, and evolution of the database. The DBA must also ensure the integrity

and security of the data in the database, but this job is made easier because the data is collected together within a single integrated structure.

Two important benefits result from these advantages: firstly, investment in developing applications is preserved. It will not be necessary to change applications programs when the database is changed to be more efficient, or to accommodate new applications. Secondly, investment in storing data is preserved. Data will not have to be re-stored in some other form for new applications.

There are also costs incurred when applying the database approach:

1)  Additional software is required to support the database approach. This will include the DBMS itself, software to extend programming languages so that they may access the database, special database languages and tools for building database applications, and various special programs for database organisation and maintenance.
2)  For large–scale database applications (such as Examples 1.1 and 1.3), organisational changes will be necessary. A DBA must be established to manage the database. The DBA is responsible for database design and administrative tasks. The latter include authorising access to the database, monitoring and coordinating database usage and security, and ensuring adequate response times. Programmers, analysts, and users will have to be trained.

The above expenses may be prohibitive for certain applications which are relatively independent of other applications and which process small amounts of data.

## DATA MODELS

Some DBMSs may be better suited than others for specific types of application. DBMSs differ according to the types of logical data structures they support for representing information as data and the operations that are supported by the DBMS languages. A collection of logical data structures from which databases can be constructed, together with the set of operations which can be used to manipulate databases and the rules which ensure that databases are plausible, is called a data model. Different DBMSs can be classified according to the data model they implement. Data models are explained and discussed in the next chapter.

## 1.3 SUMMARY

An **organisation** can be viewed as a system of activities co-ordinated by a flow of information. The **information system** is the underlying system concerned with maintaining this information flow.

Formally communicated information is represented as **data**. An organisation's **database** is the set of data which is recorded within the organisation at any one time. Database usually refers specifically to the data that is stored on computers.

The conventional **file–oriented approach** is to build computer systems to support specific activities, or applications. This approach is unstable because of the changing nature of activities, the need to share data, and the dependence of the programs on the structure of the files.

The **database approach** is to treat the database as an entity in its own right, and to design it to model the organisation. A special program called a database management system (DBMS) is used to manage and provide access to the database. Selective logical views are defined for each application. The **database administrator** (DBA) is responsible for managing the database.

The advantages of the database approach are independence of applications from changes in the representation of the database, or its evolution. Also, central control of data provides better data security and integrity.

The ways in which data can be structured and manipulated by a database are defined by its **data model**. Some data models are inherently more expressive than others.

## EXERCISES:

(1.1)    Explain the relationship between an organisation, its activities, and its database.

(1.2)    Describe three database applications, in addition to Examples 1.1 to 1.4, given in this chapter.

(1.3)    Distinguish between data and information, giving examples of each.

(1.4)    A small business comprising a potter, a salesman, and a secretary makes and sells china pots. Give examples of the informal and formal information flow which may occur within this organisation.

(1.5)    Identify problems that may occur when a small business implements its information system in a file-based fashion.

(1.6)    Keywords in the definition of the database approach are natural, shareable, and duplication. Explain the significance of each of these words in this definition.

(1.7)    Give examples of the entities, attributes, and relationships that the pottery business in Exercise 1.4 would wish to represent within a database.

(1.8)    Distinguish between logical and physical data structures.

(1.9)    What is the role of a database management system with respect to the logical and physical representation of information as data.

(1.10)   Explain how the 3-level database architecture in Figure 1.4 provides data independence.

(1.11)   With reference to Examples 1.1 to 1.4 explain if a database administrator is required and what her role should be.

(1.12)   The directors of a small engineering company currently store all of their data in files. You have been asked to advise them on the desirability of using a database management system. Write a short report setting out the potential advantages and disadvantages of changing to database technology.

# 2

# AN OVERVIEW
# OF THE
# OBJECT DATA MODEL

A data model is a set of structures with which a database can be constructed, operations that can be used to manipulate databases, and rules that ensure that databases are at least plausible. DBMSs differ according to the data models they support for representing and manipulating information as data. This chapter explains the concept of a data model, reviews the evolution of data models through to the present day, and provides an overview of object data modelling which forms a basis for object database technology. The object data model described is the one defined in Object Database Management Group's object database standards (ODMG) [Cattell 97] which is becoming the de facto standard, and is referred to simply as the Object Data Model. The ODMG languages for implementing the Object Data Model are described in subsequent chapters.

Section 2.1 gives a basic outline of what an object data model is. A brief history of data models is given in Section 2.2. Section 2.3 is a more detailed overview of the Object Data Model. Finally, a summary is given in Section 2.4.

This chapter is preliminary to a detailed study of the ODMG Object Data Model in subsequent chapters.

## 2.1 WHAT IS THE OBJECT DATA MODEL?

The Object Data Model is a particular type of data model. Data models are theoretical models which describe ways in which information can be represented and manipulated as a database. Theoretical models can be found in almost all areas of human endeavour. They are used to categorise and possibly simplify or approximate parts of the real world that are being studied. For example, weather forecasters use theoretical models to analyse and predict the consequences of various conditions on the weather system. Economists use theoretical models to analyse the effects of economic changes upon economies. A theoretical model is a set of concepts, operations, and rules, often expressed in a mathematical form, which behave in a way that mimics the behaviour of that which is being modelled.

A data model has three aspects relating to the way information is modelled as data. The structural part of a data model is the set of structures with which a database can be constructed, the manipulative part is the set of operations by which databases can be manipulated, and the integrity part is the set of rules that constrain a database to be plausible. Parallels to these parts can be found in programming languages. The structural part of an object data model corresponds to the programming language facilities for defining types, variables, and constants; the manipulative part corresponds to the executable instructions in the programming language with which we perform calculations using the variables and the integrity part corresponds to the rules that constrain the programmer, such as not being allowed to alter the value of something declared to be a constant.

A data model has two important roles.

1) It is the basis for DBMSs. A DBMS implements the structures, operations, and rules defined in the model.
2) It may be used to describe and analyse database systems. This facility enables the database designer and researchers to reason about database systems without actually having to build them.

The Object Data Model prescribes the capabilities of a particular type of DBMS, an object DBMS (ODBMS), by defining the logical data structures that it should support, and the operations with which it should be possible to manipulate object databases using the ODBMS's languages. An ODBMS implements the model's rules to constrain the use of the structures and operations, such that object databases are at least complete and self-consistent.

The quality of a theoretical model can be judged by how accurate and complete a representation it provides of the things it models, and the extent to which its predictions correspond to what happens in reality. For example, a weather model which predicts rain when in fact there is a drought is a poor model. Similarly, the quality of a data model must be judged on the basis of how well it can represent and model information and its behaviour. In this respect, the Object Data Model is an improvement over previous data models. It can capture more of the meaning of the information represented in a database than previous generations of data models. This is because the Object Data Model can represent both complex information structures and complex operations that occur. It will be seen that previous generations of data models have limited facilities for representing complex information structures and cannot represent complex operations.

## 2.2 A BRIEF HISTORY OF DATA MODELS

The evolution of database technology has taken place over the last three decades. It is an example of one form of progress in computing technology, whereby some aspect is factored out and more sophisticated ways of handling that aspect are developed. In the case of database technology, the aspect that has been factored out is the representation and manipulation of information as data.

In the first stage of the evolution of database technology, were the early programming languages (of the 1950s), such as assembler languages and machine code. These provided no separate treatment of data and the processes by which it was manipulated. For instance, assembler language programs would often modify their own instructions to turn them into other instructions. Later programming languages (in the 1960s onwards), such as COBOL and FORTRAN, introduced separate facilities for data definition and for specifying the procedures that used the data. A COBOL program, for example, is divided into separate parts, called the data division, and the procedure division. Still later (in the mid-1960s onwards), the introduction of database technology provided facilities for the definition and management of data separate from the programs which use the data. Database technology allowed persistent data, i.e., data which must be retained even after a program that creates it or uses it has terminated, to be stored and managed as a central resource which could be shared by many programs.

## STRUCTURE AND BEHAVIOUR

Database technology has continued to evolve, in response to a need for more sophisticated ways of managing, administering, and using data. In particular, data models have evolved to capture more of the meaning of the information represented. This need can be explained in terms of the semantic gap. The semantic gap occurs because of the mismatch between the database designer's understanding of the information that she wishes to represent and that which can be represented using the data model of the database technology being used. Data models have evolved to reduce the semantic gap.

The first two generations of data models were concerned mainly with representing the meaning of data in terms of the structure of the information represented. The third generation of data models, which includes the object data model, in addition represented the meaning of data in terms of the behaviour associated with the information represented.

The structural meaning of data is concerned with the entities it represents and the ways in which they are interrelated. For example, the information that Bruddersfield Bikes (Example 1.1) uses must describe its customers, its products, and the sales orders placed by the customers, where each sales order is related to a particular customer and to the set of products ordered by that customer. This sort of knowledge can be represented by combining and linking data values in ways which correspond to these structures. The structure of the information represented by a database is called its structural semantics.

Information can also be analysed in terms of behaviour, i.e., the things that can happen to the entities it represents. For example, information about Bruddersfield Bikes must also describe: the placing of an order; producing, storing, and delivering ordered products; and receiving payment for products ordered. The behaviour of an entity can be represented as procedures or programs which operate upon the data which represents that entity. The behaviour of an entity which is represented by procedures associated with a particular data structure is called its behavioural semantics.

## FIRST GENERATION DATABASE TECHNOLOGY

The first generation of database technology was based upon the network data model (as defined by the CODASYL Database Task Group [DBTG 71]) and the hierarchical data model (as implemented by the IBM IMS database management system) [Tsichritzis 76]. In these models, information is represented as collections of interlinked records. Different types of record are used to represent different types of entity. The fields of a record represent facts about an entity, and links between records represent relationships between the entities. There can be different types of record–to–record links to represent different types of relationship. The hierarchical model allows records to be linked to form tree structures (e.g., Figure 2.1 (a)), and the network model allows records to be linked into network structures (e.g., see Figure 2.1 (b)). The records themselves are defined in the same way that file records are defined in conventional programming languages, such as COBOL, FORTRAN, or C.

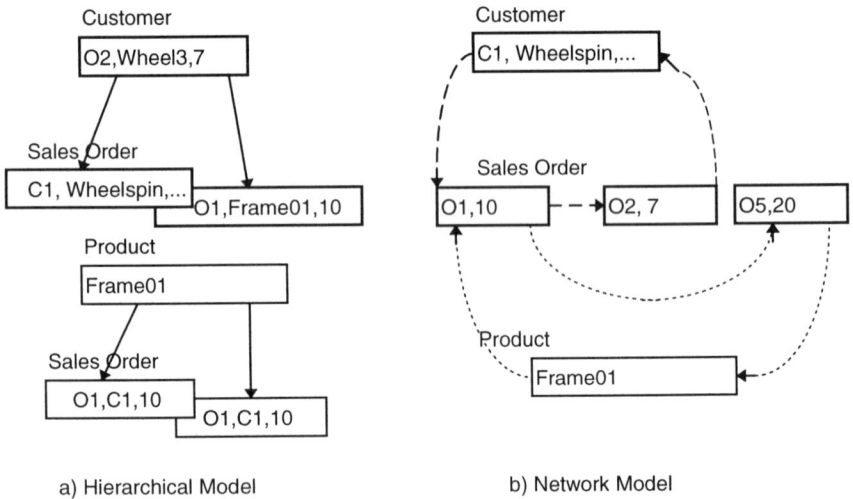

a) Hierarchical Model                    b) Network Model

Figure 2.1 Example databases using first generation models

The hierarchical and network data models both include operations for locating, reading, and writing records. Records can be located by specifying their properties or their relationship to other records to which they are linked and which have already been located. Both the hierarchical and network DBMSs can therefore be viewed as extensions to conventional file handling facilities, whereby, in addition to opening and closing files, and reading and writing records, programs can also "find" records by navigating the inter–record links.

These first generation data models have a number of limitations:

1) There is no clean separation between the logical structure of the data and the way in which it is physically implemented. Consequentially, the interface between programs and the DBMS is complicated, and a knowledge of how the linked records are implemented often has to be written into the programs. There is therefore only limited data independence (see Section 1.2, The database management system).

2) The database languages manipulate only one record at a time. It is therefore necessary to program the way in which the records in the database are to be navigated (i.e., the loops and decisions needed to select and access the records required) using a conventional programming language within which the database language instructions are embedded.

3) There is no theoretical foundation for hierarchical and network data models. This impeded research.

The first generation data models are quite expressive, in that they can represent different types of entities and relationships as different types of records and record–to–record links, i.e., they have quite a rich structural semantics. However, they have no facilities for representing the processes, i.e., the behaviour, associated with the entities. The behavioural semantics has to be represented within application programs that use the database.

First generation database systems are still in use today (an international standard network database language, NDL, was introduced as recently as 1986 [ANSI 86a]). The reason for their longevity is that the poor separation of logical and physical structures (i.e., the poor data independence) allows programmers and database designers to design systems which are highly efficient for specific applications, but also results in excessively complex systems. Rewriting such systems using more up–to–data technology may therefore require more investment than can be justified, given that the old systems still operate effectively. Systems of this type, which were written using old technology, and which are too large and complex to rewrite, are called legacy systems.

The problem of finding ways of allowing legacy systems to operate alongside systems developed using more up–to–date technology is an open problem, and is currently the focus of much research [Brodie 92].

## SECOND GENERATION DATABASE TECHNOLOGY

The second generation of database technology is based upon the Relational data Model [Codd 70]. The relational model was first published in 1970, by Edgar Codd, who was then a researcher at IBM's San Jose laboratories. Codd described the relational model as a theoretical model for large shared databanks. The relational model represents all information as tables of data values (see Figure 2.2).

Customer

| Customer_ID | Customer_name | ... |
|---|---|---|
| C1 | Wheelspin | ... |
| ... | ... | ... |

Product

| Part_number | Part_name | ... |
|---|---|---|
| Frameo1 | ... | ... |
| ... | ... | ... |
| Wheel3 | ... | ... |
| ... | ... | ... |

SalesOrders

| Order_number | Customer_ID | Part_No | Quantity | ... |
|---|---|---|---|---|
| O1 | C1 | Frame01 | 10 | ... |
| O2 | C1 | Wheel3 | 7 | ... |
| ... | ... | ... | ... | ... |
| O5 | C4 | Frame01 | 20 | ... |
| ... | ... | ... | ... | ... |

Figure 2.2  Example database using the relational model

A table is used to represent some type of real world entity, or a type of relationship between entities, and the rows represent occurrences of the entities or relationships. A column represents a property or attribute of the entity or relationship, and the values in a row therefore represent the properties of a particular occurrence of an entity or relationship. In the Relational Data Model, all information is visible as data, and relationships between rows are represented by storing the same value in each of the related rows.

A strength of the relational model is that it has a precise mathematical definition, and therefore provides a theoretical model for database systems. A table in a relational database is, in fact, a representation of a mathematical relation, and the operations which manipulate the tables are based upon the corresponding mathematical operations upon relations. The relational model therefore represents an important stage in the development of database technology; the mathematical rigour with which the model was defined made possible a more rigorous study of issues such as the design of databases and database languages.

In particular, the relational model includes an algebra for manipulating the tables, which provided the basis for a new generation of database languages, epitomised by SQL [ANSI 86b, ANSI 89, ANSI 92]. (An example SQL query is given in Figure 2.3).

```
select Customer_name, Order_nunmber, Part_number, Quantity
from Customer, SalesOrder
where Customer.Customer_ID = SalesOrder.Customer_ID
order by Customer_name,Order_number;
```

| Customer_name | Order_number | Part_number | Quantity |
|---|---|---|---|
| ... | ... | ... | ... |
| Wheelspin | O1 | Frame01 | 10 |
| Wheelspin | O1 | Wheel3 | 7 |
| ... | ... | ... | ... |

Figure 2.3 SQL query on the Example 2.2 relational database and resulting table

The algebra can define whole tables as the result of applying operators to other tables. The operators of the algebra approximate to copy, cut, and paste operations with which new tables can be composed from the rows and columns of others. Relational database languages are said to be relationally complete if they can express all operations that can be expressed in the relational algebra. This provides a basis for query languages, such as SQL, which are both set–oriented and declarative. By set–oriented we mean that statements in the language can manipulate whole tables of values at a time rather than one record at a time, as is the case with first generation database languages. By declarative, we mean that the language allows queries to be expressed without having to state how they must be executed. SQL, for example, does not include programming loops and decisions with which to navigate from one record to another; instead, statements in SQL define a new table by specifying its columns, identifying from where the data is to be extracted, and specifying conditions that must be true for data in the new table.

The attractions of the relational models are:

1) Mathematical rigour. The model is defined with mathematical rigour, and therefore provided a formal specification of the logical properties of relational DBMSs.
2) Simplicity. All information is represented in the relational model using one simple logical structure, the table. All information is visible as data values, and database languages are based upon simple cut, copy, and paste operations on columns and rows.

Both first and second generation data models are concerned solely with representing the meaning of data in terms of the structure of the information represented, i.e. the structural semantics; the behavioural semantics has to be represented within the programs which use the data.

However, the relational model is poorer at representing structural semantics than the first generation models. In a relational database there is only one logical data structure, the table, and so there is no discrimination between the different types of information represented. For example, entities and relationships between entities are both represented in the same way—as tables. This Spartan simplicity contrasts with first generation models, in which different types of entity and relationship are respectively represented as different types of record and different types of linkage between records. The major advance of the relational model was, however, the introduction of an algebra for manipulating a database, and a theoretical foundation for database technology. The relational algebra means that much more can be done in a single instruction, and the theoretical rigour has paved the way for research into database systems.

After the introduction of the relational model in 1970, it took a decade and a half of research and development before relational database management systems were readily available and of industrial standard. Since the mid-1980s relational technology has become commonplace in all sizes of computer, and has sufficient performance and reliability for large scale applications. Relational database technology is currently the state–of–the–art.

Many of the weaknesses of relational databases stem, not from the relational model itself, but actually reflect the weaknesses of particular implementations of relational theory [Codd 85, Date 86]. However, the relational model does have a number of inherent limitations which make it inappropriate for many applications.

Structural limitations: All information is represented in a relational database as tables of atomic values. This restriction is called first normal form and tables which conform are said to be normalised. The benefit is the simplicity of the technology and the generality of its application; tables are a very easily understood and versatile way of presenting information. However, this tabular presentation is inappropriate for representing the complex structures which exist in the real world. For instance, the relational model is unsuitable for design applications where it is necessary to represent complex designs, wherein each component is also a complex design. In the relational model complex structures must be represented by a number of separate tables interconnected by common values, and applications must then combine data from many tables to retrieve all the information about one entity.

---

*EXAMPLE 2.1*

*The museum (Example 1.3) has a small library of archeological books. The catalogue of these books is to be kept in a database system. Each book has an identifier, the ISBN, a title, and author or authors, as well as other attributes. The relational model gives us a way of representing the information about a book that works well when there is only one author—each book is represented by a single row of a book table (see Figure 2.4 (a)). However, many books have multiple authors, so in general each book has a list of authors. The relational model does not allow us to represent directly books with this more complex structure; attributes cannot have complex structures, and so we cannot have the author attribute shown in Figure 2.4 (b). The only way the book can be successfully modelled is by moving the authors out into a separate table. The complete information about a book must then be re–assembled by joining rows of the book and author tables where they have a common ISBN (see Figure 2.4 (c)).*

| ISBN | AUTHOR | TITLE |
|---|---|---|
| 0300024258 | Cunliffe,B | Excavations at Portchester Castle |

Figure 2.4 (a) Simple relational model of book with one author

| ISBN | AUTHORS | TITLE |
|---|---|---|
| 0300024258 | Cunliffe,B | Excavations at Portchester |
| 0231036582 | Ingersoll,D Yellen,JE Macdonald,W | Experimental Archeology |

Figure 2.4 (b) Unnormalised relational model of book

| ISBN | TITLE |
|---|---|
| 0300024258 | Excavations at Portchester |
| 0231036582 | Experimental Archeology |

| ISBN | AUTHOR | AUTHOR_SEQ |
|---|---|---|
| 0300024258 | Cunliffe,B | 1 |
| 0231036582 | Ingersoll,D | 1 |
| 0231036582 | Yellen,JE | 2 |
| 0231036582 | Macdonald,W | 3 |

Figure 2.4 (c) Normalised relational model of book

There are two undersirable consequences of this structural limitation. Firstly, it is hard to perceive the structure of the information in this flattened and fragmented form. Secondly, programs which process the structure will tend to be complex and inefficient, because of the need to re–combine the tables and to repeatedly apply queries, for example, so as to descend to the deeply nested parts of a structure. For such applications, we need better ways of representing complex information structures.

Behavioural limitations: Relational database languages express only a small subset of the ways in which data can be manipulated. In order to define complex computations upon data it is necessary to use other programming languages. Relational languages are said to be relationally complete, because they can express everything that can be expressed in the algebra of the relational model, but are not computationally complete, because they cannot express arbitrary complex computations. The advantages gained from restricting the expressiveness of relational languages is that they can both have sufficient power to express a useful set of data manipulation operations and be sufficiently restricted to make optimised query processing possible. The disadvantage is that it is not possible to express complex operations associated with the data purely within a relational language. To do this, instructions of the relational language must be included within programming languages, such as C, Pascal, or Ada. Even once complex operations on data have been expressed using a combination of database language and some other computationally complete programming language, those procedures are not a part of the database. Rather, they are part of the application programs that use the database. The database supports only structural semantics, not behavioural semantics.

## THIRD GENERATION DATABASE TECHNOLOGY

The above limitations of first and second generation data models are currently being addressed by researchers, standards committees, and database product developers, and a third generation of database technology is now emerging [Atkinson 90, Stonebraker 90, Scheck 91]. There are two dominant third generation data models. These are the object–relational model and the object (or object–oriented) data model (the subject of this book).

The concepts incorporated in object data models are taken from conventional database technology, and also from object–oriented programming languages, such as C++ and Smalltalk. Object data models allow more information to be represented by incorporating the facility of object–oriented programming languages, whereby users can extend the type system to include new types specially tailored to their applications. For example, a designer of a sales order processing database can create types to represent information about products and customers, in addition to the basic built–in types, such as integer and character. The main features of object data models are overviewed in the following section, and explained in detail in subsequent chapters.

Object–relational data models are an evolutionary approach, since they adapt and enhance the relational model. This contrasts with object data models, which may be seen as revolutionary, since they replace the relational model. Extensions to the relational model have been defined to allow direct modelling of complex structures, e.g., by allowing tables to be nested (the nested relation or non–first–normal–form models [Scheck 91]) and by extensions to the relational algebra to increase its expressive power. Many of the extensions have also been influenced by object–oriented technology, and incorporate many features associated with object data models. (A brief review of object–relational data models is given in Section 10.2, Object–relational databases.)

Object data models (and to a lesser extent object–relational models) are more expressive than those of the previous generations. They provide a richer representation of the structure of the information represented by the data than is possible using first or second generation models. Also, they provide facilities for representing within the database the behaviour of the information represented by the data (see Figure 2.5); with first and second generation models it is necessary to represent the behaviour of information as application programs.

Object data models exist in a confusing variety of forms, with different and sometimes contradictory terminologies and definitions [Nelson 91]. This is a consequence of the newness of the technology, and the fact that object database concepts have evolved from a variety of object–oriented programming languages, rather than from a single theoretical model, as was the case with relational databases. Object databases are still the focus of much research and are still evolving. Not surprisingly, there is as yet no official object database standard. However, clear definitions of the object data model are now emerging.

The "Object-Oriented Database System Manifesto" [Atkinson 90] was an early attempt to clarify what an object database is. More recently, object database system vendors have attempted to introduce some conformity by proposing the ODMG standards for an object data model and object database languages [Cattell 97]. ODMG is a consortium of object database system vendors. Though ODMG standards currently have no official status, the influence of the ODMG standards is likely to be considerable. This is because the members represent a significant portion of the object database systems market, and are all committed to producing "ODMG compliant" products. The ODMG standards are therefore likely to dominate the object database market and become a de facto standard.

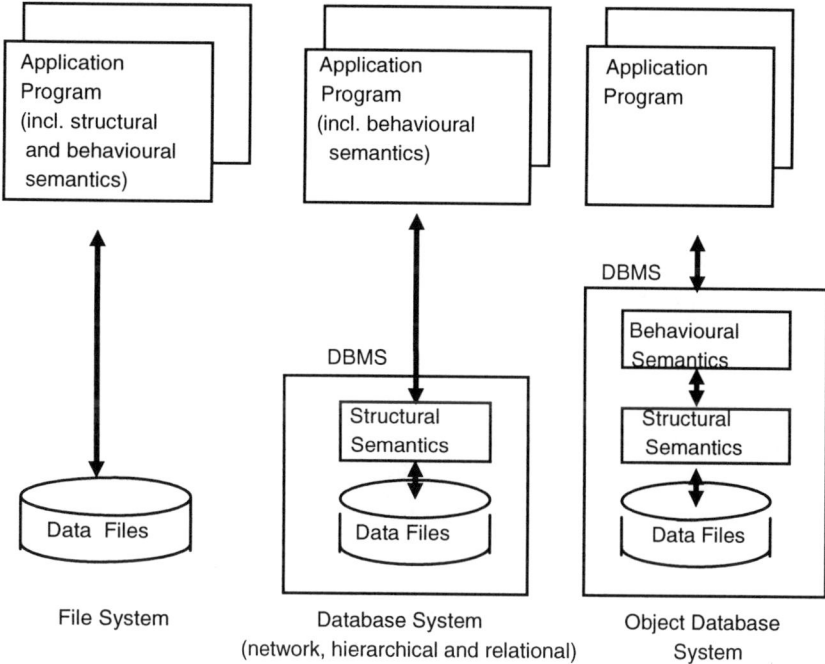

Figure 2.4 The evolution of data models

## 2.3 AN OVERVIEW OF THE OBJECT DATA MODEL

This section provides an overview of the Object Data Model as a preliminary to a detailed study of the model and its languages. We do this by presenting and explaining an example object database which characterises the important features of the model. This example represents the (simplified) sales order processing information used by Bruddersfield Bikes (Example 1.1).

---

*Bruddersfield Sales Order Processing System: The information processed by this system is about customers, salespersons, the products manufactured and sold by the company, and the sales orders for products placed by the customers.*

*A sales order records the quantities of products ordered from Bruddersfield by one of their customers and the Bruddersfield's salesperson through whom the order was placed.*

## ENTITIES AND OBJECTS

We begin by considering the information that must be represented. When designing an object database, information is analysed in terms of the **entities** it describes, the ways in which they are interrelated, and their behaviour. Entity is a very general term, which refers to anything which is uniquely identifiable and about which we wish to record facts.

Entities are represented in an object database as a special structure, called an **object**. An object database is a collection of objects, each of which represents an entity which is of interest to the organisation that the database serves.

An object is a combination of data which represents the **state** or value of the entity that the object represents and procedures which represent its **behaviour**. The data is called the object's state and the operations are its behaviour. The procedure which implements a particular operation on an object is called a method.

### EXAMPLE 2.2

*An object database in which an employee called Mick Ridley is represented will include an object to represent him. This object will have a state, which comprises data values, including the character string "Mick Ridley" to represent his name. The object will also have a behaviour, which comprises methods, for example to represent the processes for paying, promoting, demoting, and dismissing him.*

The entity and object in Example 2.2 are depicted in Figure 2.6. The notation used here is that of the Unified Modelling Language (UML) [Booch 95, Booch 96] for designing object–oriented systems and will be used throughout this book. The object is represented as a box. The name of the type of object, Employee, is given in the top half. This name is underlined to show that the box represents an actual object rather than properties of many objects. The values contained by the object, i.e., its state, are listed in the bottom half.

Figure 2.6 Object diagram for Mick Ridley

The procedures associated with an object act as that object's **interface**, and are the only means by which the data values can be accessed and manipulated. The facility by which data and procedures are integrated within an object is called **encapsulation**.

The entities in the sales order processing application are:
- employees of the company, and salespersons in particular;
- the customers who place orders;
- the sales orders placed by the customers;
- the products that the customers can order.

These entities must be represented as objects in the object database.

The state of an object represents the properties of the entity modelled by the object. There are two types of property that can be represented:

1) **attributes**, the values of which represent facts about the entity modelled. For example, the state of an employee object will include attribute values which represent the employee's name, address, date of birth, etc.

2) **relationships**, the values of which represent the associations between the entity and other entities represented in the object database. For example, the state of an object which represents a sales order will represent relationships with the objects which represent the customer who placed the order, the salesperson who took the order, and the ordered products.

An object is very much like a miniature database system. Conventionally, a database system comprises a database within which relevant information is represented as data and a set of applications programs which are executed to make use of the data in the database. The data within the database represents the state of the organisation and the application programs its behaviour. If we constrain the database such that it describes just one entity within the organisation, and the applications programs model the operations on that particular entity, we have an object. The miniature database system becomes the object, the database itself becomes the state of the object, and the applications programs become the procedures which provide the interface to the object (see Figure 2.7). An object database is an interrelated collection of such objects, each one representing an entity of interest to the organisation that the object database serves.

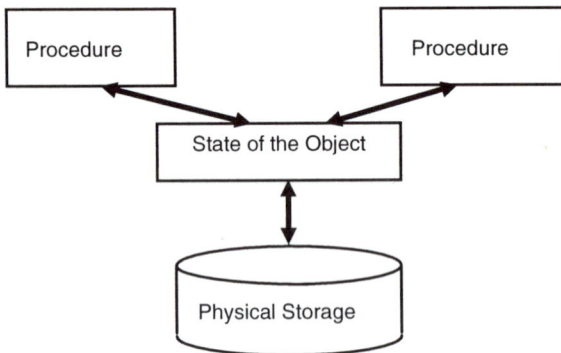

Figure 2.7 Object as a miniaturised database

## TYPES AND CLASSES

Many objects may share the same set of characteristics; their states can take data values from the same set of possible values and they can be manipulated using the same set of operations. Objects with the same characteristics are said to be of the same **object type**. An object type definition defines the possible states and behaviour of objects of that type. Objects of a particular type are called **instances** of that type, and the set of instances of a type is called the type's **extent**.

---

*EXAMPLE 2.3*

*All employee objects have the same characteristic; they can take state values from the same "pool" of possibilities and share the same operations. We therefore* *say that employee objects have the same **type**. Each employee object is an instance of the employee object type, and the set of all employee objects is the employee object type's extent.*

An example declaration of an object type is given in Figure 2.8. The details of the declaration will become clear in the following sections; here we give an outline explanation.

```
class SalesPerson (extent customers
                   keys    name, number) : Employee
{
        attribute String sales_person_number;
        attribute Money  value_of_orders_taken;

        relation List<SalesOrder> has_taken
                inverse SalesOrder:: taken_by
                {order_by SalesOrder::number}

        Boolean take_order (in String product, Integer
                Quantity, String customer_number);
        Money   get_commission ();
}
```

Figure 2.8. An example object type definition

The example object type defined in Figure 2.8 has a name, SalesPerson, and defines a set of properties. The properties include a set of attributes (sales_person_number, value_of_orders_taken), the values of which represent facts about the entities represented by objects of this type, and a set of relationships (has_taken, taken_by), the values of which represent associations between objects of this type and other objects. The type also has a set of operators (take_order, get_commission) which may be applied to objects of this type. The attributes and relationships define the state and the operations define the behaviour.

Note also that the type definition defines the ways in which an object of that type can be used, but not how it is implemented; a type definition defines only the interface to objects. For a type to be used in an object database, it is also necessary for the database designer to provide an implementation. The implementation will define the representation, i.e., data structures used to implement the state and procedures that implement each operation. These procedures are called **methods**.

A type can be implemented in many ways. An implemented type is called an **implementation class** or simply a **class**. Since there may be many implementations of a type, there can therefore be many implementation classes with the same type. This facility is useful, particularly when accessing multiple databases, as in the museum (Example 1.3), where the same type may be implemented in alternative ways in different object databases.

Figure 2.9 is a type diagram for the sales order processing object database, in which each box represents an object type, and the connecting lines represent relationships between object types.

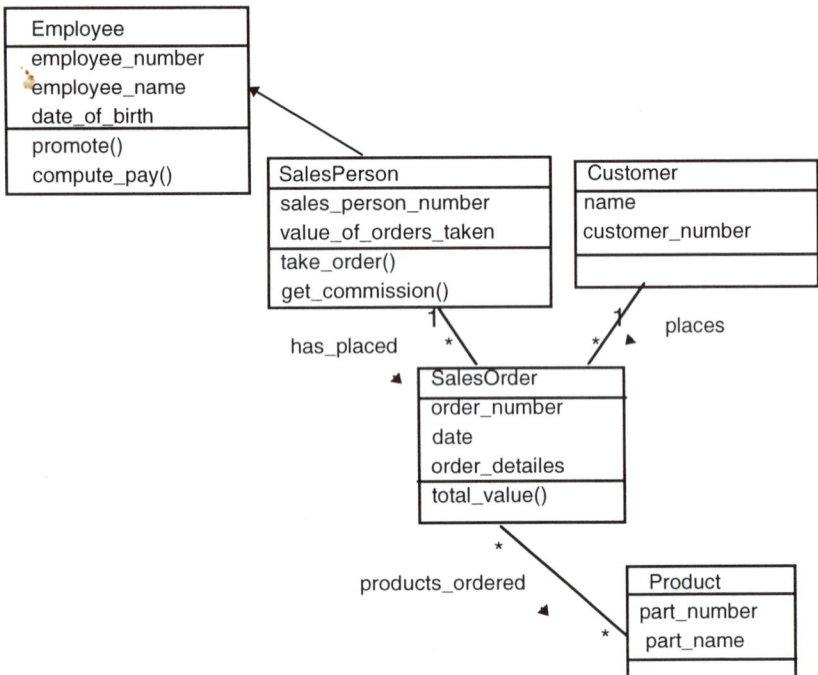

Figure 2.9 Type diagram for sales order processing database

When designing an object database we compose diagrams like this in order to create a model of the part of the world that is relevant to the application; each type represents a sort of entity that is of interest. The name of each type describes the entities represented and is the first name in each icon—Customer, SalesPerson, etc. Under each type name is the list of attributes (which are part of the state) and a list of operations, which are the behaviour. Relationships between objects are represented by the lines that connect the type icons. The numbers and asterisks (an asterisk means many) at each end of each connecting line shows how many objects can be involved in an instance of the relationship. Connecting lines are also annotated with names and arrows. These are the names of the **relationship paths** in the direction of the arrow. The arrow from SalesPerson to Employee denotes a special type of relationship—a SalesPerson is a specialised type of Employee.

---

*EXAMPLE 2.4*

*A sales order is related to the customer who placed it and the salesperson through whom the order was placed. These relationships are represented in Figure 2.8 by the lines connecting the SalesPerson icon to the SalesOrder icon, and the SalesOrder icon to the Customer icon. The line from SalesPerson to SalesOrder has a name, has_placed. This is the path name of the relationship from SalesPerson objects to SalesOrder object (the direction of the path is shown by the arrow head). This line is also annotated with 1 and  *. This indicates that each occurrence of the has_placed relationship associates 1 SalesPerson object with possible many (\*) SalesOrder objects. Similarly, the line from SalesOrder to Customer is annotated to show that each occurrence of the places relationship associates one Customer object to possibly many SalesOrder objects.*

---

Each object therefore has a type and is a member of one of the classes that implement that type. An object is organised into three parts (see Figure 2.10):

1) its **state**, which is the data it carries. Each object will have a collection of state variables the values of which are the object's state;
2) its **interface**, which is the collection of operations by which the state of the object can be accessed and modified;
3) the **implementation**, which is the code that implements the operations.

The state and interface are defined by the object's type, and the implementation by its class.

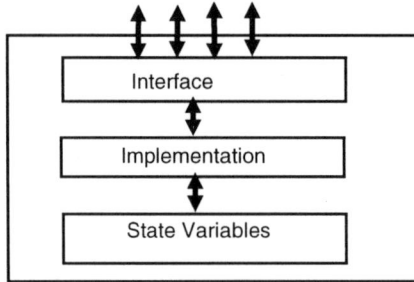

Figure 2.10 Organisation of an object

The designer of an object database must define classes to represent each relevant entity type, by specifying the state variables, the operations, and the ways in which they are implemented.

As can be seen, the object data model contrasts with previous data models. In first and second generation data models entities are represented by values in records (or rows in tables), which are accessed directly using the database language. The behaviour of the entities has then to be modelled in the application programs which manipulate the data values. In an object data model, the records exist only as the states of objects, and the values can only be accessed by executing the object's procedures which model the entity's behaviour.

## OBJECT IDENTITY AND COMPLEX OBJECTS

Objects can be combined to model entities with complex structures. This is done by including objects which represent components of an entity within the state of the object which represents the composite entity. Objects composed from other objects are called **complex objects**.

---

### EXAMPLE 2.5

*The state of a complex object which represents a Bruddersfield Bikes sales order may contain a collection of objects which represent each of the individual orders on that sales order.*

---

In practice many objects in an object database may represent composite entities with shared components.

---

*EXAMPLE 2.6*

*Bruddersfield Bikes publishes a number of product lists, but the same product often occurs in more than one list. The product lists can be represented by complex objects, the states of which include objects which represent the products. However, the states of two different product list objects may include the same product object.*

---

Representation of shared components is possible because each object is uniquely identifiable by an object identifier which is automatically assigned to it when it is first created. Object identifiers can never be altered or reused to identify other objects. This makes it possible to create objects which are collections of other objects, because the state of one object can include the object identifiers of other objects (or even of itself!).

In general, object identifiers can be included in the state of one object to represent a relationship with other objects. For example, the relationship between a customer and the sales order she places can be represented by including the customer object's identity in the state of each of the sales order objects and/or by including the set of object identifiers for the customer's sales order objects in the customer object's state.

## INHERITANCE

Objects in an object database can be instances of many types simultaneously. This feature models the fact that real world entities can also be classified in many ways. For example, Barry Eaglestone can be classified as a person, as an employee, and as a mammal. Some of these entity classifications are more general than others. For instance, "Barry Eaglestone is a person" is a more general statement than "Barry Eaglestone is an employee". A consequence is that Barry has the specific properties of an employee, but also inherits all of the properties of a person. Similarly, objects in an object database inherit properties of the general types to which they belong, as well as having properties of the most specific types.

This form of property inheritance is illustrated in the sales order processing example. In Bruddersfield Bikes, a salesperson is a special type of employee, and so will have all the properties of an employee (name, address, employee number, etc.) but also additional properties (commission earned, etc.). This relationship is modelled in the object database design, depicted in Figure 2.9. The arrow from SalesPerson to Employee represents that the type implemented by the SalesPerson class (from which the arrow starts) inherits all of the properties of the type of the Employee class (to which the arrow points). We say the SalesPerson object type is a **subtype** of the Employee object type, and the Employee type is a **supertype** of the SalesPerson type. A consequence of this is that all SalesPersons objects are also Employees objects (though not all Employees are SalesPerson objects).

The effect of implementing **subtype/supertype relationships** can be seen in the type definition in Figure 2.8. In this definition we show that SalesPerson is a subtype of Employee in the first line by including the name of the pointed–to class after the colon. A consequence is that all the attributes, relationships, and operations defined in the Employee type definition are automatically added to the SalesPerson definition, i.e., they are **inherited**.

In this example, SalesPerson has only one supertype, but it is also possible for real world entities to be special cases of many more general entities. For example, a senior salesperson may be considered to be a salesperson and also a manager. The SeniorSalesPerson object type would then need to inherit properties of both the Manager and SalesPerson object types. This situation can be modelled in an object database by multiple inheritance. Many supertypes can be defined in a type definition, and the subtype inherits the properties of all of its supertypes.

Inheritance is considered by many to be the most important feature of object data models. Its importance is that it allows object definitions to be reused when new object classes are added to the object database. In the above example (see Figure 2.8) it is not necessary to redefine the properties of Employee objects in the SalesPerson type definition. These are automatically inherited and their implementation is therefore reused in the SalesPerson class. Furthermore, existing applications programs, written to access Employee objects, will automatically access all objects which are instances of the subtypes of Employee, including those which were undefined when the application program was first written.

## 2.4 SUMMARY

The Object Data Model is a **data model**, which is a special type of theoretical model. A data model defines the structures, operations, and integrity rules of a database.

There are now three generations of data model: (1) the **network** and **hierarchical** data models; (2) the **relational** model; and (3) **object– relational** and **object** models.

An object database is a collection of **objects,** each of which represents an entity of interest.

An object has a **state** (attributes and relationships with other objects), and **behaviour** (operations by which it can be accessed and manipulated).

Objects with the same state and behaviour characteristics are defined by an **object type**. An object is an **instance** of its type. The set of instances of a type is called the type's **extent.**

To be of use a type must be implemented—the state and behaviour must be implemented as data structures and procedures. The data structures are called the representations and the procedures are the methods. A type and its implementation is called an **implementation class.**

**Inheritance** is a special type of relationship that can exist between object types, whereby one type is a subtype of another and therefore inherits all of its characteristics.

Classes, their attributes, relationships, and operations, can be represented in a **class diagram.**

## EXERCISES:

(2.1)  Explain how a data model provides a basis for a "natural representation of information as data" as prescribed in the database approach.

(2.2)  Explain the purpose of the structural, manipulative, and integrity parts of a data model.

(2.3)   What is meant by the structural semantics?

(2.4)   What is meant by behavioural semantics?

(2.5)   What is meant by the semantic gap?

(2.6)   What advantage is gained by using a first generation database system, rather than a file system?

(2.7)   What advantage is gained by using a second generation database system, rather than a first generation database system?

(2.8)   What advantage is gained by using a third generation database system, rather than a second generation database?

(2.9)   The basic component of an object database is the object. Describe the parts of an object, and explain how it can be used to represent structural and behavioural information about an entity, such as yourself.

(2.10)  Distinguish between object type and object implementation class.

(2.11)  Describe how objects in a database could represent information about a family with two parents, two children, and a dog. In your answer you should describe:

   (i)    the object types and classes—attributes, relationships, operations, methods, and inheritance relationships;

   (ii)   the database objects, themselves.

(2.12)  Extend the class diagram in Figure 2.8 to include additional information concerning employees who work in the Bruddersfield Bikes' factory. Each of these employees works on one or more production processes. Each process is part of the manufacture of one or more products.

# 3

# THE STRUCTURAL PART OF THE OBJECT DATA MODEL

This chapter describes the structural part of the Object Data Model. The structural part is the set of building blocks (objects, types, and classes) for constructing an object database. These building blocks were introduced in the overview of the Object Data Model given in Chapter 2. Here they are described in greater detail and illustrated using the Bruddersfield Bikes' sales order processing object database. The notation used in this chapter is similar to the Object Definition Language, ODL, that is used to implement actual object database systems. ODL is described in detail in Chapter 4. A diagrammatic language for representing the building blocks is also used and will be described in greater detail in Chapter 8 as a language for designing object databases.

Section 3.1 describes the basic building block of an object database, the object. Objects with the same characteristics can be categorized into types. Object types are explained in Section 3.2. Section 3.3 explains how objects can be combined to model structurally and behaviourally complex entities. Finally Section 3.4 gives a summary.

## 3.1 THE OBJECT

### ENTITIES AND OBJECTS

The basic building block (or modelling primitive) of an **object database** is called the **object**. Information represented in an object database takes the form of a collection of objects.

An **object database** contains a collection of **objects**, each of which represents one of the **entities** that are of interest to the organisation that the object database serves.

Entities are things about which we wish to record facts and which are distinguishable, one from another (see Section 2.3, An overview of the Object Data Model, entities and objects). Furthermore, entities have behavioural characteristics, i.e., there are things that can happen to an entity during its life. Each object has the following structure in order to represent the characteristics of an entity:

1)  **Identity**–a unique and unalterable **object identifier** assigned to the object. This models the fact that entities represented by objects are uniquely identifiable.
2)  **State**–the state of an object is the set of values that it contains. The values represent facts about the entity represented by the object, including facts about associations with other entities.
3)  **Behaviour**–the behaviour of an object is the set of operations that can be applied to it. These operations are designed to model the ways in which the entity that the object represents can behave.

---

*EXAMPLE 3.1*

*The object which represents the Bruddersfield Bikes customer, Grafts Ltd, will have an object identifier, which was automatically assigned when it was created. This identifier distinguishes that object from all other objects. The object will have a state which comprises values representing facts, such as the customer's name, address, and telephone number. It will have a behaviour which consists of a set of operations that can be applied to the object to model activities such as placing a sales order, making a payment for products delivered, or changing address.*

---

In addition to identity, state, and behaviour, it is possible to assign to an object one or more meaningful **object names** by which it can be referred to. For example, it may be convenient to create a **named object**, called MD, which represents the managing director of Bruddersfield Bikes.

Objects are used to represent entities which exist outside of the object database, such as customers and products, and other entities which exist within the object database, such as values and object types (object types are explained later, in Section 3.2, Object types).

## REAL WORLD ENTITIES

Objects are used to represent entities which exist outside of the object database and are relevant to the operation of the organisation that the object database serves. For example, Bruddersfield Bikes will represent its customers, products, and employees as objects within its object database. These types of entity are called **real world entities** because they exist within the world in which the organisation must operate (its Universe of Discourse). Real world entities may be physical (i.e., things you can touch, such as customers and products) or abstract (i.e., concepts, such as appointments, processes, and agreements).

---

## EXAMPLE 3.2

*Let us suppose that Bruddersfield Bikes currently has:*
* *four salespersons (Smith, Brown, Jones, and Green);*
* *five customers on its books (Grafts Ltd, King Cans PLC, Grange Moore Motors, Harding Bros, Faulties);*
* *a range of four products: (P10, P25, P25/4, and P25/6);*
* *three outstanding sales orders:*
    * *Harding Bros have ordered 100 of P10 and 1,000 of P25/6s, the order was taken by Jones.*
    * *Faulties have ordered 500 P25s, through Jones.*
    * *Graft Ltd have ordered 200 P25s, through Green.*

*The Bruddersfield Bikes object database must therefore include 16 objects to represent the 16 real world entities listed above, as shown in Figure 3.1. Of the above entities, the salespersons, customers, and products are physical, whereas the sales orders are abstract.*

---

## DATABASE ENTITIES

Objects are also used to represent entities which exist only within the object database, referred to as **object database entities**. Three examples are as follows:

1) Objects represent the **values,** such as numbers and text, which are used within the object database to model facts about entities

represented by other objects. For example, a Bruddersfield Bikes product may be represented as an object, in which case the value that represents the price of that product will also be represented by another object.

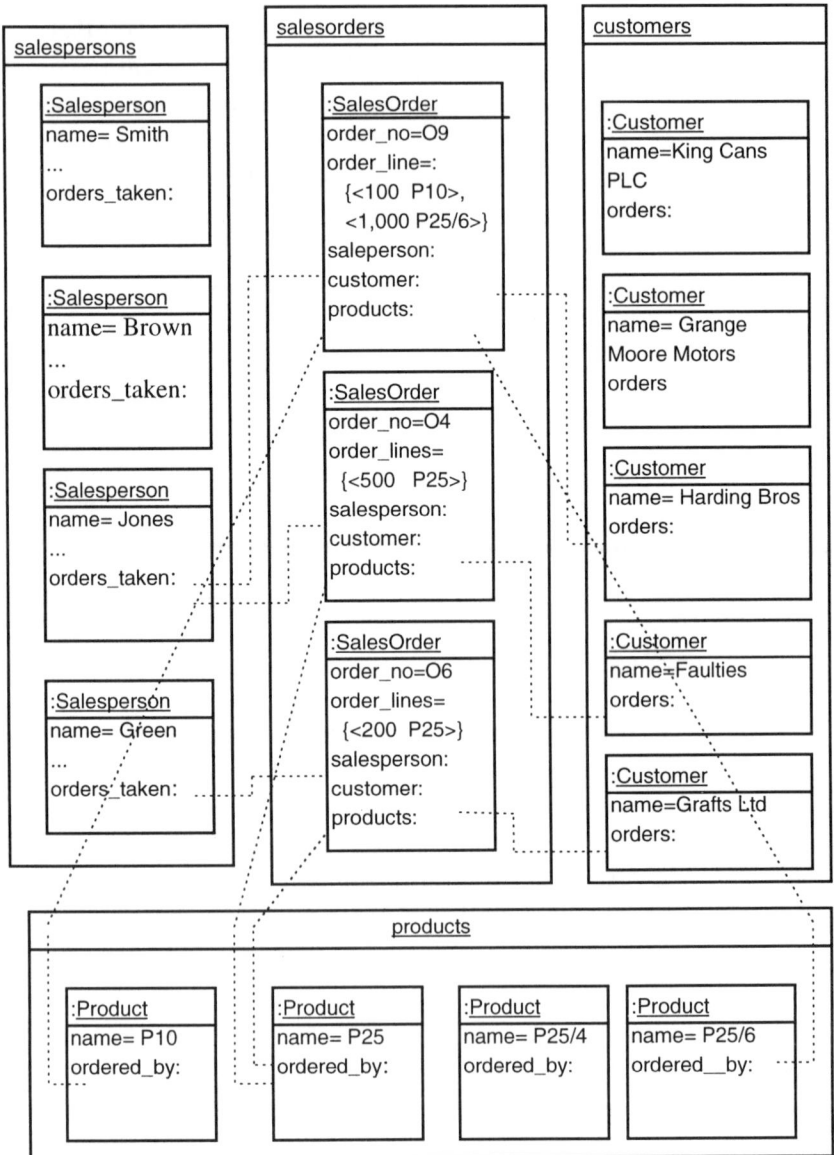

Figure 3.1 An example object database which represents the real world entities in Example 3.2 (Objects are represented by the boxes and relationships between them by the dotted lines)

2) Objects represent **entities** that model the different types of object that an object database may contain. For example, an object in the Bruddersfield Bikes object database will represent the characteristics of the objects used to represent their customers.

3) Objects represent **entities** that model certain exceptional events that can occur within the object database system, such as a request to create a sales order object for a non–existent product. This type of object database entity is called an **exception**. The operations that can be applied to an exception object are the procedures that are executed when the event occurs.

## MUTABLE OBJECTS AND LITERALS

Though the Object Data Model has a single abstraction, the object, which is used to represent all information, there is an important difference between objects which represent **values** and other types of object. The state of an object which represents a value cannot be changed, whereas the state of other types of object can. The former are called **literals** (or **immutable objects**) and the latter are called **mutable objects,** or just **objects**.

> A **mutable object** is an object which can change its own state. A **literal** is an object which cannot change its own state.

A literal is a container for a fixed value and serves the same purpose as a constant in programming languages, whereas a mutable object is a container for facts about an entity, the properties of which may change over time. The immutability of literals is therefore a sensible restriction, since the represented values will not change. A consequence is that the state of a literal also acts as its object identifier (a literal does not have a separate identifier). Individual literals are therefore referred to by their state. For example, the literal that represents the number 25 is simply referred to as 25. The Object Model includes pre–existing literals (the designer of the object database does not need to define them) which represent all of the values typically available in a programming language for use as constants.

It is necessary to represent entities (other than values) as **mutable objects,** since this enables us to modify an object's state so as to model changes which occur to the entity represented.

---

## EXAMPLE 3.3

*The object which represents Bruddersfield Bikes' customer, Grafts Ltd (in Example 3.1), must be a mutable object, so that it can be changed to model changes that occur to Grafts Ltd This mutable object will contain within its state a number of literals which represent facts about Grafts Ltd., such as their name, address and telephone numbers. These literals are replaced by other literals when the object's state is changed, for example, to represent a change of name or address.*

---

## ENCAPSULATION

The bringing together of representations of both **state** and **behaviour** within an object is called **encapsulation**. Encapsulation achieves two things. Firstly, it provides a representation of the meaning of data contained in the object database, in terms of both the structure and the behaviour of the entities modelled. Secondly, encapsulation ensures that data is used only in ways that are consistent with its meaning. The operations provide the interface to the object, and so the state can only be accessed and manipulated by executing appropriate operations. The operations therefore act like a "suit of armour"—they protect the data from being accessed or altered in ways that are contradictory to the behaviour of the entity represented by the object.

The behaviour and state of an object are closely related. The operations which define the behaviour of an object are to do with:

1) Deriving information from the state in a convenient form. For example, an operation on an employee object may extract the age of the employee represented, by performing a computation on the employee's date of birth, which is part of the object's state.

2) Making changes to the state in order to model changes that happen to the entity represented by the object. For example, a promote operation on an employee object will change the salary value in the object's state, to reflect the new salary of the promoted employee.

The following sections explain the identity, state, and behaviour of objects in greater detail.

## THE IDENTITY OF AN OBJECT

Each object is uniquely identifiable from all other objects. When an object is first created, it is assigned a value to identify it. This value is called its **object identifier**.

> An object's **object identifier** is an automatically assigned and unchangeable value that uniquely identifies that object and distinguishes it from all other objects.

The object identifier is separate from the object's state and is not visible to the user or database programmer. It provides a means of referencing objects within the system. The use of object identifiers will become clear when object database programming languages are discussed in Chapters 6 and 7.

Object identity is an important property of an object, since it means that an object remains the same object, even when its state takes a completely new set of values. Conversely, since an object's identity is independent of its state, it is possible for us to represent different entities which have the same properties.

---

*EXAMPLE 3.4*

*Suppose an object is created to represent a salesperson who has just been recruited to Bruddersfield Bikes, and the object state comprises the employee's name and address. Later the employee marries and moves to a new house. Both the name and the address are therefore altered, but the object is still the same object—its identity remains the same. This is consistent with the changes to the real world entity that is represented by the object. Though the recorded state of the entity has changed completely, it is still the same entity.*

---

Object identifiers can be used to represent associations between objects. In particular, objects can represent entities comprising many parts, possibly with shared components.

---

*EXAMPLE 3.5*

*Two objects represent different Bruddersfield Bikes products, a bicycle and a tricycle. A third object represents the front wheel fork which is a part of both products. Both of the product objects therefore include the value of the front wheel fork object identifier as part of their respective states to indicate that they have a component in common (see Figure 3.2).*

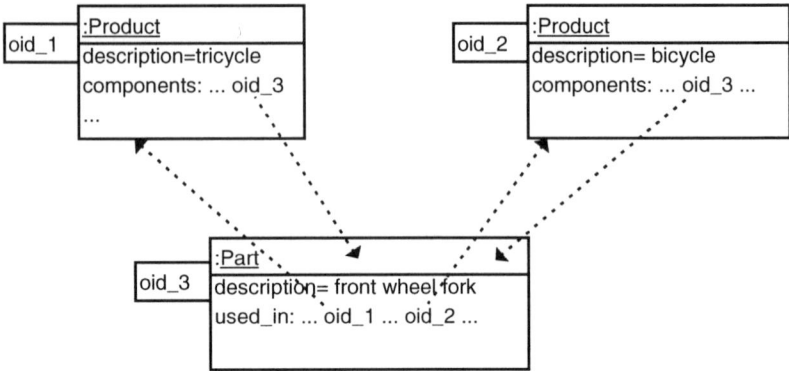

Figure 3.2 This diagram represents how object identifiers can be used to represent entities with a shared component. The objects represent the entities in Example 3.5. The diagram represents the objects as boxes, each with a unique identifier, oid_1, oid_2, and oid_3. Note that the object identifiers of related objects are contained in the object states

The fact that an object's identity is distinct from its state means that concepts of object equivalence and object equality are different. Two objects are **equivalent** if they have the same object identity (that is, they are equivalent if they are the same object) but are **equal** if they have the same state values (but possibly different identities). We can also distinguish between **shallow** and **deep equality**–objects have shallow equality if their states contain the same values (when we exclude references to other objects); they have deep equality if their states contain the same values and if the corresponding objects to which they are related also contain the same values.

### EXAMPLE 3.6
*Two objects record the names of two different salespersons. However, since both employees are called James Last, the states of the two objects are the same. The objects are therefore **equal**, but are not **equivalent** since they have different object identifiers. The two salesperson objects are related to other objects which represent the sales orders they have each take. Since they are related to different*

*sets of sale order objects, with different state values, the salesperson objects have* **shallow equality** *but not* **deep equality**.

The Object Data Model supports two additional but optional means of uniquely identifying objects. Objects can be assigned unique meaningful names, as previously described (see Section 3.1, The object: entities and objects). Designated values contained in the object state, i.e., **object keys**, can be used to identify objects, as is explained in the following section.

## THE STATE OF AN OBJECT

An object's state can be thought of as the set of values that the object contains. Each value represents a **property** of the entity represented by the object. An object state can carry two types of property:

- **attributes**–i.e., values which represent facts;
- **relationships**–i.e., values which represent associations with other objects.

## ATTRIBUTES

An object's state may carry a number of attributes, each of which represents a fact about the entity represented by that object. Each attribute has a descriptive name and a value. An attribute's value is represented by a literal.

### EXAMPLE 3.7

*The state of an object which represent Bruddersfield Bikes customer, Grafts Ltd, includes an attribute called name, the value of which is the literal that represents the character strin, "Grafts Ltd". In many cases, the value of an attribute will change over a period of time. For example, the value of the name attribute will be changed if Grafts Ltd changes its name to Grafts & Son Ltd. Each new name is represented by a different literal which replaces the previous value of the name attribute.*

An attribute exists only as part of an object and is not an object in its own right. An attribute therefore has no object identifier—it can be referred to only by first referring to the object that contains it.

Optionally, certain attributes can be designated as **object keys**. The values of an object key will distinguish each object from other similar objects, even when the values of all other properties are the same. Often there is an obvious choice of key, since certain properties represent the names or identifying numbers of the entities modelled by the objects. For example, the product number attribute is an obvious choice of key for the objects which represent products. Key values must be explicitly specified and maintained by the end–user of an object database system, but object identifiers are automatically assigned and maintained.

## RELATIONSHIPS

An object's state may include **relationships**. A relationship represents an association between the entity represented by that object and entities represented by other objects. Each relationship is given one or two descriptive names and has a value. The first name labels the relationship path from the object to the associated object(s) and the optional second name labels the inverse relationship path, from the associated object(s) to the object. The value of a relationship comprises the object identifiers of the associated objects.

---

## EXAMPLE 3.8

*A customer is associated with the sales orders she places. The state of the object which represents a customer will therefore include a relationship which associates it with the relevant sales order objects. The relationship value in the state of the customer object will comprise the object identifiers of all of the objects which represent sales orders placed by that customer, and the inverse relationship value of each of those sales order objects will contain the object identifier of the customer object. The relationship path from the customer object to the sales order objects and the inverse relationship path from the sales order objects to the customer object will each have a name, orders_placed and placed_by, for example. (These and other relationships are represented by dotted lines in Figure 3.1.)*

---

A relationship (like an attribute) is not an object in its own right. It does not have an object identifier, and can only be referred to by first referring to the object that contains it.

## THE BEHAVIOUR OF AN OBJECT

An object's behaviour is defined by a set of **operations.** These operations define all the things that can be done to that object and therefore define the object's **interface**. The object operations provide the only means by which an object's state can be accessed and manipulated, and are used to model the ways in which the entity represented by the object behaves.

---

**EXAMPLE 3.9**

*The behaviour of an object that represents a salesperson comprises a set of operations which model the ways in which a salesperson behaves. For example, the behaviour will be defined by operations which access, and possibly modify, the state of the salesperson object to represent what happens when the salesperson is paid, or takes a sales order from a customer.*

---

When executed, an operation can receive certain objects as **parameter values** and will return an object as the **operation value**. For example, a promote operation on an object which represents an employee may take, as a parameter value, a character string literal which describes the new post to which the employee has been promoted, and will return a Boolean literal (i.e., one which takes the value true or false) which indicates whether the operation has executed successfully or not. Another operation, age, which determines the age of an employee, will not receive any parameter values but will return a number computed from the value of the date of birth attribute in the object's state.

In general, there are two types of operation:

1) **update operations**, which modify the state of an object. Update operations model changes that happen to the entity represented by the object, such as a customer's change of address, or adding a new telephone number to a list;
2) **retrieval operations**, which query the state of an object. These are necessary in order to determine the current state of the world in which the organisation that the object database serves must operate. Retrieval operations could be used, for example, to determine the credit status of a customer, prior to accepting his sales order.

The Object Data Model currently does not distinguish between update and retrieval operations, and this can cause problems. For example, a **side effect** of retrieving the value returned by an update operation is that the state of an object is changed, even if the user is interested only in the returned value. This means, for example, that hypothetical questions, such as "what would Ridley's salary be if we promote him to Head of Department? ", need to be handled carefully.

An operation can also be associated with one or more **exception objects**. An exception object represents an exceptional event that can occur when operations are executed, such as executing the promote operation on an employee object, but to a non–existent post. An operation can terminate by executing one of the operations of the relevant exception object when an exceptional event occurs. Exceptions are typically used to handle error conditions.

### BUILT–IN PROPERTIES AND OPERATIONS
In addition to those properties and operations defined by the object database designer, there are others which are built into the Object Data Model. For example, there are built–in operations to provide general services for all objects (to delete objects, or test for object equivalence), attributes (to assign and retrieve the attribute values), relationships (to create, delete, modify, and traverse relationships), and operations (to execute them and to terminate execution in various ways).

## 3.2 OBJECT TYPES
Objects which have the same characteristics can be catagorised into **object types**. The term type will be familiar to programmers. In programming languages, such as Pascal, C, C++, Smalltalk, or Java, every variable is assigned a type. The type of a variable defines the set of values that the variable can be assigned and the operations that can be applied to it. For example, if a variable called ivar of type integer is to be used in a Pascal program, it must first be declared as:

```
    integer      ivar;
```

This declaration signifies that ivar may take any of the set of integer values that can be represented, and that the integer operations supported by Pascal, (+, -, *, etc.) can be applied to ivar.

Similarly, objects which have the same characteristics, i.e., they can take state values from the same set of possibilities, and the same behaviour, i.e., the same operations can be applied to them, can be categorised as belonging to the same object type. Each object is an **instance** of the object type on which it was defined. The set of all instances of an object type is called the object type's **extent**. New objects are created using a operation called **new** on an object which is an instance of a special type called **ObjectFactory**. (ObjectFactory is one of a number of built–in object types which provide general object database services.)

---

### EXAMPLE 3.10

*The Customer object type will define the characteristics of objects which represent customers. The individual objects are instances of the Customer object type. Their characteristics will include properties and operations. The object properties will include attributes, such as name, address, and telephone number, and relationships, such as the association between a Customer object and relevant SalesOrder objects. The characteristics will also include the operations that can be applied to Customer objects, such as place_order, change_address, change_telephone_number, and make_a_payment. The Customer object type extent contains all objects of type Customer.*

---

Categorisation of objects into types is also illustrated in Figure 3.1. Note that the top part of each box that represent an object specifies the object type, i.e., Customer, SalesPerson, SalesOrder, or Product. These type names are underlined to show that the boxes represent actual objects, i.e., an instance of the named object type, rather than the object type itself. Object type extents are represented in the figure by the boxes which contain all objects of a particular type. The top part of each extent box specifies the extent name, i.e., customers, salespersons, salesorders, and products.

An object type defines the external appearance and behaviour of the objects which are its instances, rather than the way in which they are implemented. An object type has only one interface, but may be implemented in many different ways. An object type together with an implementation is called an **implementation class**.

In programming languages, types are chosen so as to best characterise the information represented by the program variables. For example, if a program must count occurrences of something, the variable used will be of type integer, because we are only interested in whole numbers. Similarly, object types are defined so as to best characterise the information being represented—an object type is used to model as closely as possible the entities represented by its instances. An advantage of this is that object types constrain users from manipulating objects in ways which are inconsistent with their meaning.

The Object Data Model provides an extensible type system—the model includes a number of built–in types, and from these the object database designer can construct the set of new types which best model the information that is to be represented. A primary aim of an object database designer is to define the set of types which best mimics the bit of the world which the object database will represent.

When designing an object database it is necessary to define an object type for each set of similar entities that are to be represented in the database. For example, in the Bruddersfield Bikes sales processing object database (see Figure 3.1) it is necessary to define object types for representing salespersons, customers, products, and sales orders. When the object database is actually implemented and used, it is populated with instances of those object types.

The set of object type definitions for a database is called the **object database schema**. The purpose of the object database is to stores objects which are instances of the types described in its schema, such that they can be shared and used by all relevant users.

## DEFINITION OF AN OBJECT TYPE

The definition of an object type specifies the appearance of the type to its users, i.e., the types of value its instances can contain (state), and the operations that can be applied to them (behaviour). However, a type definition does not specify the way in which the type is implemented. The implementation is specified separately, using a programming language extended to include object database facilities (see Chapter 7).

An object type's definition must specify values for properties of the object type and the characteristics, i.e., the properties (attributes and relationships) and operations, of the objects which are instances of that object type. An object type definition is therefore in three parts:

- **type properties;**
- **instance properties;**
- **instance operations.**

Note that an object type definition does not provide a complete definition of the object type, since it does not define what the operations on instances do. It is necessary to examine the code that implements an operation to establish exactly what that operation does.

The Object Data Model distinguishes between two aspects of an object type.

1) **The type's interface**—this first aspect is the object type's abstract appearance, i.e., the features of the type by which users can interact with its instances. A definition of these features is called an **interface definition**. An interface of an object type defines only information relating to the behaviour of the type's instances. It does not provide the additional information necessary to create instances of the type. The term **interface** is therefore used to refer to an object type which cannot be instantiated. Interfaces can be useful, even though it is not possible directly to create instances of them, because their characteristics can be utilised by other object types (see Extends relationships).

2) **Object creation**—the second aspect is the ability to create objects which are instances of the object type. A type which can be instantiated is defined by a **class definition**. A class definition defines both the state and behaviour of the object type. It include state–specific information, not included in an interface declaration, such as the name of the type's extent and the instance properties used as object keys. The term **class** refers to an instantiatable object type

(Note the Object Data Model has different meanings for the terms class and implementation class. The former is an instantiable object type, whereas the latter is an object type together with its implementation.)

Classes and interfaces refer only to mutable objects, not literals. Many literal types are built into the Object Data Model to represent values, such as numbers and text. Other structured literals can be defined which are combinations of other literals. These are defined by **literal definitions**. A literal definition defines objects which are formed by combining other objects (see Section 3.3, Representation of composite entities). A literal definition defines only information relating to the state of the composite objects, i.e., it specifies the component object types and the way in which they are combined, but does not specify any operations upon them.

## NOTATIONS FOR DENOTING OBJECT TYPES

We shall use two notations for describing object types, one graphical and the other textual. The graphical representation is used primarily in the design of object databases (see Chapter 8). An object type can be represented graphically as a box, as shown in Figure 3.3.

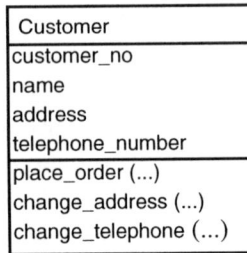

```
┌─────────────────────────────┐
│ Customer                    │
├─────────────────────────────┤
│ customer_no                 │
│ name                        │
│ address                     │
│ telephone_number            │
├─────────────────────────────┤
│ place_order (...)           │
│ change_address (...)        │
│ change_telephone (...)      │
└─────────────────────────────┘
```

Figure 3.3 A graphical representation of an object type

The **object type box** is subdivided into three: the top part gives the type name and properties; the middle part describes the instance attributes; and the bottom part describes the instance operations. (The Figure 3.3 example provides only a sketch of an object type. However, this notation also allows us to include more detailed information, such as the types of the attributes and details of the operation parameters.)

The general style of the textual notation that we will use for denoting object type definitions is illustrated by the example class definition in Figure 3.4.

```
class Customer
(        extent customers
         keys   customer_no,  (name,address)
{
         attribute String        customer_no;
         attribute String        name;
         attribute String        address;
         attribute Integer       telephone_no;
```

Figure 3.4 An example ODL interface declaration

```
relationship Set<SaleOrder> orders_placed
        inverse SalesOrder::placed_by;
Boolean place_order (in OrderDetails new_order)
        raises (no_such_product);
Boolean change_address (in String new_address
Boolean change_telephone (in Integer
        new_telephone_number)
        raises (no_such_telephone_number);
}
```

Figure 3.4 An example ODL interface declaration—completed

This textual notation is based on the **Object Definition Language** or **ODL** described in Chapter 4. ODL is an object database language and is used in conjunction with other computer languages to implement actual object databases. The specific role of ODL is to define database schemas.

The details of the definitions in Figure 3.4 are not important at this stage and will be explained later. However, note that the general structure, and also that of the object type box, corresponds to the three parts of an object type definition, i.e., type properties, instance properties (attributes and relationships), and instance operations.

Note also that the following conventions are used:

1) we have chosen to embolden the keywords, such as **attribute** and **relationship** so as to distinguish them from names devised by the object database designer.
2) type names start with upper case letters; other names start with lower case.

In general, the textual notation provides precise definitions of object types for implementation purposes and the graphical notation provides summary representations for explanatory and design purposes.

## LITERAL TYPES

Literals are immutable objects and are used to represent values (see Section 3.1, The object: mutable objects and literals). In general, literal object types do not need to be defined. A set of literals (corresponding to the constants which are pre–defined in most programming languages) automatically exists within the Object Data Model. Similarly, the object types for the different categories of literal pre–exist and need not be defined. The Object Data Model includes **simple** (or **atomic**) **literal types** such as:

- **Integer**—these are whole numbers, e.g., 1, 2, -5, -19. (Integer literals may be **long** or **short, signed** or **unsigned.**)
- **Float**—these are decimal numbers, e.g., 1.52, -0.3456, 2.000. (Floating point literals may be single (**float**) or double (**double**) precision.)
- **Boolean**—these are the values true and false.
- **Char**—these are single characters, e.g., a, b, c, d, e, @, #, !.
- **String**—these are character strings, e.g., "Eaglestone", "Ridley".
- **Octet**—these are bit strings and are used to represent "raw" untyped data.

In addition, more complex values can be represented by combining literals defined on the above atomic literal types. For example, a date can be formed by combining the numbers which represent the day, month, and year. The Object Data Model's built–in **structured literal types** include the following:

- **Date**—e.g., 22 03 1995.
- **Time**—e.g., 22:30.
- **Timestamp**—e.g., [22 03 1995, 22:30].
- **Interval**—e.g., [22:30, 23:00].

The ways in which objects can be combined to represent structured entities will be discussed later (see Section 3.3, Representation of composite entities).

New literal types can be defined (other than those based on characters and numbers) using **Enumeration** (or **enum**). Enumeration is called a **type generator** because it is not a type, but can be used to create a new type. This is done by specifying the set of values contained in the type. For example, the declaration:

```
enumeration Sex {male, female}
```

creates a new type called Sex which can have two instances, i.e., the literals, male and female.

The object database designer can define other new literal types, for example, to represent employee number values, by combining the above built–in literal types.

## INHERITANCE

Object types which can be instantiated are defined by **class definitions**, whereas an **interface definition** defines an object type which cannot be instantiated. A class definition specifies the characteristics of the type instances, either explicitly or by specifying other object types from which characteristics are **inherited**. A class can inherit characteristics from other object types in two ways:

1) **Subtype/supertype relationships**—a class or interface definition can inherit behaviour from one or more interfaces.
2) **EXTENDS relationships**—a class can extend another class (its extender class) ,in which case it inherits both behaviour and state from that class.

The following analogy provides a general explanation of the differences between classes and interfaces and the above two types of inheritance.

Consider the situation where vehicles are designed and manufactured. We can describe two different types of vehicle, performance cars and vans, by defining their controls and facilities for the driver. These descriptions are analogous to object type definitions, since they describe how the vehicles (the objects) can be used without explaining how they will be constructed (the implementations). Furthermore, these descriptions are too general to provide a specification for building an actual car or van (instantiating the type). The descriptions are therefore analogous to interfaces.

If we now wish to design an actual vehicle, a high performance commercial vehicle, we must provide additional details, including details of the vehicle's construction (its implementation). The description of a vehicle (a type definition) from which we can build actual vehicles (objects) is analogous to a class. The high performance commercial vehicle that we have specified includes features of a performance car and also of a van—this is analogous to inheritance of behaviour from interfaces using subtype/supertype relationships (e.g., a performance commercial vehicle is a subtype of performance car and also of van).

If we later wish to create special editions of the performance commercial vehicle, we must extend its description (the class definition) in various ways to include additional characteristics, such as a sunroof or spotlights. A vehicle built using an extended description will be an extended version of the performance commercial vehicle (it will be a performance commercial vehicle with added or refined characteristics). This is analogous to a class inheriting characteristics from another class via an EXTENDS relationship.

Inheritance through subtype/supertype and EXTENDS relationships is described in detail in the following subsections.

### SUBTYPE/SUPERTYPE RELATIONSHIPS

Object types can be related by subtype/supertype relationships. Two object types are related in this way if one (the subtype) is a refinement of the other (the supertype). This type of relationships is called an **is_a** or a **generalisation–specialisation** relationship. For example, if Person is a supertype of Employee we can say Employee *is_a* Person. Alternatively, we can say that Person is a generalisation of Employee and Employee is a specialisation of Person.

A subtype may have more than one supertype automatically **inheriting** all of their characteristics (operations, attributes, and relationships). This means that any operation that can be applied to an instance of a particular type can also be applied to instances of its subtypes. In other words, instances of a subtype inherit the behaviours of instances of it supertypes.

The supertypes of a class must be interfaces, i.e., types defined by interface definitions, not class definitions. However, an interface may also have other interfaces as its supertypes. A class cannot have subtypes. (If we wish to specialise a class in some way then we must use the EXTENDS relationships described in the following subsection.) Subtype/supertype relationships therefore provide a mechanism by which a class (an instantiable object type) can inherit and implement the behaviours of zero, one, or more general interfaces (uninstantiable object types).

Inheritance from more than one supertype is called **multiple inheritance**. There is a potential problem with multiple inheritance—what happens to a subtype if two of its supertypes have characteristics with the same name? The Object Data Model resolves this problem by simply not allowing this situation to occur. The database designer is responsible for avoiding this form of naming conflict.

---

*EXAMPLE 3.11*

*As an example of multiple inheritance, consider the following situation. Bruddersfield Bikes give special discounts to members of staff. This situation can be represented by a Employee_Customer class, with two supertype interfaces, Employee-IF and Customer-IF. (Note our convention of using the suffix, "-IF", to denote an interface, rather than a class.) Instances of Employee_Customer therefore will have all of the characteristics from both Employee-IF and Customer-IF. In addition they will have their own special characteristics, such as a staff_discount_card attribute. Other classes may also inherit characteristics from the interfaces. For instance, the TradeCustomer class will be a subtype of Customer. Inherited operations, such as place_order and make_payment, will have different implementations for Employee_Customer and TradeCustomer.*

---

A subtype/supertype relationship is denoted graphically by linking object type boxes with an arrow which points from the subtype to the supertype. For example, Figure 3.5 represents the situation described in Example 3.11. The five object types, Person-IF, Customer-IF, Employee-IF, Employee_Customer, and TradeCustomer, are represented by the boxes. The connecting arrows show that Person-IF is a supertype of both Customer-IF and Employee-IF, or conversely, Customer-IF and Employee-IF are subtypes of Person-IF. Customer-IF and Employee-IF are supertypes of Employee_Customer. Customer-IF is also a supertype of TradeCustomer.

We specify the supertypes in the object type declaration. The supertypes are listed after naming the object type. In the above example, Person-IF, Customer-IF, and Employee-IF must be defined as interfaces (a supertype must be an interface, not a class), Employee_Customer and TradeCustomer are classes (which can be instantiated). The first lines of the interface and class definitions of the four object types in Figure 3.5 will therefore be:

```
interface Person-IF
interface Employee-IF : Person-IF
interface Customer-IF : Person-IF
class Employee_Person:Employee-IF,Customer-IF
class Trade_Customer : Customer-IF
```

A consequence of subtype/supertype relationships is that an object may have many types. Though an object can be defined on only one class, the object is automatically also an instance of its supertypes and therefore is a member of the extents of the supertypes—the extent of a type is a subset of the extent of each of its supertypes.

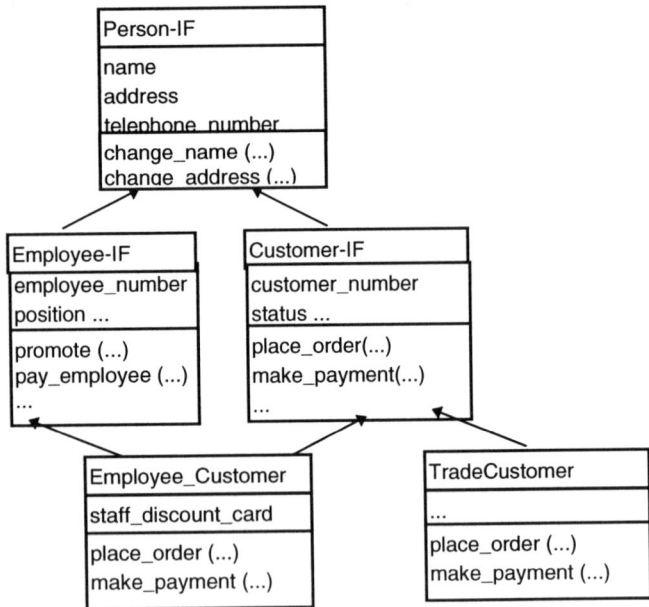

Figure 3.5 The object type graph for Employee_Customer

A subtype/supertype relationship signifies the following:

1) An object subtype automatically **inherits** all of the attributes, relationships and operations of the object types which are its

supertypes. For example, both Customer-IF and Employee-IF inherit the characteristics of Person-IF; i.e.:
- attributes—name, address, and telephone_number;
- operations—change_name, change_address, etc.;
- any relationships defined for Person.

2) An object subtype can have **additional characteristics**. For example, Customer-IF has customer_number and status attributes and a place_order operation, in addition to those characteristics inherited from Person-IF.

3) An object subtype can **refine** the characteristics it inherits from its supertypes by redefining them. For example, the Employee_Customer type redefines the inherited Customer-IF operations, place_order, and make_payment, because these procedures are different for a customer who is also an employee.

4) An object is defined on a class but is also an instance of each of its supertypes. For example, an object which represents a customer who is also an employee will be defined on the Employee_Customer type, and will therefore be an instance of Employee_Customer and of its supertypes, Employee, Customer, and Person, by virtue of the subtype/supertype relationships.

5) An object is a member of the extent of the type upon which it is defined, and also of the extents of each of its supertypes. An instance of Employee_Customer is a member of the Employee_Customer extent and also the Customer-IF, Employee-IF, and Person-IF extents.

Some subtype/supertype relationships are built into the Object Data Model itself. For example, the user–defined mutable object types implicitly inherit the characteristics of the most general object type, **Object** (see Figure 3.6). A consequence of the built–in relationships in Figure 3.6 is that all user–defined mutable objects inherit characteristics which are common to all mutable objects, including the operations:

1) **delete**—when an object executes the delete operation it destroys itself;

2) **same_as?**—this operation takes an object identifier as a parameter, and returns true if that is the identifier of the object; otherwise false;

3) **copy**—creates a new equivalent object, i.e., one with the same type and state.

```
┌─────────────────────────┐
│Object                   │
├─────────────────────────┤
│...                      │
├─────────────────────────┤
│delete ( )               │
│same_as? (...)           │
│copy (...)               │
└─────────────────────────┘
```

```
┌──────────────────┐      ┌──────────────────┐
│Customer          │      │SalesOrder        │
├──────────────────┤      ├──────────────────┤
│...               │      │...               │
├──────────────────┤      ├──────────────────┤
│...               │      │...               │
└──────────────────┘      └──────────────────┘
```

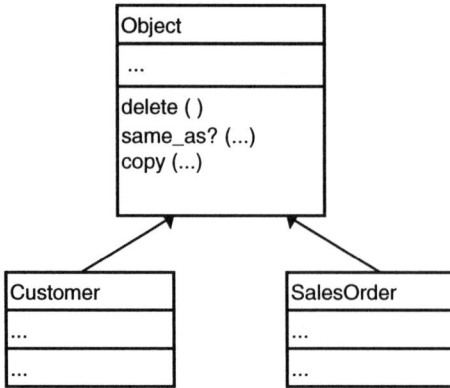

Figure 3.6 Built–in subtype/supertype relationships

The full built–in type hierarchy is given in Figure 3.13 at the end of this chapter as part of Section 3.5, Summary.

### EXTENDS RELATIONSHIPS

The Object Data Model also includes another form of inheritance between object types, called the **EXTENDS relationship**. EXTENDS works in a similar way to subtype/supertype relationships, but with the restriction that it relates only classes and supports only single–inheritance. EXTENDS allows classes to be specialised. A class which extends another class will automatically inherit all of the characteristic (attributes, relationships, and operations) of the extender class (or superclass). In addition the extended class (or subclass) may define its own attributes, relationships, and operations.

Unlike the subtype/supertype relationship, where multiple inheritance is allowed, the EXTENDS relationship allows an object class to extend just one object class. This restriction is a pragmatic one which avoids inefficiencies and ambiguities which arise when one instantiable type inherits from many other instantiable types (these will be familiar to C++ programmers).

EXTENDS and subtype/supertype relationships are useful in those cases where objects have similar states but different behaviours. For example, consider the situation where customers are represented by a class called Customer. We can extend the Customer class to form TradeCustomer and PrivateCustomer classes, since both will include characteristics such as customer number, as well as specialised characteristics. (In this way we reuse the Customer class definition.) In addition, behaviour associated with the extended classes can be inherited respectively from the interfaces, Business-IF and Person-IF, using subtype/supertype relationships (see Figure 3.7).

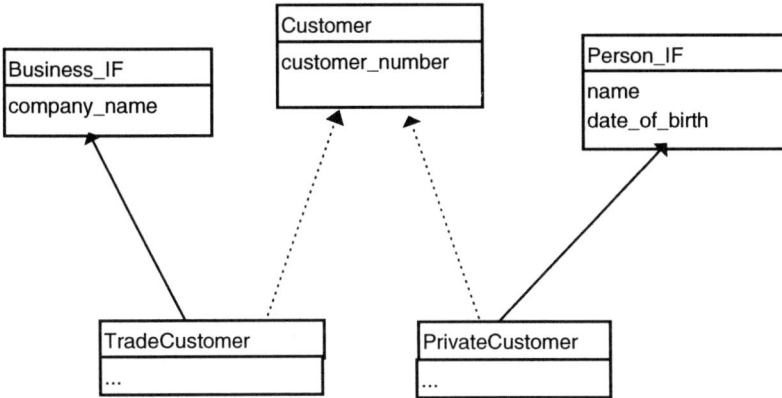

Figure 3.7 Example uses of the EXTENDS and subtype/supertype relationships.

A keyword, **extends**, is used in the textual notation to specify an EXTENDS relationship within a class definitions. For example, the class definitions for the object classes, TradeCustomer and PrivateCustomer, in the above example will start with the following declarations:

```
class TradeCustomer extends Customer
     : Business_IF

class PrivateCustomer extends Customer
     : Person_IF
```

## LATE BINDING

Late binding is a mechanism whereby the above inheritance relationships can be used to allow very general queries to be applied to objects in a very specific way.

Every operation within a type definition must have a unique name, but the same operation name can be used in other type definitions. This has already been illustrated in Example 3.11 where, for instance, Customer-IF, TradeCustomer, and Employee_Customer all have an operation called place_order. Giving different operations the same name is called **operation overloading** and is often a useful thing to do. For example, different procedures for placing an order are needed for a trade customer and for a customer who is also an employee.

Operation overloading is exploited when an operation is invoked upon each object in a collection which contains objects of different types, using a technique called **operation name resolution** or **late binding**. Late binding enables the ODBMS to choose which implementation of an operation is to be executed on an object-by-object basis. The operation that is executed is the one defined for the most specific type of the object to which the operation is applied. The most specific type is the class on which it was defined, since that class will specify *all* of the characteristics of the object.

Operation name resolution works in the following way:

Consider the situation where salaried and waged employees are represented respectively as instances of the Salaried and Waged classes, which both extend the Employee class (see Figure 3.8).

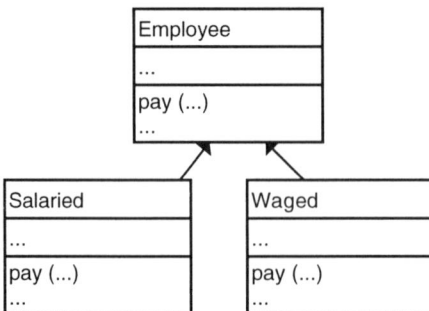

Figure 3.8 An example subtype/supertype hierarchy

Both classes, Salaried and Waged, inherit the pay operation from the Employee class. This operation computes the pay for an employee, but the operation is redefined for Salaried and Waged, since pay is computed differently for these two categories of employee. The Employee implementation of pay is used to calculate payment for staff who are neither waged nor salaried, such as casual labour. We therefore have three operations, each with the same name, pay. This is an example of operation overloading.

A consequence of the EXTENDS (subclass/superclass) relationships (in Figure 3.8) is that each instance of Salaried has two types, Salaried and Employee—Salaried the most specific type, Employee the most general. Similarly, instances of Waged have two types, Waged and Employee.

In order to compute the pay of employees we can treat all of the objects which represent them as being instances of Employee, and invoke the pay operation on objects in the Employee extent. The procedure could therefore be as follows:

```
for all members, e, of Employee extent
      compute pay by executing e::pay()
```

However, different implementations of this operation must be executed for different Employee objects, depending on whether they were defined on Waged or Salaried. The selection of which implementation of the pay operation is to be executed is made by the ODBMS for each object, on the basis of its most specific type. In this way, the Waged implementation of the pay operation will be executed for objects defined on Waged and the Salaried implementation for objects defined on Salaried, even though the pay operation of Employee was invoked.

Subtype/supertype relationships and EXTENDS relationships are advantageous during the design and evolution of an object database:

1) Subtype/supertype and EXTENDS relationships can be used by the object database designer to model certain types of entity. For example, they can be used to model special case entities (e.g., a customer is a special case of a person) or entities which aggregate together the characteristics of other entities (e.g., a customer who is also an employee). An advantage is that the definitions of the supertypes are **reused** in the subtype definitions—they do not have

to be redefined. This can ease the problem of extending or modifying an object database to meet changing requirements.

2) Operation overloading and name resolution mean that new specialisations of types and their operations can be defined without disrupting existing applications. In the above example, addition of a new class, PartTimeEmployee, could be integrated into the object database by making it an extention of Employee, and redefining the pay operation. The existing procedure for computing pay for all employees would not then need changing.

## CLASSES, INTERFACES, AND INHERITANCE—A SUMMARY

- A **class** is an instantiable object type.
- An **interface** defines the instance of an abstract type (one which can not be instantiated).
- An **EXTENDS relationship** allows a class to be extended to include additional specialised characteristics.
- A **subtype/supertype relationship** allows a class or an interface to inherit behaviour from one or more interfaces.
- **Late binding** allows the most specific implementation of an operation to be executed for an object. The most specific operation is that defined by the type which species *all* of the object's properties, i.e., the class on which the object was defined.

## OBJECT TYPE PROPERTIES

Object types are themselves entities within the object database system and are represented as objects. This type of object is called a **meta object**, because it describes the characteristics of other objects. The data contained in meta objects is called **metadata** (data about data). The meta objects collectively define the **object database schema** and are used by the ODBMS to define and access objects contained in the object database. The metadata is stored in a **Schema Repository** for use by tools and application programs. Objects in the Schema Repository are accessed in the same way that other objects, such as those that represent customers and sales orders in the case study object database are accessed. (Those interested should refer to [Cattell 97] for detailed specifications of the meta objects of the Object Data Model.)

The meta objects which represent an object type have properties of their own. The values for these are specified in the **type properties** part of a class definition. The following properties can be specified.

1) **supertypes**—the supertypes of an interface or class (see the previous section, Subtypr/supertype Relationships);
2) **extender**—the class that is extended by the specified object type (see previous section, EXTENDS Relationships);
3) **extent**—the name of the object type's extent. The extent of an object type is the collection of its instances. Naming the extent is optional. If the extent is named, the convention is that the object type has a singular descriptive name, e.g., Customer, and the extent has the plural name, e.g., customers;
4) **keys**—the instance properties that are to act as object keys. The value of a key will be unique for each instance of the object type (see Section 3.1, The object: attributes).

Type properties are specified in a class declaration as illustrated below:

```
class Employee_Customer extends Employee
      : Customer_IF
(      extent        employee_customers
       key           employee_number,
                     (name, address))
```

Note that the extender object type is specified after the object type name, followed by the supertypes. The extent name is, by convention, the plural of the type name. Also by convention, the type name starts with an upper case letter, and the extent (which is an object, not a type) starts with a lower case letter. There can be many keys, each of which may be simple, i.e., comprising one property (e.g., employee_number), or complex, i.e., comprising a set of properties (e.g., name and address).

The above type properties, with the exception of the supertypes, concern a type's state (i.e., its instances), rather than its behaviour. Accordingly, they are specified in class definitions and not in interface definitions. The header of an interface definition will specify only the supertypes (which concern behaviour inherited from other types).

## INSTANCE PROPERTIES

An object type's instance properties are the attributes and relationships of the instances of the object type (these must be specified in both interface and class definitions).

Each **attribute** has a name and a type which defines the set of values that can be assigned to the attribute. All attributes have literal types. The notation for defining attributes within an object type interface declaration is illustrated in the following example.

---

### EXAMPLE 3.12

*The instance properties of an object type which represents employees will include attributes to represent the numbers used to identify each employee within the company, the employees' names, and dates of birth. The instance properties part of the Employee object type interface or class declaration will therefore include the following attribute specifications:*

```
attribute Integer        employee_number;
attribute String         employee_name;
attribute Date           date_of_birth;
```

*Note that Integer, String, and Date are literal types, and employee_number, employee_name ,and date_of_birth are attribute names.*

---

**Relationships** associate objects with other objects in order to represent associations between the entities they model. There are two ways of looking at an association. For example, a marriage association can be viewed from the perspective of the husband or the wife. Similarly, there are two ways of viewing an inter–object relationship—a relationship which associates Husband and Wife objects relates a Husband object to an associated Wife object, but also relates the Wife object to the Husband object via the **inverse relationship**, as shown below:

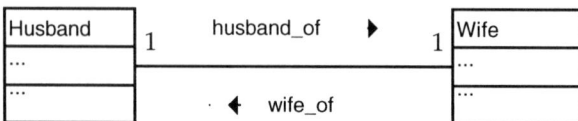

Note that the diagrammatic representation depicts relationships as lines which link the participating object type boxes. The paths are named and arrow heads indicate the direction of each path. Numbers at each end of a relationship line indicate how many objects can participate in an instance of the relationship (the above example represents monogamous marriage, i.e., a one–to–one relationship).

The specification of relationships within object type interface declarations reflects this two–way perspective of associations. Each relationship is defined as a property of an object type, not as an object in its own right. Relationships themselves are unnamed, but the paths by which a relationship can be traversed are named. Each relationship declaration therefore specifies one or two descriptive (path) names. One of the names is used to label the path, provided by the relationship, to the associated object(s). Optionally, a second name labels the path, provided by the inverse relationship, from the associated object(s). Only the named paths can be navigated by programs.

As an example, consider the relationship which associates objects of types Employee and Project. This relationship could have the names works_on and project_team, respectively, to name the relationship paths from each Employee object to the related Project object(s), and the inverse relationship paths from each Project object to the related Employee object(s). This is an example of a many–to–many relationship, since employees may work on many projects, which in turn may have teams of many employees. This many–to–many relationship also allows for situations where employees are not assigned to any projects and where certain projects do not yet have a project team.

A relationship must be specified within the definition of the object type(s) from which it defines a path. The relationship specification will declare the name of the relationship path, and optionally the name of the inverse relationship path. The relationship specification will also declare the relationship type. A relationship type is the type of the associated object or collection of objects. The value of a relationship can be thought of as the object identifier(s) of the associated object(s). The following example illustrates how a relationship is declared in an object type interface declaration.

---

*EXAMPLE 3.13*

*A sales order is associated with the customer who placed that order. The state of the object which represents that sales order will therefore include a relationship which associates it with the relevant Customer object. This is an example of a many–to–one relationship, since many sales orders can be related to one customer. This relationship is defined within the interface or class definition, for SalesOrder, as:*

> **relationship** Customer placed_by
> **inverse** Customer::has_placed;

---

Note that the relationship definition in Example 3.13 specifies the type of the relationship as Customer, i.e., the type of the object to which instances can be associated. The definition gives the paths from SalesOrder objects to associated Customer objects a name, placed_by, and also names the inverse relationships, has_placed, by which Customer objects are associated with the SalesOrder objects. The name of the inverse relationship is preceded by Customer:: to show that it is defined in the interface declaration for the Customer object type.

This relationship in Example 3.13 is represented graphically in Figure 3.9. The symbols at either end of the relationship line (* and 1) show that it is a many–to–one relationship, i.e., each instance of the relationship can relate many SalesOrder objects to one Customer object.

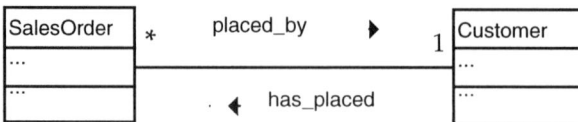

```
┌────────────┬──┐          placed_by      ▶   ┌─┬──────────┐
│ SalesOrder │* │                              │1│ Customer │
├────────────┴──┤                              ├─┴──────────┤
│ ...           │                              │ ...        │
├───────────────┤          ◀  has_placed      ├────────────┤
│ ...           │                              │ ...        │
└───────────────┘                              └────────────┘
```

Figure 3.9 The SalesOrder/Customer relationship

The number of instances that can participate in a relationship is called the relationship **cardinality**. Relationship cardinalities can be:
- one–to–one (e.g., between a married couple);
- one–to–many (e.g., between a mother and her children)
- many–to–many (e.g., between parents and their children).

## INSTANCE OPERATIONS

Each instance operation has a name and a type. An operation type defines the types of the objects accepted as parameters and the type of the object returned by the operation—the operation value. The type of an operation is called its **operation signature**. In addition, each operation has a meaning or **semantics**. The semantics of an operation is a declaration of what it does when it is executed. For example, the signature of an operation, add, that adds two integers, x and y, and returns the sum, z, can be expressed as:

$$\text{add} : (\text{x: integer, y: integer}) \rightarrow \text{z: integer}$$

The meaning of this add operation is defined by the code that implements it, or by some formula which establishes the relationship between what goes into the operation and the result, e.g., $z - x = y$.

The Object Data Model does not include any formal (mathematical) way of specifying operation semantics—it is necessary to inspect the code that implements an operation to find out exactly what it does. However, the Object Data Model does require that operation signatures are declared as part of the relevant object type definitions.

The declaration of the signature for the above add operation is as follows:

```
Integer add (in Integer x, in Integer y);
```

Note that the type of the object returned by the operation precedes the operation name. Also, each of the operation parameters has a name, a type, and is preceded by **in** to indicate that it is an input parameter. Example 3.14 further illustrates operation signatures.

---

## EXAMPLE 3.14

*The behaviour of the objects of type Employee comprises operations which model ways in which an employee behaves. For example, the behaviour will be defined by operations which access and possibly modify the state of an Employee object to represent what happens when the employee is promoted or paid. The definition of the Employee type may therefore include the following operation definitions:*

```
void promote
(in String new_position_in_company)
        raises (no_such_position);
Money compute_pay
(in Integer hours_worked, overtime);
```

*Note that promote returns a value of type void, which means that no value is returned when promote is executed. The input parameter is an object of type String, named new_position_in_company. The compute_pay operation returns an object of type Money, and takes two objects of type Integer, called hours_worked and overtime as input parameters. Note also that the raises clause of the definition of promote associates this operation with the no_such_position exception. Exception objects are used to model exceptional events.*

---

In Example 3.14 there are only input parameters, i.e., the parameters are used only to pass information to the operations. It is also possible for operations to return results as parameter values, in which case the parameter declaration is prefixed with the keyword **out.** Parameters which are both used to pass information to the operation and by which the operation returns information are prefixed **inout.**

## 3.3 REPRESENTATION OF COMPOSITE ENTITIES
### STRUCTURED OBJECT TYPES

Entities often have complex structures—an entity may be an assembly of many other interrelated entities. For example, a bicycle produced by Bruddersfield Bikes is a combination of the wheels, pedals, frame, etc. In the preceding sections we have seen how objects may represent associations between entities as relationships (see Section 3.1, The object: relationships). However, relationships provide a poor representation of composite entities—using relationships, a single composite entity must be represented as a collection of separate objects linked together, rather than as a single composite object. For such cases, the Object Data Model supports **structured objects**. A structured object represents a composite entity in a more natural way, as a single object. The state of that single object contains the component objects. This contrasts with the objects previously described, which are called **atomic objects** because they are not constructed from other objects. The state of an atomic object comprise only attributes and relationships, which are not objects.

Both literals and mutable objects can be either structured or atomic objects, as can be seen from the built–in subtype/supertype relationships shown in Figure 3.10.

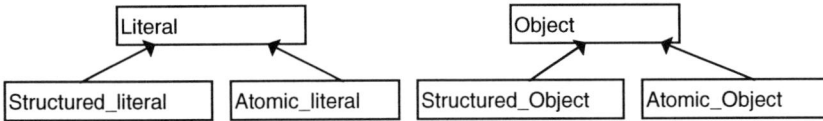

Figure 3.10 Built–in subtype/supertype relationships

The Object Data Model supports various ways of combining objects within the state of a structured object. Component objects can be combined to form sets, bags, lists, arrays and structures (or tuples). The characteristics of these constructs are illustrated in Figure 3.11 and explained below.

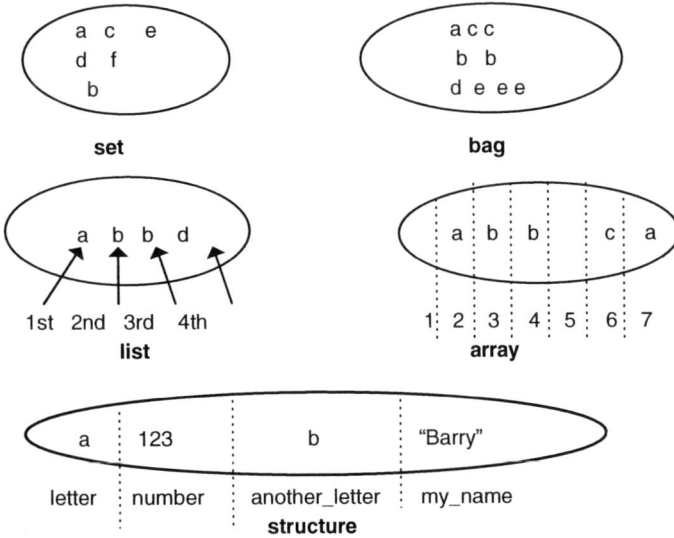

Figure 3.11 Structured types

In general, these forms of object combinations can be grouped into two categories:

Sets, bags, lists, and arrays are each collections of varying numbers of objects of the *same* type.

1) a set is an unordered collection of distinct objects—an object can occur only once in a set;

2) a bag is an unordered collection of not necessarily distinct objects—the same object can occur more than once in a bag;

3) a list is an ordered collection of not necessarily distinct objects—a list has a first object, second object, etc., and the same object can occur more than once in a list;

4) an array is a collection of indexed objects—an array can be thought of as a list of object containers which can be referred to by their position or index in the list. Each container may be empty or may contain an object.

The Object Data Model also includes a special type of set–object, called a **dictionary**. Dictionary–objects are basically lookup tables. They are sets of pairs of objects, the first acting as a key by which the second can be accessed. For example, a dictionary–object could represent a telephone directory, using Person / Telephone_number object pairs. A dictionary–object is therefore a special type of set–object, a set of structures.

A structure (or tuple) comprises a fixed number of objects, possibly of *different* types. A structure can be thought of as a fixed number of named slots, each of which can contain an object of some specified type.

The structured object types can be used freely to model complexly structured entities. This is illustrated in Figure 3.11, which includes a list of characters, "Barry", within the structure.

Structured object types are defined using **type generators**—a type generator is not an object type, but when it is provided with appropriate parameter values. A type generator creates a new object type (see also Section 3.2, Literal types, where Enumeration, another example of a type generator, was described). The Object Data Model has built into it a number of **structured object type generators**. Each of these defines a family of object types. For example, the **Set** type generator defines the family of all object types where the instance states are sets of objects, e.g., sets of SalesPerson objects or sets of Integer literals. Structured object type generators can be thought of as the "glue" with which objects can be stuck together to form models of complex things.

## COLLECTION OBJECT TYPES

The state of an instance of a collection–object type is a collection of objects, all of the same type. Five collection type generators are built into the Object Data Model. These are:

1)  **Set<T>**—for object states which are sets, i.e., unordered collections, of distinct objects of type T;
2)  **Bag<T>**—for object states which are bags, i.e., unordered collections, of objects of type T;
3)  **List<T>**—for object states which are lists, i.e., ordered collections, of objects of type T;
4)  **Array<T>**—for object states which are arrays, i.e., ordered and indexed collections, of objects of type T.
5)  **Dictionary<T>**—for object states which are sets of object pairs.

A collection–object type is specified by providing the type generators with the type of the objects that can be included in the collection. For example, a set–object type, Customers, an instance of which contains a set of objects of type Customer, is defined as follows:

```
type Customers :  Set<Customer>
```

Note that the definition includes the name of the collection–object type defined, Customers; the type generator, **Set**; and a parameter which specifies the type of object that can be included, Customer.

Set–, bag–, list–, array– and dictionary–object types are all specialised types of collection (see Figure 3.12).

The Object Data Model therefore defines them as subtypes of collection–object types. A collection–object type is, however, an **abstract type**. That is, you cannot define objects directly on a Collection type, such as **Collection<Customer>**. Instead, you could define them on one of the more specific collection–object types, such as **Set<Customer>**. The general features that would exist in **Collection<Customer>** are then inherited by virtue of the subtype/supertype relationship. The purpose of having the abstract type generator, **Collection**, is to define the properties and operations which are common to all collection–object types so that they can be inherited by them. In addition to the characteristics inherited from a Collection supertype, set–, bag–, list–, array–, and dictionary–object types each have their own special characteristics.

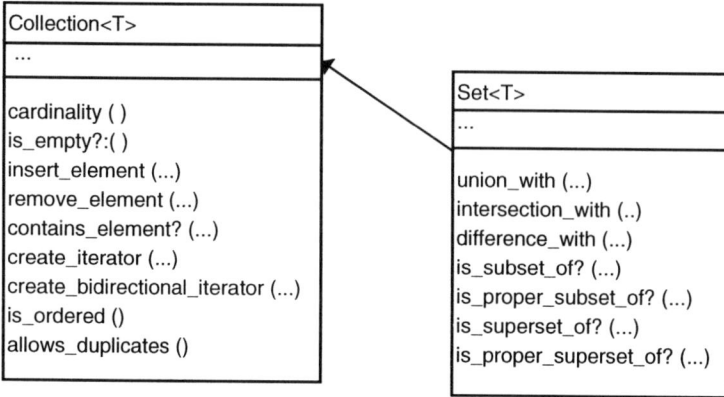

```
┌─────────────────────────────────────┐
│ Collection<T>                        │
│                                      │
│ ...                                  │──────┐
├─────────────────────────────────────┤      │      ┌──────────────────────────────────┐
│ cardinality ( )                      │      └──────│ Set<T>                           │
│ is_empty?:( )                        │             │                                  │
│ insert_element (...)                 │             │ ...                              │
│ remove_element (...)                 │             ├──────────────────────────────────┤
│ contains_element? (...)              │             │ union_with (...)                 │
│ create_iterator (...)                │             │ intersection_with (..)           │
│ create_bidirectional_iterator (...)  │             │ difference_with (...)            │
│ is_ordered ()                        │             │ is_subset_of? (...)              │
│ allows_duplicates ()                 │             │ is_proper_subset_of? (...)       │
│                                      │             │ is_superset_of? (...)            │
│                                      │             │ is_proper_superset_of? (...)     │
└─────────────────────────────────────┘             └──────────────────────────────────┘
```

Figure 3.12 The subtype/supertype relationship between Set and Collection types

The meanings of the **Collection**<T> object types operations, listed in Figure 3.12, are as follows:

1)  **cardinality**—returns the number of elements in the collection–object;
2)  **is_empty**—returns true if the collection–object does not have any elements;
3)  **insert_element**—inserts a specified object into the collection–object;
4)  **remove_element**—removes a specified object from the state of the collection–object;
5)  **create_iterator**—creates a pointer for iteratively pointing to each object in the collection–object's state (from first to last);
6)  **create_bidirectional_iterator**—creates an iterator which can be moved forwards or backwards to point to different objects in a collection–object;
7)  **is_ordered** and **allows_duplicates**—these test the properties of the collection, i.e., are the elements ordered and distinct?

When processing a collection–object it is often necessary to process each of the objects contained in its state, one at a time. To do this we must create an iterator object, using the create_iterator operation of the relevant collection–object (see above). An iterator object acts as a pointer to the object in the collection that is currently being processed. Its operations allow us to access the next, first, or last object, test if there are still more objects to be processed, and reset or delete the iterator.

Collection–objects are created using the new_of_size operation on the CollectionObjectFactory object.

## SUBTYPES OF COLLECTION OBJECT TYPES
The characteristics of the Collection type are inherited by all types of collection–object, i.e., set–, bag–, list–, array–, and dictionary–object types, but each specific collection type will also have its own special characteristics.

## SET OBJECT TYPES
A set is an unordered collection of distinct objects of the same type. A set–object comprises a set of other objects. A set–object type is created using the Set type generator as illustrated in the following example.

---

### EXAMPLE 3.15
*The following specifies a type called SalePpersons, instances of which represent sets of salespersons.*

```
type SalesPersons: Set<SalePerson>;
```

*The state of an instance of the SalesPersons type will comprise a set of instances of the SalesPerson type.*

---

A set–object type, **Set<T>**, inherits operations from **Collection<T>** (as shown in Figure 3.11). In addition, the set–object type has specific set operations which will be familiar to anyone who has studied set theory. These operations include, for example, set union, intersection, and difference. The meaning of these operations are covered later when the manipulative part of the Object Data Model is described (see Chapter 5).

## BAG OBJECT TYPES
A bag is an unordered collection of objects of the same type, but not necessarily distinct. A bag–object type is defined using the Bag type generator, as illustrated in the following example.

---

*EXAMPLE 3.16*

*The state of an instance of the  bag–object type, Telephone_calls, defined below, will be a bag of objects of type TelephoneNumber:*

```
type Telephone_calls: Bag<TelephoneNumber>;
```

---

Note that a bag is used in the above example, rather than a set, so that the same telephone number can occur more than once in a Telephone_calls object, for example, to record that a caller has telephoned more than once.

The special bag operations defined for bag–object types, in addition to the inherited Collection operations, implement operations on bags, i.e., bag union, intersection, and difference (see Chapter 5).

### LIST OBJECT TYPES

A list is an ordered bag. Objects in the list are in a sequence; there is a first, second, third, ... and the same object can occur more than once in the list, in different positions. All objects in the list are of the same type. A list–object type is defined using the List type generator as illustrated in the following example.

---

*EXAMPLE 3.17*

*The following defines a type, MachineFaults, an instance of which contains a list of objects of type MachineFault:*

```
type MachineFaults : List <MachineFault>;
```

*Note that the MachineFaults type allows the same MachineFault object to occur more than once within an instance, and in specific positions within the list. The ordering of MachineFault objects makes it possible, for example, to store them in chronological order within a MachineFaults object.*

---

In addition to the operations inherited from the collection–object type, a list–object type has a number of operations which exploit the fact that a list has an ordering. These include operations for storing, replacing, deleting, or retrieving objects at specific positions within a list.

## ARRAY OBJECT TYPES

An array is a collection of objects in which each object is stored at a particular position. However, positions in the array may be empty. An array may be thought of as a list of containers for storing objects. All objects in the array must be of the same type. An array–object type is defined using the Array type generator, as illustrated in the following example.

---

*EXAMPLE 3.18*

*The following defines a type, MachineWorkSchedule, instances of which contain an array of Process objects:*

```
type MachineWorkSchedule : Array <Process>;
```

*An instance of MachineWorkSchedule can store Process objects at different positions in the array that it contains. This feature could be used, for example, if each position in the array corresponded to a particular time interval during a day. An empty position would then indicate that the relevant machine was idle for the associated interval, whereas a Process object would indicate what the machine was being used for at that time.*

---

In addition to operators inherited from a Collection type, an array–object type also has operations to access objects at specified positions in the array, and to re–specify the number of positions in the array.

## DICTIONARY OBJECT TYPES

A dictionary is a set of structures, each of which is an object pair. The first object within each pair is unique within the dictionary. A dictionary may be thought of as a list lookup table; the first object in a pair acts as a key for accessing the second.

---

*EXAMPLE 3.19*

*The following defines a type, ProductList, instances of which contain a set of Product_Number, Product_Name object pairs:*

```
type ProductList : Dictionary
        <Product_Number, Product_Name>;
```

*An instance of ProductList can store a dictionary of product names which can be accessed by specifying a product number.*

In addition to operators inherited from a Collection type, a dictionary–object type also has operations which can add or remove an object pair (a dictionary entry), access an object (the second in a pair) by specifying its key (the first), or test if a key is present in the dictionary.

## STRUCTURE OBJECT TYPES

A structure can be thought of as a fixed number of named slots, each of which can contain an object of a particular type. A slot's name is used to refer to the object it contains. Each slot has a type which specifies the type of object it can contain. Different slots may have different types. This contrasts with collection–objects, which must contain objects of the same type. A structure–object type is defined using the **Structure** type generator, as illustrated in the following example.

### EXAMPLE 3.20

*The following defines a structure–object type, CustomerDetails, each instance of which can contain three objects: the first, called forenames, is of type **List<String>**; the second, called family_name, is of type **String**; and the third, called customer_number, is of type Integer.*

```
type CustomerDetails : Structure <
     forenames : List<String>,
     family_name :String,
     customer_no: Integer >
```

The operations defined for types created by the Structure type generator allow us to: create and initialise structure–objects; to assign objects to structure element;, to remove objects from structure elements; to retrieve objects from specified elements; and to make copies of a structure–object. (The Object Data Model also includes a number of built–in structure–object types: **date, interval, time,** and **timestamp.**)

## COMBINING STRUCTURES AND COLLECTIONS

Example 3.19 illustrates how Collection and Structure types can be combined to represent complexly structured entities. The object type, CustomerDetails is a Structure type but includes within it an element of type List<String>. In general, the structured–object type generators can be freely combined so as to generate types with structures inside structures, such as lists of bags of sets of structures.

The choice of collection or structure type is at the discretion of the object database designer, but in general, the collection used should most closely model the properties of the entity collection being represented in the object database. The characteristics of collections and structures are summarised in Table 3.1.

Table 3.1 Properties of structured types

|  | Set | Bag | List | Array | Dictionary | Structure |
|---|---|---|---|---|---|---|
| Same type | Yes | Yes | Yes | Yes | Yes | No |
| Ordered | No | No | Yes | Yes | No | No |
| Unique | Yes | No | No | No | Yes | No |
| Indexed | No | No | No | Yes | No | No |
| Named | No | No | No | No | No | Yes |

## 3.5 SUMMARY

All entities are represented as **objects**. Each object has an **identity, state** and **behaviour**, and may optionally be assigned meaningful **object names**. Values are represented by objects which cannot change their state, called **literals**. Other entities are represented by **mutable objects** which can change their state. The integration of state and behaviour within an object is called **encapsulation**.

Objects with the same characteristics can be categorised into **object types**. An object type together with an implementation is called an **implementation class**. An object type can be defined in one of three ways. An **interface declaration** specifies the behaviour of a type. A **class definition** defines the behaviour and state of a type. A **literal definition** defines only the type's state. A programmer can define objects on a class, but not on an interface. Each object is an **instance** of the object type on which it was defined. The collection of all instances of an object type is called its **extent**.

**Literal types** are built into the Object Data Model. There are predefined **atomic literal types** (for numbers, characters, text, etc.), and a number of **structured literal types**, constructed from the simple literal types (date, timestamp, etc.). In addition, new literal types can be created using the **enumeration** type generator.

Object types are related by **subtype/supertype relationships**, whereby, a subtype **inherits** the characteristics of its supertypes. Object types can also be related by **EXTENDS relationships** by which one type inherits the state of another. **Operation overloading** and **operation name resolution** allow an operation to be implemented differently for different object types, and for the most specific implementation to be executed. An object is an instance of all of its supertypes, as well as the type on which it was defined. Accordingly it is a member of its **supertype's extents**. Many object types and subtype/supertype relationships are built into the Object Data Model. The full hierarchy of built–in types is given in Figure 3.13.

An **interface declaration** defines the **type properties** (supertypes, extent and keys), **instance properties** (attributes and relationships) and **instance operation**. An object type can be represented either graphically or textually, for example, using the **Object Definition Language (ODL)**.

Objects can be **atomic** or **structured**. The state of a structured object contains other objects. The state may be a collection, i.e., a set, bag, list or array, of objects of the same type, or a **structure** (or tuple) comprising named slots each of which can contain an object, usually of different types. Structured types are created using type generators.

```
Literal
        Atomic_literal
                long
                short
                unsigned long
                unsigned short
                float
                double
                octet
                Character
                Boolean
                string
```

Figure 3.13 The Built–in type hierarchy

```
Collection_literal<T>
        Set<T>
        Bag<T>
        List<T>
        Array<T>
        Dictionary<T>
Structure_literal< ... >
        Date
        Time
        Timestamp
        Interval
        structure<...>
Object_type
        Atomic_object
        Collection_object<T>
                Set<T>
                Bag<T>
                List<T>
                Array<T>
                Dictionary<T>
        Structure< ... >
                Date
                Time
                Timestamp
                Interval
```

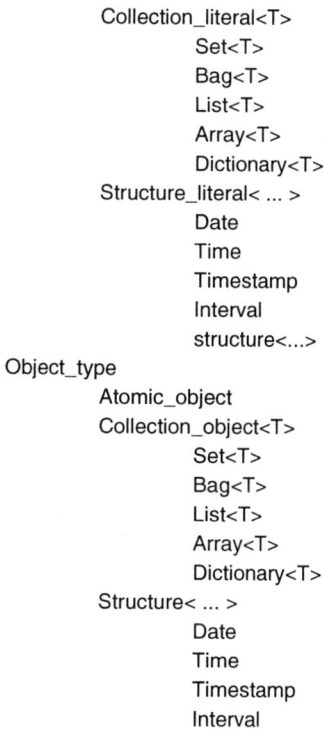

Figure 3.13 The built–in type hierarchy

# EXERCISES:

(3.1)    What is meant by "the structural part of an object data model"?

(3.2)    What is the single modelling primitive of the Object Data Model?

(3.3)    What is meant by an entity, in the context of object database design? What is the relationship between an entity and an object?

(3.4)    Identify three types of characteristic that an object has.

(3.5)    Describe three ways by which an object can be identified.

(3.6)    Give three examples of real world entities and of database entities that you would expect to represent in an object database for a football club.

(3.7)    How are values represented in an object database?

(3.8)    What is the fundamental difference between a literal and a mutable object?

(3.9)    Why would you choose to represent a product within a sales order processing object database as a mutable object?

(3.10)   What is meant by encapsulation?

(3.11)   Detail two main advantages of encapsulation.

(3.12)   How does an object database ensure that all objects are uniquely identifiable, and why is this necessary?

(3.13)   Give examples of objects which are equivalent, which have shallow equality, and which have deep equality.

(3.14)   How are object identifiers used to represent associations between entities?

(3.15)   An object's state can have two types of property. What are they?

(3.16)   Explain the difference between an object key and an object identifier.

(3.17)   Distinguish between a simple and a complex key. Give examples of each for objects which represent voters on an electoral register.

(3.18)   An attribute has a name and a type. What is the significance of an attribute's type?

(3.19)   Does an attribute have an object identifier?

(3.20)   Describe how you would represent two entities, a husband and a wife, and the marriage association between them in an object database.

(3.21)   What is the value of a relationship?

(3.22)   A relationship itself does not have a name, but can be referred to by one or two associated names. What are their significance?

(3.23)   What is meant by the behaviour of an object?

(3.24)   Explain the difference between update and retrieval operations.

(3.25)   What is an exception object, and what is it used for? Give an example application of an exception.

(3.26)   Explain how an operation on a Stock object, which represents a bin in a warehouse, would use parameters and the operation value to update the object state when the contents of the bin are added to or removed.

(3.27)   The Object Data Model does not distinguish between operations which update the object's state and those which simply return a value derived from the state. Give an example of where this can be dangerous.

(3.28)   The Object Data Model includes built–in object properties and operations. Which of these are common to all mutable objects?

(3.29)   What does an object's type signify? What are the advantages of typing objects?

(3.30)  If you are designing an object database for the administration of a football club, name four object types that you must specify.

(3.31)  Why is an object type definition also called an interface?

(3.32)  What is meant by an extensible type system?

(3.33)  An interface definition for an object type has three parts. What are they and what do they signify?

(3.34)  How does a class definition differ from a type definition? What are their respective uses.

(3.35)  Describe a Person object type, with name and address attributes, and marry and divorce operations, using both the diagrammatic and textual languages (as a class definition).

(3.36)  Give examples of built–in atomic and built–in structured literal types?

(3.37)  Define an enumerated type for representing the days of the week.

(3.38)  Explain, with the aid of a type diagram, how subtype/supertype relationships can represent the members of an orchestra (strings, wind, brass, and percussion players) as objects, but with a single declaration of properties which are common to all types of player.

(3.39)  What is meant by multiple inheritance?

(3.40)  With the aid of a type diagram, show how you can use multiple inheritance to represent a player manager of a football team (i.e., a team manager who is also a player) in an object database for administration of a football club.

(3.41)  What is the potential problem that multiple inheritance can cause, and how is it resolved in the Object Data Model?

(3.42)  Explain how subtype/supertype relationships allow definitions to be reused when an object database is extended. Illustrate your answer by considering the changes to an object database for administration of an orchestra which has changed from a string orchestra to a full symphony orchestra.

(3.43)  What is meant by operation overloading and operation name resolution?

(3.44)  Illustrate how operation overloading can be used in an object database for a computer aided design system to provide a uniform way of displaying objects (represented in various ways, i.e., as bit maps, text, and vectors) on a workstation screen.

(3.45)  All mutable objects are objects. Explain how this fact is represented within the built–in types of the Object Data Model.

(3.46)  Explain how the EXTENDS relationship differs from the subtype /supertype relationship. What are their respective uses?

(3.47)  Explain how EXTENDS and subtype/supertype relationships could be used to represent horses and cattle, which are respectively transport and food. Assume the existence of three object types, Animal, Means_Of_Transport, and Type_of_Food.

(3.48)  Conventionally, what would you call the extent of a SalesPerson object type, and what would it contain?

(3.49)  Which properties could you use as keys for an object type which represents company cars owned by Bruddersfield Bikes Ltd?

(3.50)  Declare attributes of a Customer type to represent the customer's maximum credit, their loyalty card number, and their account number.

(3.51)  Relationships in the Object Data Model are unnamed, so how do we refer to them?

(3.52)  What are the cardinalities of the following relationships?
   (i)     between products and their component parts;
   (ii)    between books and borrowers in a library;
   (iii)   between books and their author(s);
   (iv)    between books and their titles;
   (v)     between books and their publishers.

(3.53)  Define object types, using both the textual and diagrammatic notations, to represent each of the relationships in the previous question.

(3.54)  In what way does an interface declaration for an object type provide an incomplete definition of the type?

(3.55)  An object type is itself represented as an object. What are the properties of an object which represents an object type?

(3.56)  Declare an operation on a Product type which will return the value of the price attribute.

(3.57)  Declare an operation on a Customer type which will change the department of an employee by assigning a new value to the department attribute. The exception, no_such_department, will be raised if the specified new_department parameter is invalid.

(3.58)  What is an abstract type, and what is it used for?

(3.59)  Define a structure–object type and a set–object type, both to represent three addresses. Explain the differences between the types, and discuss their suitability for the application.

(3.60)  What are the consequences of  Set<T> being a subtype of Collection<T>?

(3.61)  What is an iterator object, and what is its use?

(3.62)  Define a set–object type and a bag–object type, both to represent collections of committee member names. Explain the differences between these two types, and discuss their suitability for this application.

(3.63)  Define an object type which represents a list of sets of bags of integer literals.

(3.64)  Define a structure–object type for representing the title, author(s), and publisher of books.

(3.65)  Define an Array type and a List type, both to represent entries in a diary. Explain the differences between these two types, and discuss their respective suitability for the diary application.

(3.66)  The managing director of a small company has expressed to you the view that a database is simply a collection of files, so what is all this fuss about. Write her a short report explaining how the Object Data Model differs from files.

# 4

# THE OBJECT DEFINITION LANGUAGE, ODL

This chapter describes the Object Definition Language, ODL. ODL is one of a collection of languages which are used together to implement object database systems. The purpose of ODL is to define object types which conform to the Object Data Model described in Chapter 3 (using a notation similar to ODL). In this way ODL enables application programs to access and utilise the contents of object databases. The other languages used to implement object databases and object database applications are described in later chapters (see Chapters 6 and 7).

The ODL language described here is part of the ODMG object database standards [Cattell 97], and is likely to becoming a standard feature of ODBMSs. This is not yet the case, partly because of the inertia between publication and acceptance of standards and their implementation within the products on the market—many ODBMSs, at the time of writing this book, still support their own idiosyncratic languages for defining object type interfaces, often based upon object–oriented programming languages such as C++, Smalltalk, or Java. Some object database languages are even based upon programming languages which do not themselves contain object–oriented features, such as $O_2C$, which is an extended version of C. However, most of the object database features that can be described using ODL are general to object databases and similar features will be found in other object definition languages.

Section 4.1 gives an introductory overview of ODL as an object database language. Section 4.2 then provides a practical guide in the form of an extended tutorial which navigates the reader thorough the various features of ODL and their uses. Finally, Section 4.3 gives a summary.

## 4.1 WHAT IS ODL?

Traditionally, database management systems support a number of computer languages to implement the different aspects of database systems. One language, called the **data definition language, ddl**, is used to define the database structures and another language called the **data manipulation language, dml**, is used to manipulate the data stored in the database. Actual database systems are typically constructed by embedding ddl and dml statements within conventional programming languages. It is often also possible to use the dml on its own as a **query language** for ad hoc queries to the database.

An alternative approach is also common, particularly among relational database systems. This second approach is to have a single database language which includes both data definition and data manipulation facilities, i.e., it acts as both, ddl and dml. An example is the standard relational database language, SQL [ANSI 86b, ANSI 89, ANSI 92] which includes commands for creating, modifying and removing data structures from a database, and also for querying and updating the data stored in those structures.

ODBMSs which conform to the ODMG standards follow the first strategy—different languages are used to implement object types, to define their interfaces, and to utilise them within applications. The language for defining interfaces to object types is called the **Object Definition Language** or **ODL**, and can be thought of as a ddl for object database systems. In addition, an ODMG–compliant ODBMS will support a dml called the **Object Query Language** or **OQL** (also defined in the ODMG standards), which can be used as a stand–alone query language. Other programming languages, such as C++, SmallTalk, and Java, can be used in conjunction with ODL and OQL to implement the object types and the object database applications programs (OQL is described in Chapter 6 and the ODL/OQL bindings with other programming languages are detailed in Chapter 7).

The role of ODL is summarised in Figure 4.1. Note that ODL code is sandwiched between the applications programs and the object database—ODL can be thought of as providing programs with a window into object databases. ODL is used to describe a set of object types, for use by applications, and is programmed in a ddl, whereas the applications manipulate instances of the object types, and are programmed using the dml. A ddl description of all or part of an object database is called a **schema** and defines metadata, i.e., data about the data stored, whereas the applications, written using the dml, manipulate the data itself.

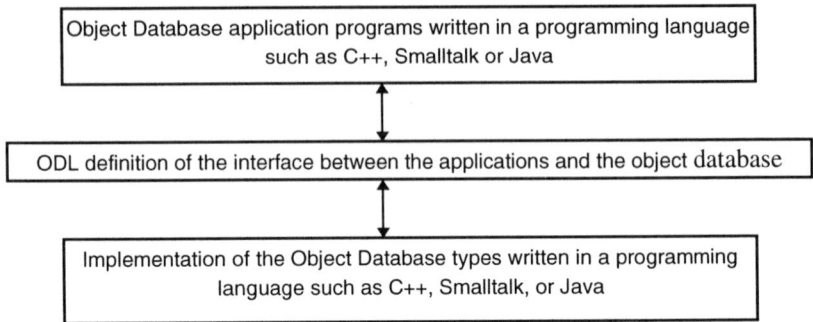

```
┌──────────────────────────────────────────────────────────────┐
│ Object Database application programs written in a programming language │
│                  such as C++, Smalltalk or Java               │
└──────────────────────────────────────────────────────────────┘
                              ↕
┌──────────────────────────────────────────────────────────────┐
│ ODL definition of the interface between the applications and the object database │
└──────────────────────────────────────────────────────────────┘
                              ↕
┌──────────────────────────────────────────────────────────────┐
│ Implementation of the Object Database types written in a programming │
│            language such as C++, Smalltalk, or Java           │
└──────────────────────────────────────────────────────────────┘
```

Figure 4.1 The relationship between ODL and other programming languages

Figure 4.2 shows the division of functions between the programming language and ODL. ODL supplies the object database with metadata, which is stored as a collection of objects (meta objects) which represent database entities (see Section 3.1, The object: database entities). The ODL also supplies applications programs written in other programming languages with interfaces to the object types that they must access and manipulate.

The facility whereby ODL, OQL, and a particular programming language can be used together is called a **binding**. ODL / OQL bindings have been defined to enable applications to be created using various programming languages, currently C++, Smalltalk, and Java (see Chapter 7).

The approach on which ODL is based contrasts with that of **persistent object–oriented programming languages**, where a programming language is extended to provide "object database"–like capabilities by making the objects defined and manipulated by the programs persistent [Aitkinson 96]. A persistent object continues to exist, even after the program that created it has terminated, until it has been explicitly deleted. The aim of a persistent object–oriented programming language is therefore to create a single programming environment for both applications and database programming.

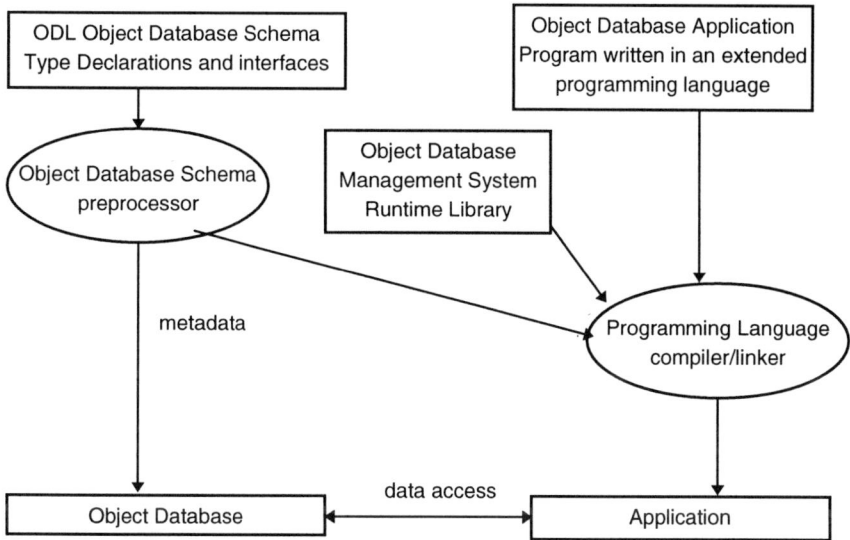

Figure 4.2 The relationship of ODL to an object database schema and applications

Persistent object–oriented programming language systems and object database systems can be viewed as being complementary. The former are appropriate for systems where the application and the object database are tightly integrated (such as Example 1.4), whereas object database systems are more appropriate for systems where the data is viewed as a separately administered resource, sharable by many applications (as in Example 1.3).

An advantage of having different database languages to implement different aspects of an object database system is that the object databases can be defined in a way which is independent of the languages that have been used to implement the object types and applications. Different languages may be appropriate for different types of application. For example, image processing applications of the museum object database in Example 1.3 are best implemented using programming languages with advanced image processing features, whereas other applications in this system require only the features of conventional languages. Two further advantages of the independence of ODL from specific programming languages are, firstly, the ability to port object database systems from one programming environment to another, and secondly, the ability to operate many object database systems together, even when different languages have been used to implement them. This latter point is important if we are to realise the potential for global access to information sources now made possible through the Internet and the World Wide Web. (The use of object databases within distributed environments, such as that provided by the Internet, is discussed in Section 10.6, Multidatabases.)

The ability to define interfaces to objects in a way which is independent of the languages that are used to implement or utilise them has a general use in distributed object–oriented environments. This ability makes it possible for many applications to share and utilise objects which provide general services. The **Object Management Group (OMG)** (not to be confused with the Object <u>Data</u> Management Group (ODMG)) has defined standards which address this general requirement. The OMG standards include an architecture for **object request brokers** (the Common Object Request Broker Architecture (CORBA)) [OMG 91] and an object interface definition language called IDL. An object request broker acts like a telephone exchange, by which messages can be passed to and between objects stored in a distributed environment. The ODL builds upon the standards defined by the OMG—ODL is an extension of IDL. (Object request brokers are discussed in greater detail in Section 10.6, Multidatabases.)

## 4.2 ODL

This section is a tutorial which guides the reader through the features of ODL, progressing from the general structure of an ODL schema, through to detailed descriptions of the language features for defining each of its components. The tutorial provides progressively more detailed ODL examples mainly based upon a simplified version of the Bruddersfield Bikes sales order processing object database (see Figure 4.3).

The general ODL syntactic rules, i.e., the rules for forming statements in ODL, are given using a notation called Extended BNF (Backus–Naur Form), in which:

- the symbol '::=' can be read as "is defined as";

- the parts of an ODL statement are described in angular brackets (e.g., <type definition>), or as they appear in the statement itself;
- square brackets are used to denote optional parts of an expression. An asterisk after the closing square bracket, ']*', indicates the optional part can occur many times;
- a vertical line is used to separate alternative parts of an expression.

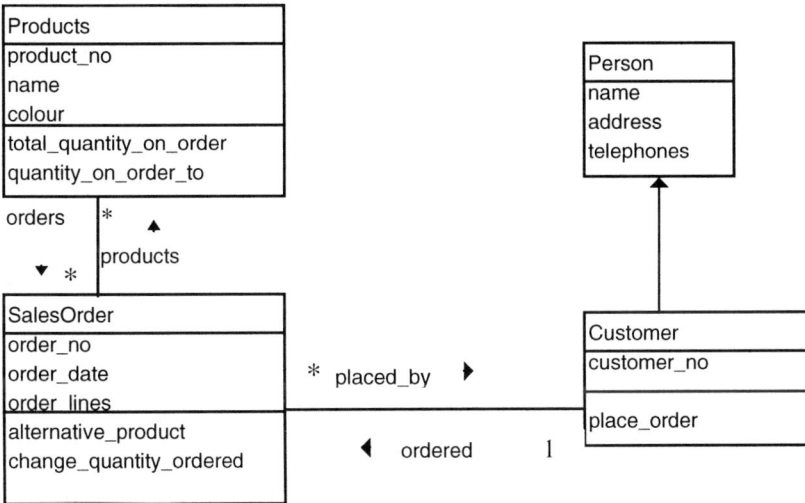

Figure 4.3 Type diagram for the sales order processing object database

The following two example Extended BNF definitions illustrate the use of these features. The first defines the syntax of an ODL clause which defines an instance property (an attribute or relationship).

```
<property declaration> ::=
      <attribute declaration>
      | <relationship declaration>
```

The above definition means that a property declaration is defined as either an attribute declaration or a relationship declaration. The next example Extended BNF definition provides more detail about how an attribute declaration is composed.

```
<attribute declaration> ::=
     [ readonly ] attribute <type definition> ;
```

The above definition means that an attribute declaration may optionally start with the keyword, **readonly**, followed by the keyword, **attribute**, followed by a type definition, and finally it will terminate with a semicolon, ';'.

The purpose of this chapter is to explain the language features of ODL, its expressiveness, and its use. However, this book is not intended to serve as a programmers' manual for actual ODBMSs and does not define the ODL syntax down to the finest detail—for that level of detail readers must refer to appropriate programmers' manuals.

## THE STRUCTURE OF AN ODL SCHEMA

The purpose of an ODL schema is to enable application programs and tools to create, access, and manipulate the contents of an object database. The schema is therefore primarily a list of **object type definitions** for each relevant object type that the database designer has designed.

Most of the object type definitions in a schema will be defined by **class definitions**. This is because instances of classes can be directly created by the programmer—a **class definition** defines the behaviour and state of an object type.

---

*EXAMPLE 4.1*

*The schema for the Bruddersfield Bikes sales order processing object database introduced in Example 1.2 will include class definitions for object types which represent customers, products, and sales orders, since objects of these types will be created to populate the object database.*

---

In some cases an object type is an abstract type—it has no instances defined on it, but instances are defined on its subtypes. In those situations the object type may be defined by an **interface definition**. An interface definition defines only the behaviour of an object type—a type defined as an interface cannot be directly instantiated.

---

*EXAMPLE 4.2*

*The Bruddersfield Bikes sales order processing object database schema, introduced in Example 1.2, may include an interface definition, Person_IF, for an object type which represents people in general. This would be an abstract type, since Person_IF objects would not be directly created, but there would be instances of the subtypes of Person_IF, such as Customer and Employee.*

The object type definitions in a schema may be for **persistent** and **transient** objects. A persistent object is retained within the object database, even after the program which created it has terminated, whereas a transient object is created by a specific program for its own use and is automatically destroyed when the program terminates.

### EXAMPLE 4.3

*A program which allows users to query stock levels of specified products must access objects of type ProductStock, which represent information about products stored within the warehouses. The program will also create and manipulate objects of type ProductReport, which contain the results of individual stock level queries. Instances of ProductStock must be **persistent** because they must be maintained to provide a continuous record of stock levels, whereas instance of ProductReport are **transient**, because they are of use only to the program while it is processing the relevant queries.*

In addition to the object type definitions (classes and interfaces), a schema will include definitions of types, constants and exceptions, not built into the Object Data Model, for use within the object type definitions or by the programs which use the schema.

The overall structure of an ODL schema is illustrated by the Bruddersfield Bikes' sales order processing object database, given in Figure 4.4. The object types represented in this schema are those also shown in Figure 4.3.

Figure 4.4 Example object database schema

```
1       module SalesOrderProcessingSchema
2       {
3           const pcode_length = 5;
4           const ccode_length = 6;
5
6           deftype Struct OrderLine
7               {String <pcode_length> product_no;
8               Long quantity;}
9
```

Figure 4.4 Example object database schema—continued

```
10          exception no_such_customer
11          {
12              String<ccode_length> customer_number;
13              String error_code;
14              String error_message;
15          }
16
17          interface Person_IF
18          {
19              attribute String name;
20              attribute Struct Address
20                  {String street, town,
21                      district, country, postcode}
22              attribute List<Unsigned Short>
23                      telephones[14];
24          }
25
26          class Customer: Person_IF
27          (extent customers
28              key customer_no) : persistent
29          {
30              readonly attribute String<ccode_length>
31                  customer_no;
32              relationship List<SalesOrder>
33                  orders_placed
34                      inverse SalesOrder::placed_by;
35              SalesOrder place_order
36                  (in List<OrderLine> details;)
37                      raise (product_doesnt_exist);
38          }
39
40          class Product
41          (extent products
42              key product_no,(name,colour)) :persistent
43          {
44              attribute String<pcode_length>
45                  product_no;
46              attribute String name;
47              attribute String colour;
48              relationship Set<SalesOrder>
49                  has_been_ordered
50                      inverse SalesOrder::ordered;
51              Long total_quantity_on_order? ();
52              Long quantity_on_order_to?
53                  (in String<ccode_length> customer_no)
54                      raises (no_such_customer);
55          }
```

Figure 4.4 Example object database schema—continued

```
56
57          class SalesOrder
58          (extent sales_orders
59              key order_no) : persistent
60          {
61              attribute String order_no;
62              attribute Date order_date;
63              attribute List<OrderLine> order_lines;
64              relationship Customer placed_by;
65              inverse Customer::places;
66              relationship Set<Product> ordered;
67              void alternative_product
68                  (in String<pcode_length> new_product,
69                   replaced_product)
70                  raises (no_such_product);
71              void change_quantity_ordered
72                  (in String<ppcode_length> product_no;
73                   in Short new_quantity;)
74                  in raises (no_such_product);
75          }
```

Figure 4.4 Example object database schema—concluded

Before looking in detail at the schema's component parts, there are points we can observe concerning the overall structure of an ODL schema.

1) The main part of the schema (lines 16–75) is a list of interface and class definitions, each of which starts with the keyword **interface** or **class**. These declare the object types in the object database.
2) The interface definitions are preceded by a few object type, constant and exception declarations, which start, respectively, with the keywords **deftype**, **const**, and **exception**;
3) The schema as a whole forms a module (denoted by the keyword module) called SalesOrderProcessingSchema. The purpose of packaging code up into a module is that it enables large sections of code to be referred to by some meaningful name.

An ODL schema is a list of definitions of interfaces, classes, literals, types, constants, exceptions, and modules.

```
<ODL schema> ::= <definition>
       [ <definition> ]*

<definition> ::=
       | < interface definition >
       | < class definition>
       | <literal definition>
       | < type declaration>
       | < constant declaration >
       | < exception declaration>
       | < module declaration >
```

As in conventional programming languages, ODL has a block structure whereby things are defined within structures, i.e., within interfaces, classes, exceptions, and modules. These structures can be nested one inside another. For example, declarations in Figure 4.4 are nested within classes, which are in turn nested within a module.

A name declared within a schema must be unique only within the structure in which it is declared. The part of a schema within which a name is guaranteed to provide a unique reference to the thing it names is called its **scope**. For example, the schema in Figure 4.4 includes two declarations of attributes called name (lines 19 and 46). Their scopes are the Person interface and the Product class definitions, respectively.

The above example illustrates how a name can be ambiguous from outside of its scope—a reference to an attribute called name could mean the name of either a product or a customer. It is therefore often necessary to qualify a name by prefixing it with the name(s) of the structure(s) within which it was declared. For example, we can refer to the two name attributes as `Customer::name` and `Product::name`. If we wish to refer to the name attributes from a different module we must also prefix the module name in order to assure uniqueness, for example, `SalesOrderProcessingSchema::Customer::name`. Note the use of the double colon ': :' to separate the different scope names.

The schema in Figure 4.4 contains examples of scoped names. For instance, line 34 refers to the placed_by relationship of the SaleOrder type from within the Customer class definition. We must therefore prefix the relationship name placed_by with the scope name, SalesOrder, i.e., `SalesOrder::placed_by`. We use scope names to refer to an object type from outside of its scope.

## OBJECT TYPE DECLARATIONS

Each **interface** and **class definition** defines the external appearance of objects of a particular type, i.e., their state properties (attributes and relationships) and the operations that can be applied to them. The ways in which the state properties and operations are implemented are not part of the definition and are defined elsewhere (see Chapter 7). An interface or class definition defines how an object can be used, but not how it works, in the same way that operating instructions for a car will specify how to drive it, but not how its internal combustion engine makes it go.

An **interface definition** defines the behaviour of an object type and must therefore specify the following information:

1)  the name of the object type;
2)  the names of the supertypes of the object type;
3)  characteristics of objects which are instances of that object type, i.e., attributes, relationships, and operations.

However, an object type defined as an interface cannot be directly instantiated—we cannot define objects to be instances of it. If we wish to directly create instances of an object type we must define it as a class. A **class definition** will include the above information and also additional information needed to create new objects:

4)  properties of the object type, i.e., the extent, keys, and the class that it extends (if any).

### CLASS DEFINITION

The syntax for a class definition is illustrated in the following example, taken from the schema in Figure 4.4.

---

EXAMPLE 4.4

*The following ODL is a class definition for an object type, Customer, instances of which represents customers of Bruddersfield Bikes.*

```
1          class Customer : Person_IF
2          (extent customers
3            key customer_no)
4          {
5            attribute String<ccode_length>
6                customer_no;
7            relationship List<SalesOrder>
8                orders_placed
9                inverse SalesOrder::placed_by;
10           SalesOrder place_order
11               (List<OrderLine> details;)
12               raise (product_doesnt_exist);
13         }
```

*The above ODL specifies that:*

1) *the class specified is for the Customer object type (line 1);*
2) *Customer is a subtype of the object type Person_IF (line 1);*
3) *the extent, i.e., the collection of instances, is called customers (line 2);*
4) *the attribute, customer_no, is a key, i.e., each instance of Customer is uniquely distinguishable from other instances of Customer by the value of customer_no (line 3);*
5) *the state includes an attribute of type String<ccode_length>, called customer_no (lines 5–6);*
6) *the state includes a relationship between instances of Customer and sets of instances of SalesOrder (lines 7–9)—the relationship from Customer to SalesOrder is called orders_placed (line 8), and the inverse relationship from SalesOrder to Customer is called placed_by (line 9);*
7) *the behaviour is an operation called place_order (lines 10–12), which takes an object of type List<OrderLine> as its parameter, and returns an object of type SalesOrder;*
8) *The place_order operation raises an exception (line 12), product_doesnt_exist, in exceptional circumstances.*

---

Example 4.4 includes only one of each type of instance characteristic (one attribute, one relation, and one operation). Class instances will typically have many of each.

The example illustrates the general form of a class definition. Note that the class has two main parts, and terminates with a semicolon ';'.

1)  The first part, the **class header**, defines the object type properties and is mainly contained in rounded brackets, ( ... ).
2)  The second part, the **class body**, defines instance characteristics and is contained in curly brackets, { ... }.

```
<class definition> ::=
    <class header> <class body> ;
```

## CLASS HEADER

Object types are themselves represented as objects and therefore have properties—the properties of an object type include its supertypes, extender class, extent, and keys. The purpose of the class header is to specify values of those properties. The general form of a class header is:

```
<class header> ::=
        class    <object type name>
        [ extends <object class name> ]
        [ <supertypes> ]
        [ <type properties> ]
```

Note that square brackets denote the optional parts of a class header, i.e., extender class, supertypes, and type properties. Minimally, a class header can be just the keyword **class**, followed by the name of the object type.

## SUPERTYPES AND EXTENDER CLASSES

A class may inherit from other object types in two ways.

1)  A class may have zero or one extender classes (see Section 3.2 Object types: EXTENDS relationships). This means that it inherits the behaviour and state of the extender class.

2) An object type (a class or interface) may also have zero, one, or more interfaces which are its **supertypes** from which it inherits behaviour (but not state, since an interface cannot be instantiated).

The way in which the extender class and the supertypes are specified in ODL is illustrated in the following example.

---

*EXAMPLE 4.5*

*One way of representing customers who are also employees is as a Customer_Employee class. This class is a special type of customer, and so it extends the Customer class. It also has two supertype interfaces, Employee_IF and AccountHolder_IF, from which it inherits bahaviour. The header of the ODL class definition for Customer_Employee must therefore start with the following definitions:*

```
class Customer_Employee
        extends Customer
            : AccountHolder_IF, Employee_IF
```

---

The name of the extender class is specified in a class definition and is preceded by the keyword **extends.** The names of an object type's supertype interfaces are listed in a class or interface definition and are separated from the object type name (or the extends declaration) by a colon. If there is no extender class, then **extends** in omitted. If there are no supertypes, then the colon is omitted. As is common in programming languages, ODL separates items in a list with commas.

```
<extended class> ::= extends <object class name>

<supertypes> ::=
    : <object type name> [ , <object type name> ]*
```

Note the use of the ']*' symbol, to show that ', <object type name>' is optional but can occur many times, as in Example 4.5.

*TYPE PROPERTIES*
Optionally, a class may specify values for the following type properties:
- the **extent** name;
- the instance properties that are used as **keys.**

The extent of an object type is the collection object which contains its instances. The convention is to name the extent as the plural of the type name and to start the extent name with a lower case letter because it is a variable rather than a type. For example, the extent of the type Customer will be named customers. Naming the extent is optional.

Keys of an object type are instance properties, the values of which will be different for each instance. Keys are typically attributes which represent the names and numbers used to identify the entities represented, such as employee numbers and product names. An object type may have zero, one, or more keys, and the keys may comprise a single property or a set of properties.

Extents and keys are declared within an ODL class definition as illustrated in the following example, taken from Figure 4.4.

---

*EXAMPLE 4.6*
*Instances of the object type, Product, are contained in an extent called products.*
*Instances of Product can be uniquely identified by the product_number attribute*
*value or by the combination of the product_name and colour attribute values.*
*The ODL class definition must therefore include the following declaration:*

```
( extent products
  keys product_number, (product_name, colour) )
```

---

The type properties declaration is contained in rounded brackets and comprises the extent declaration, followed by the keys declaration.

```
<type properties> ::=
        ( [ extent   <extent name> ]
          [ key[s]    <key> [ , <key> ]* )
```

Either the extent or keys may be omitted, since not all object types have a named extent or keys. Keys can be simple (a single property), e.g., product_no, or complex (a set of properties), e.g. name and colour:

```
<key> ::= <property name>
      | ( <property name> [ , <property name> ]*
      )
```

## INTERFACE DEFINITION

The syntax for an interface definition is illustrated in the following example.

---

### EXAMPLE 4.7

*The following ODL is an interface definition for an object type, Employee_IF. In this example, Employee_IF is an abstract type (it is not directly instantiated). It is defined so that other types which represent special type of employee (e.g., FactoryWorker and SalesPerson) can inherit characteristics common to all employees, such an employee number.*

```
interface Employee_IF: Person_IF
{
    attribute String employee_number;
    relationship Department works_in;
    . . .
}
```

*The above ODL specifies that the interface is for the Employee_IF object type, which is a subtype of the object type Person_IF. The state includes an employee number attribute and a relationship to the object which represents the department within which the employee works. If written out in full, there would also be operations, such as hire, fire, and pay.*

---

Note that the syntax of an interface definition is the same as that of a class specification. The only difference is that an interface definition cannot include the type properties (extender class, extent, and keys) which may be used when creating instances.

Like a class definition, an interface definition has two main parts, and terminates with a semicolon ';'.

1) The first part, the **interface header**, defines only the object type name and its supertypes.
2) The second part, the **interface body**, defines instance characteristic and is contained in curly brackets, { ... }. The body of an interface definition has exactly the same syntax as the body of a class definition.

```
<interface definition> ::=
<interface header> <class or interface body> ;
```

## A CLASS OR INTERFACE BODY

The body of a class and that of a interface definition both have the same syntax. The body follows the header declarations described in the previous sections and is contained in curly brackets, { ... }. It is used to declare the instance characteristics, i.e., the attributes, relationships, and operations of the objects which are instances of the object type. ODL does not prescribe the order in which these declarations should occur, but it is good practice to partition the list such that all of the attributes are declared, then all of the relationships and finally all of the operations.

The general form of the body of an object type definition is:

```
<class or interface body> ::=
        {<characteristic declaration>
        [ , <characteristic declaration> ]*
        }
```

Each characteristic declaration in the definition body defines an attribute, relationship, or operation. In addition, characteristic declarations can define the types, constants, and exceptions used in the other characteristic declarations.

```
<characteristic declaration> ::=
        | <attribute declaration>
        | <relationship declaration>
        | <operation declaration>
        | <type declaration>
        | <constant declaration>
        | <exception declaration>
```

## ATTRIBUTES

Attributes can be thought of as the values that an object contains. When defining the interface or class for an object type it is necessary to declare, for each attribute, its name and the type of value that it can have. ODL also allows us to specify restrictions on access to certain attributes—for example, an attribute can be designated **readonly**, in which case the attribute's values can be accessed but cannot be altered by programs which use the schema.

The way in which attributes are declared in ODL is illustrated in the following example, taken from Figure 4.4.

---

### EXAMPLE 4.8

*Instances of the Customer class represent Bruddersfield Bikes' customers. The attributes include a customer number, and the customer's name, address, and telephone numbers. The sales office applications must access Customer instances and may record changes to a customer's name, address, or telephone numbers, but these applications should not alter a customer's identification number. The class definition for the Customer object type will therefore include the following attribute declaration:*

```
1       readonly attribute String<ccode_length>
2           customer_no;
```

*The name, address, and telephones attributes are inherited from the Person_IF interface, which is a supertype of Customer. Person_IF therefore includes the following attribute declarations:*

```
3       attribute String name;
4       attribute Struct Address
5           {String street, town,
6               district, country, postcode;};
7       attribute List<Short> telephones;
```

---

Note that the general form of an attribute declaration is:

```
<attribute declaration> ::=
    [ readonly ] attribute
    <attribute type>    <attribute name> ;
```

Example 4.8 illustrates the expressive range of attribute declarations. In particular, note the following points:

1) Optionally, a declaration my be prefixed with **readonly** to indicate that it can be accessed but not altered (line 1 of the code in Example 4.8).
2) Attributes must be defined on literal types (in the example the literal types used are **Unsigned Short** (short integer) and **String** (character string)).
3) An attribute can be defined on an array type; this can be specified in an attribute declaration by specifying the array size after the attribute name (as in lines 1–2).
4) Type declarations can be simple atomic literals (line 2) or structured literals (e.g. lines 4–6).

The attribute type specifies the type of values that the attribute may have. An attribute must have a literal type, but it can be atomic, structured, or enumerated. The attribute declaration may include the type definition or may refer by name to a type defined elsewhere in the schema.

```
<attribute type> ::= <atomic literal type>
          | <structured type>
          | <enumerated type>
          | <type name>
```

The **atomic literal** types defined in the ODL language include, for example, integer, character, and Boolean types (other atomic types definable in ODL can be found in the appropriate reference manual). Integer, character and Boolean types are specified in ODL as follows:

```
<atomic literal type> ::= Short  |  Long|
        Unsigned Short  |  Unsigned Long  |
        Char  |  Boolean  |  ...
```

The meanings of the above atomic literal types are:
- **Short, Long, Unsigned Short, Unsigned Long**—these are integer types, respectively, single and double precision, and single and double precision unsigned.
- **Char**—this is the character type. An attribute of this type will take a single character as its value.
- **Boolean**—an attribute of this type will take true or false as its value.

The object database designer can also invent his or her own atomic literal types, if those built into the Object Data Model do not suffice. New atomic literals, called **enumerated types**, are defined using the **Enum** type generator. **Enum** must be provided with the type name, followed by the list of its values (in curly brackets, '{ ... }'). For example,

```
attribute Enum EmployeeType {salaried, waged}
     status;
```

declares an attribute called status with an enumerated type called EmployeeType, the values of which are salaried and waged.

The values of structured literal types are collections or structures of other literals and are defined using the type generators introduced in Chapter 3, i.e., **Set**, **Bag**, **List**, **Array** (or **Sequence**), **Dictionary**, **Date**, **Time**, **Timestamp**, **Interval**, and **Structure**.

The ODL for defining collection types, i.e., set, bag, list, array, and dictionary types, requires the type generator and then the type of the elements of the collection, in angular brackets, '< ... >'. For example, the ODL,

```
attribute Set< Unsigned Short[8] >
     department_employees;
```

defines an attribute called department_employees, with a set–object type. The set–object type is defined using the **Set** type generator. Its parameter specifies that the set elements are of type **Unsigned Short[8]**, i.e., each element is an array of eight single precision unsigned integers.

When specifying an array (or sequence) type, we can optionally specify the number of elements in the array (or sequence). For example,

```
attribute Array < Boolean, 20 >
     questionnaire_return;
```

defines an attribute called questionnaire_return with an array type. The array has twenty elements of type Boolean.

Though listed as an atomic literal type, **String** can also be viewed as a special case of a sequence—a string is a sequence of elements of type **Char** and is used to represent text. When using the **String** type generator the element type is not specified (it is always **Char**), but optionally the string length can be specified. For example,

> **attribute String** < 2 >   first_two_initials;

defines an attribute called first_two_initials of type two–character string.

**Structure types** are defined using the **Struct** type generator. An instance of a structure type has named elements each of which can contain an object of a specified type. A structure type is defined in ODL as in the following example.

> **attribute Struct** OfficeAddress {
>     **String** building;
>     **Unsigned Short** room[2];
>     } location;

The above ODL declares an attribute called location with a structure type called OfficeAddress. The type has two elements. The first is called building and is of type String. The second is called room and is of type two–element–integer array.

The type generators for structured types can be used freely to define arbitrarily complex structures. For example, we could define sets of bags of arrays of structures. However, note that all attributes must be defined on literal types. This means that the lowest level elements of any structured type upon which an attribute is defined must be an atomic literal.

## RELATIONSHIPS

The body of a class or interface definition for an object type must declare the relationships that associate the type instances with other objects, so as to model associations between the entities they represent. Each relationship declaration must state:

1) the name of the path from instances to associated objects;

2) the type of the associated objects;
3) and, optionally, the name of the inverse path, from the associated objects back to the instances.

The way in which a relationship is declared in ODL is illustrated in the following example, modified from Figure 4.4.

---

*EXAMPLE 4.9*

*Objects of type SalesOrder are related to objects of type Customer and Product to represent the relationships between sale orders, the customers who placed the orders, and the products ordered. The definition of the SalesOrder class therefore includes the following relationship declarations:*

```
1       relationship Customer placed_by
2            inverse Customer::places;
3       relationship List<Product> ordered
4            inverse Product::has_been_ordered
5            order_by price, product_number;
```

*1) The first relationship declaration denotes the following: the relationship path from SalesOrder objects to Customer objects is called placed_by (line 1); the relationship type is Customer, i.e., each instance of the relationship is between a SalesOrder object and a single Customer object (line 1); the inverse relationship, from Customer objects to SalesOrder objects, is called places and is defined within the Customer definition (line 2).*

*2) The second relationship denotes: the relationship path from SalesOrder objects to Product objects and is called ordered; the relationship type is List<Product>, i.e., each SalesOrder object is related to a collection object which contains a list of Product objects; the inverse relationship is called has_been_ordered, and is declared in the Product definition; each list of Products is in product_number within price sequence.*

---

The general form of a relationship declaration is:

```
<relationship declaration> ::=
       relationship <relationship type>
              <relationship_name>
       [ inverse <inverse relationship name> ]
       [ order_by <sort keys> ];
```

Example 4.9 is contrived to illustrate all of the features of ODL for declaring relationships.

1) A relationship from an instance is to a single object which is either the associated object or a collection of the associated objects.
2) Each relationship declaration names the **inverse** relationship. The inverse relationship name is prefixed by the associated object type name with double colons in between. This is an example of a **scoped name**—the inverse relationship is defined within the scope or context of another class or interface definition. To refer to it unambiguously , the name is prefixed by the other object type name. Declaration of an inverse relationship is optional, but if it is not declared, programs are unable to traverse the relationship in the reverse direction.
3) If the relationship is to a collection object within which component objects have a sequence (such as a list, sequence, or array), it is possible to specify the attributes by which the associated object within the collection will be sequenced.

## OPERATIONS

The body of a class or interface definition for an object type must declare the operators that can be applied to instances. An operation declaration must specify:
- the operation name;
- the type of the object it returns when executed;
- the type of each of the objects that it accepts as a parameter;
- exceptions that may be raised by the operation.

An **exception** is an object which represents an exceptional event and is typically used for error handling. Exceptions are explained in detail later in this chapter. The way in which operations are declared in ODL is illustrated in the next example, taken from Figure 4.4.

---

### EXAMPLE 4.10

*The first of the following example operations can be applied to instances of the object type, Customer. The second and third can be applied to Product instances.*
- *place_order—creates a new SalesOrder object from the order details;*

- *total_quantity_on_order?—computes the total number of products of the type represented by the Product object which have been ordered by customers;*
- *quantity_on_order_to—computes the total number of products which have been ordered by a specified customer.*

*The class definition for the Customer type will therefore include the following operation declaration:*

```
1       SalesOrder place_order
2           (in List<OrderLine> details;)
3             raise (product_doesnt_exist);
```

*and the class definition for the Product type will include the following:*

```
4       Long total_quantity_on_order? ();
5       Long quantity_on_order_to?
6           (in String<ccode_length> customer_no)
7             raises (no_such_customer);
```

1) *The first declaration (lines 1–3) specifies that the operation place_order returns an object of type SalesOrder, and receives an object of type List<OrderLine> as input.*
2) *The second declaration (line 4) specifies that total_quantity_on_order? returns a literal of type Long as its result (this is the number of ordered products), and does not receive any objects as parameters.*
3) *The third declaration (lines 5–7) specifies that the value returned by quantity_on_order_to? is a literal of type Long (the number of products ordered by the specified customer), and the operation receives an object, customer_no, of type String<ccode_length>, as input (to identify the customer in question). The operation can raise the exception no_such_customer (if the specified customer does not exist). This is an example of using an exception for error handling.*

The above example illustrates the main features of ODL operation declarations. The general form is:

```
<operation declaration> ::=
    <type of object returned>
```

```
<operation name>
( [ <parameter declarations> ] )
[ raises <exceptions declarations> ] ;
```

An operation can return an object as its value. The value of an operation can be of any literal or mutable object type, atomic or structured. Some operations do not return a value. This is denoted by prefixing the operation name with the keyword **void**.

**Operation parameters** are listed in rounded brackets, ( ... ), immediately after the operation name. Each parameter has a name and a type. Like the operation value, an operation parameter's type can be a literal or mutable, atomic or structured object type. A parameter is also designated as being either input (**in**) or output (**out**) or both (**inout**) to indicate if the operation receives or returns values via the parameter.

**Exceptions** which can be raised by an operation are listed at the end of its declaration, in rounded brackets, ( ... ) preceded by the keyword **raises**.

## CONSTANT, TYPE, AND EXCEPTION DECLARATIONS

A schema may include declarations of the constants, types, and exceptions used in the class and interface definitions or for use by the programs which use the schema. These additional declarations may be included as part of an object type definition, typically at the start of the its body, or they may be included separately, typically prior to the list of class and interface declarations.

## CONSTANTS

As in programming languages, it is often useful to give constants meaningful names by which they can be referred to. The way this is done in ODL is illustrated in the following example.

---

### EXAMPLE 4.11

*The following specifies a constant called MaximumCapacity. The constant is a literal of type **Short** (short integer) and has the value 200.*

**const Short** MaximumCapacity = 200

*This constant can be used in other declarations, instead of the literal 200. For example, the following two declarations are equivalent.*

```
attribute String <MaximumCapacity> line_buffer;
attribute String < 200 > line_buffer;
```

*Advantages of using the constant are, firstly, the name given to 200 tells us something of its meaning within the schema. Secondly, if we wish to modify our system to handle larger (or smaller) lines of text, we can do this by redefining the constant, rather than changing all relevant attribute declarations.*

---

A constant declaration has the form:

```
<constant declaration> ::=
      const <literal type>
            <name of the constant> =
            <value of the constant>
```

The value of the constant can be a literal (as above) or an expression which returns a literal value, such as an arithmetic formula.

Constants can be declared as separate declarations within a schema, usually at the start, or can be embedded within the body of the interface declaration that uses them.

## TYPE DECLARATIONS

Type generators can be used to create new types. New types that are used within a schema or by the programs which use the schema can be specified by type declarations, as illustrated in the following example.

---

*EXAMPLE 4.12*

*The following ODL defines two new types. The first is called Committee, and is a set–object type, the elements of which are objects of type Employee. The second is called CommitteeOfficers, and is a structure–object type with two elements, chair and secretary, both of type String.*

```
typedef  Set<Employee> Committee;
typedef  Struct CommitteeOfficers
      {String chair, secretary};
```

*Having defined the Committee and CommitteeOfficers types, they can be used in other declarations, e.g.:*

```
attribute CommitteeOfficers wc_officers;
attribute CommitteeOfficers mb_officers;
relationship Committee on_works_committee;
relationship Committee on_management_board;
```

A type declaration has the form:

```
<type definition> ::=
      typedef <type definition> <type names>
      | <structure type declaration>
```

## EXCEPTIONS

Exceptions are objects which represent exceptional events, usually error conditions, which can occur when trying to execute an operation. When an exceptional event occurs, the operation that encountered this event terminates by executing an operation on the appropriate exception. This is called **raising** the exception. Optionally, an exception may have a state which can be used to store information about what caused it to be raised. The state of an exception is then accessible by the program that executed the terminated operation.

The form of an ODL exception declaration is illustrated in Example 4.13.

## EXAMPLE 4.13

*The following ODL declares an exception which is raised by operations which take a parameter that specifies a customer number. The exception is raised if the customer number does not correspond to that of a Customer object within the object database. The exception is declared to specify its state, which is used to store details of the error condition raised.*

```
exception no_such_customer {
      String customer_number;
      String error_code;
      String error_message; }
```

## MODULES

Parts of a schema can be packaged together to form named modules, as shown in Figure 4.4. The schema in the figure forms a single module called SalesOrderProcessingSchema. This is denoted by bounding the schema declarations with the following ODL:

```
module SalesOrderProcessingSchema
{
        . . .
}
```

The module is a general structuring device—modules can be made up from other modules, and so on. Modules have two uses. Firstly, they can be used to package together related information, such that it can be handled as a single, named entity, as in Figure 4.4. Secondly, modules can be used to establish the scope of declarations (see Section 4.2, ODL: The structure of an ODL schema). This is useful, for example, to resolve naming conflicts which arise when declarations from more than one schema are combined.

## ODL IN A DISTRIBUTED ENVIRONMENT

In a distributed environment objects may be implemented on different computers using different languages. In addition, there may be delays and uncertainties when executing operations on objects stored on remote computer systems. ODL includes a number of features (also present in IDL) which address this situation. These provide a standard way of interfacing objects, which is independent of how the objects have been implemented and which takes into account the uncertainty of invoking operations across a network, e.g., via an object request broker. Specifically, ODL includes:

1) union types—these allows schema elements to be defined upon a number of alternative types (union types will already be familiar to C and C++ programmers). This feature is useful, for example, where an attribute is defined differently on different systems.

2) Inherited characteristics can be declared again in the subtype or extended class definitions. This is useful if the supertype or extender class is implemented on a different computer, since a new implementation can then be defined.

3) oneway operations—an operation can be prefixed with the keyword **oneway**. This indicates that when the operation is invoked, it is not guaranteed to execute and there will be no response. This is useful when a remote operation is to be initiated across a slow and unreliable network.

4) context expressions—context information can be appended to an operation declaration. The context information is then sent as part of the message which invokes the operation. In this way additional non–standard information needed to execute the operation within a specific remote environment can be provided.

5) The ODMG standards [Cattell 97] also define an **Object Interchange Format (OIF)**, which is a special language for dumping and loading the contents of an object database to or from files. This is useful for exchanging information between object databaseesystems.

(Readers should refer to the OMG standards [OMG 91] for details of the above features for distributed object environments. Also, see Section 10.6, Multidatabases, for a discussion of distributed databases and mulitdatabases).

## 4.3 SUMMARY

Traditionally, DBMSs support a **data definition language (ddl)** for defining the data structures, and a **data manipulation language (dml)** for manipulating the contents of databases. The **object definition language, ODL**, is the ddl for object databases. The approach contrasts with that of **persistent object–oriented programming languages**, where languages are extended to allow the objects they manipulate to persist beyond the life of a program.

ODL is used to define the interface between application programs and objects which conform to the Object Data Model defined in the **ODMG standards**. ODL is an extension of the **interface definition language (IDL)** defined by the **Object Management Group (OMG)**.

A set of declarations defined in ODL is called a **schema**. An ODL schema contains a set of **interface** and **class definitions** for object types in an object database. Object types can be for **transient** and **persistent** objects. A schema may also include **type, constant**, and **exception** declarations. Declarations can be combined to form named **modules**. Naming ambiguities are resolved by using **scoped names**. In a scoped name, the name of a schema element, e.g., an attribute or relation name, is prefixed by the name of the containing structure, e.g., the interface or module within which it was declared.

A **class** or **interface declaration** defines the external appearance of objects of a particular type. A class defines an object type that can be directly instantiated. An interface defines one that cannot be directly instantiated.

A **class declaration** will include: the **object type name**; the names of the **extender class** (if present) and any **supertype(s)**; and the type properties, i.e., the name of the **extent** and the properties used as **keys**. An interface specification will also declare the **attributes**, **relationships**, and **operations** of the type instances. The class declaration body may also include declarations of **constants, types**, and **exceptions** used within the scope of the interface declaration.

An **interface declaration** has the same form as a class declaration, apart from omitting specification of extender classes, the type extent, and keys. Each **attribute declaration** specifies whether the type is **readonly**, its name, and its type. An attribute must have a literal type.

Each **relationship declaration** specifies the name of the relationship path and inverse relationship path, and the type of the associated object. If the relationship associates an instance with an ordered collection object, such as a list, then the declaration will also specify the properties by which the collection is sequenced.

An **operation declaration** specifies the type of the value returned by the operation, the operation name, and the name and type of each operation parameter. Parameters can be for input, output, or both. The declaration must also list the exceptions that the operation can raise.

**Constant declatrations** are used to give meaningful names to literals. New named types can be defined using **type declarations. Exception declarations** are used to declare exceptions whose state is then used to communicate what caused the exception to be raised.

ODL includes a number of additional features which are used within a distributed environment. These include **union types, oneway operations** and **context expressions**. The ODMG standards also define **an object interchange format** for interchange of information between object databases.

## EXERCISES:
(4.1)   What role does the ODL fulfil?
(4.2)   Why must an ODBMS support other programming languages, in addition to ODL? Identify each additional language and identify its purpose.
(4.3)   Distinguish between data and metadata.
(4.4)   Distinguish between persistent and transient objects.
(4.5)   What is meant by a persistent object–oriented language?
(4.6)   Identify two advantages of having a separate object definition language.
(4.7)   What is a database schema, and what purpose does it serve?
(4.8)   Identify the components of an ODL schema, explain the role of each component.

(4.9) An application which lists Bruddersfield Bikes' products would need only part of the schema in Figure 4.4. Extract from the figure a schema for this application.

(4.10) Identify the scoped names in Figure 4.4, and explain why these names had to be prefixed with a structure name.

(4.11) What is the purpose of an interface definition?

(4.12) What is the purpose of a class definition?

(4.13) Give examples of when an object type would be defined as (i) an interface and (ii) a class.

(4.14) Explain the role of each of the parts of the interface header within an interface declaration.

(4.15) Identify the role of each of the parts of the class header within a class definition.

(4.16) Declare the class header for the following object types:
    (i) an object type, SalesPerson, which is a subtype of Employee. Instances can be distinguished by the property, salesperson_number, or the combination of properties, employee_name and employee_address;
    (ii) an object type, PaySlip, with no keys;
    (iii) an abstract object type, Person.

(4.17) Write a class declaration header for a Book object type, which is a subtype of both Literature and Publication. Instances are persistent and can be identified by the ISBN attribute and by the combination of title, authors ,and publication date.

(4.18) What information does the body of a class or an interface declaration represent?

(4.19) Write attribute declarations for attributes with the following properties:
    (i) name, a string of 10 characters;
    (ii) house_number, an integer;
    (iii) customers, a set of 10 digit numerical customer numbers;
    (iv) entry_detail, a structure comprising an enrolment date and number;
    (v) entry_details, comprising a list of entry_detail structures.

(4.20) Extend the class declaration in Figure 4.4 to include the following relationships:
    (i) the child_of relationship between Customer and Person;

(ii)    the is_part_of relationship between Product and Product, to represent the relationship between a product and other products which are components of it;

(iii)    the alternative_product relationship between Product and Product;

(iv)    the husband_of relationship between Person and Person.

(4.21)    Extend the SalesOrder declaration in Figure 4.4 to include declarations of the following operations:

(i)    add_order_line, which adds a product number and quantity to the order. The operation does not return an object. The no_such_product exception is raised if the specified product does not exist;

(ii)    total_quantity_ordered, which returns the number of a specified product ordered on the sales order;

(iii)    name_of_customer, which returns the name of the customer who placed the order;

(iv)    products, which returns a list containing the products ordered (as an output parameter) and returns, as the operation value, the total number of products ordered.

(4.22)    Specify a class for an object type SalesPerson, a subtype of Person. The instance characteristics are an employee number (of type String), and a relationship with the SalesOrder instances for the sales orders taken by the salesperson. The behaviour comprises a single operation which retrieves the set of SalesOrder objects taken by the salesperson. Each SalesPerson instance is uniquely identifiable by its Employee number. (You should be able to do this by simple modifications to the ODL code in Example 4.2.)

(4.23)    Define a constant called MaxCapacity with a value of 2,000.

(4.24)    Define a type called Guests, which is an array of 2,000 string literals (use the constant defined in 4.23).

(4.25)    Define a type called EmployeeName, comprising a list of title e.g., Mr. or Dr., forenames, family name, and a list of qualifications, such as B.Sc. and Ph.D.

(4.26)    Declare a class for an object type called DepartmentMembers, with a single attribute called staff, the value of which is a list of literals of type EmployeeName (defined in 4.25).

(4.27)    What is an exception object? What is the purpose of the state and the operations of an exception?

(4.28)   Declare an exception, called Invalid_Product_Name, which communicates the invalid product name and an error code via its state.

(4.29)   Define a module called Product, containing only the Product interface declaration from the schema in Figure 4.4.

(4.30)   Explain two uses of the ODL module structure.

(4.31)   Write a brief report for the head of the information technology section of a company on ODL, and its importance in implementing object databases.

# 5

# THE MANIPULATIVE PART OF THE OBJECT DATA MODEL

The manipulative part of the Object Data Model is the set of things that can be done to object databases using the various object database languages. We can also describe these manipulations in a mathematical form, called an **object algebra**. An object algebra provides a precise way of describing and analysing object database languages, designs, and applications. It can therefore be used to investigate aspects of object database theory and technology. This chapter describes and explains an object algebra for the Object Data Model.

The description of an object algebra is deliberately informal, with the aim of providing readers with an appreciation of the style and expressive power of its operators. References are given for those who wish to study formal object data models and object algebras in mathematical detail.

Section 5.1 provides an explanation of what an object algebra is. Section 5.2. overviews an example object algebra and its operators. The ways in which this object algebra can manipulate set–objects is described in detail in Section 5.3. The algebra operators for manipulating other types of object are described in Section 5.4. Finally, a summary is given in Section 5.5.

## 5.1 WHAT IS AN OBJECT ALGEBRA?
The manipulative part of the Object Data Model is defined in the ODMG standards document [Cattell 97] as a set of object database languages which can be used to implement actual object database systems. These

are, the **Object Definition Language (ODL)** (described in Chapter 4), the **Object Query Language (OQL)** (in Chapter 6), and the object definition and manipulation language (**ODL/OML**) extensions to programming languages, i.e., C++, Smalltalk, and Java (in Chapter 7).

The syntax of ODL, OQL, and the ODL/OQL extensions to programming languages, i.e., the ways in which statements are put together, is precisely defined (using the Backus–Naur Form (BNF) notation, also used in Chapter 4). However, the meaning of statements written in these languages, the language semantics, is less clear. The semantics for each of these languages is mainly explained using natural language (English), illustrated with example code, but natural language explanations lack mathematical precision and are therefore open to different interpretations. A mathematically precise explanation would remove any ambiguities and thus ensure that different implementations of the languages are consistent. It would also provide a formal basis by which the expressive powers of different object database languages can be analysed and compared. Though an object algebra is not an object database language, it should define the things that it is possible to do using an object database language. As such, an object algebra should provide a yardstick by which the power of object database languages may be judged.

A mathematically precise description of object database manipulations is also of potential use to researchers. It can be used to investigate the properties of object database systems and object database languages without actually having to implement them. This allows researchers to study issues, such as object database design methods, the design of object database languages, and optimisation techniques for speeding up the processing of object database queries.

The absence of formal (mathematical) definitions of object database technology is partly a consequence of its rapid evolution from object–oriented programming languages and earlier generations of database technology. Researchers are currently trying to catch up with the technology. A major challenge is to establish widely accepted theoretical foundations for the object database technology which is already on the market. This contrasts with relational technology (the previous generation of database technology), where the theoretical relational data model [Codd 70] came first, and the technology which implemented it followed some years later.

There is as yet no standard formal semantics for the Object Data Model. This chapter therefore describes one from a number of published object algebras, that of the AQUA object data model [Leung 93]. AQUA has been chosen because of its strong similarity with the Object Data Model (in Chapter 3). Like the Object Data Model, AQUA has a uniform treatment of values and objects, which are respectively immutable and mutable. Also, AQUA is designed as a very general object data model and object algebra for describing a variety of specific systems.

Object algebra is to objects what conventional algebra is to numbers. In conventional algebra we can write expressions such as:

x  /  (y + 20)

This expression includes variables (x and y), a constant (20), operators (+, /) and brackets ( ( ... ) ). Once values have been assigned to the variables, the expression will have a value—if x and y are respectively assigned the values 60 and 10, the value of the expression is 2.

Expressions in object algebra are also constructed from variables, constants, and operators, but instead of numbers, their values are objects. We can therefore write expressions which represent object database queries (the value of the expression is the object which is retrieved by the query) and other manipulations, such as inserting or deleting objects, and changing the states of existing objects.

As an example, consider the following object algebra expression:

        retail_customers
        UNION[Customer]
        SET(Customer(customer_no:'C2', name:'Barry'))

This expression includes:

1)  **variables**—retail_customers is a variable of type **Set<Customer>**, and customer_no and name are variables of type **String**;

2) **constants**—'C2' and 'Barry' are constants which represents specific literal objects of type **String;**
3) **operators**—for example, UNION and SET are operators, each of which returns an object when applied to other objects.

This expression represents the insertion into an object database of a new object which represents a customer C2, called Barry. The expression's value is an object of type **Set<Customer>** which contains all of the objects contained in retail_customers and also the specified Customer object, the state of which contains the literals 'C2' and 'Barry'. The detailed meaning of this expression is not important at this stage, and will be explained as this chapter proceeds.

"Conventional" algebra defines computations that should be possible using a programming language: a programming language which can do any such computation is said to be **computationally complete**. Similarly, an object algebra defines the desirable expressiveness of object database languages. An object database language which has the expressive power of a particular object algebra is said to be **complete** with respect to that algebra.

## 5.2 THE OBJECT ALGEBRA

### A NON–MATHEMATICAL OVERVIEW

In this section we present a simple intuitive overview of the object algebra.

An object database for an organisation will contain objects which represent entities of interest to that organisation. An example is the Bruddersfield Bikes' sales order processing object database. (The ODL schema for this object database has been given in Chapter 4, Figure 4.4. An example instance given in Figure 5.1 is used throughout this chapter to illustrate the object algebra.) The entities represented are customers, products, and the sales orders placed by the customers for products.

Each application may require access to information about some of those entities and so must access and process some of the objects. For instance, a sales office application will require access to the objects which represent customers, so as to access information about addresses to which invoices must be sent.

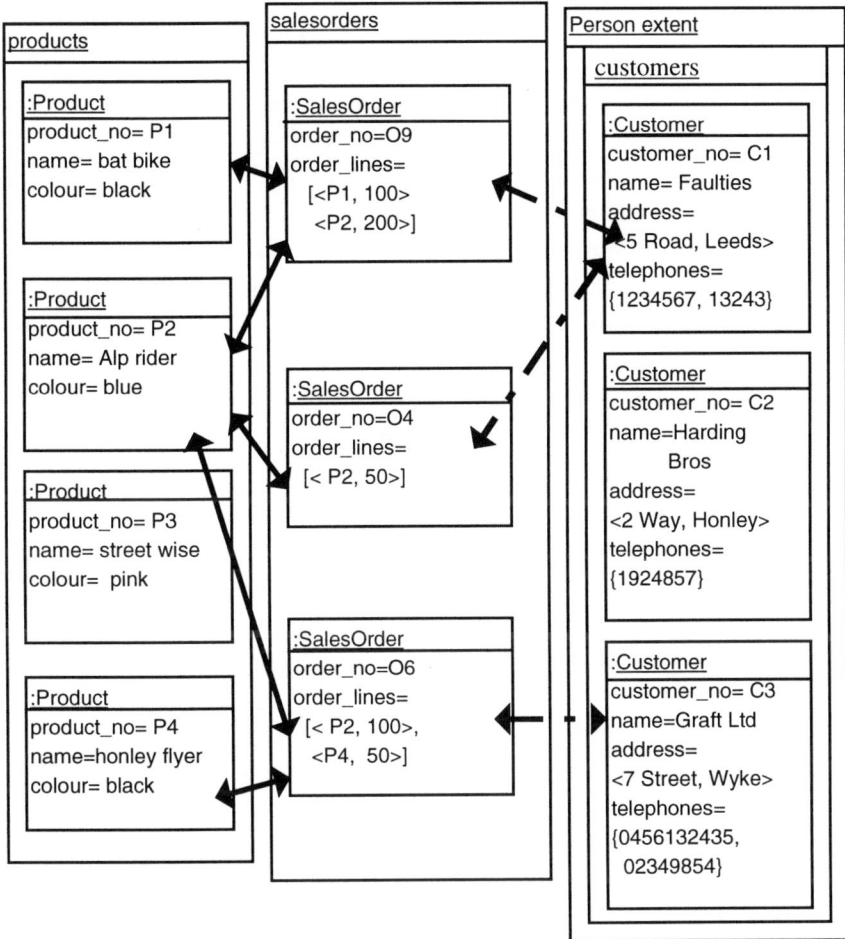

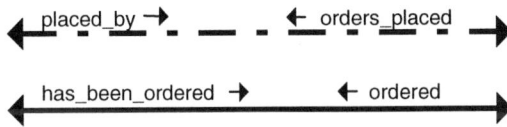

Figure 5.1 An example sales order processing object database (see Chapter 4, Figure 4.4 for the ODL schema)

Other applications must modify the object database, by creating or deleting objects and by modifying the states of existing objects, so as to reflect changes to the world in which the organisation operates. For instance, a sales office application will create objects to represent new sales orders.

In order for the object algebra to describe such applications, it must be able to express the following three general operations:

1) **Definition of the objects that are of interest**—this facility is provided by what can be thought of as a set of "pick" and "mix" operations. These create collections of "interesting" objects by "mixing" together objects which have been "picked" from existing collections. These operators can represent applications, such as a sales office application that accesses objects which represent relevant customers, products, and sales orders from the extents of the Customer, Product, and SalesOrder object types.

2) **Application of operations to objects of interest**—this is necessary in order to modify the states of objects, or to extract interesting information from them. This facility is provided by a set of operators which execute operations, such as the methods that implement the interface operations for the relevant objects. The operators can represent applications, such as in the sales office, where it is necessary to execute SalesOrder object operations in order to create objects which represent the associated delivery notes, invoices, and receipts.

3) **Return of an object which represents the required information**— the consequence of querying an object database will be the retrieval of objects which represent the required information. These objects may be newly created or may already exist, and they may be literals or mutable objects. For example, a sales office application may require details of customers with unpaid bills (i.e., a collection of existing (mutable) Customer objects) or the total value of a sales order (i.e., a literal). Accordingly, every expression in the object algebra returns an object to represent the required information.

---

*EXAMPLE 5.1*

*Consider the following problem: "Retrieve the total cost of the products ordered by Bingley Cycle Hire". The problem can be solved in three steps, corresponding to those identified above.*

1) *Definition of the objects that are of interest—the above problem is solved firstly, by a "pick" and "mix" operation, in which interesting objects are picked out of the object database. In this case, the interesting objects are those which represent the customer, Bingley Cycle Hire, the sales orders*

*placed by that customer, and the products ordered. These are picked out by searching through the extent of the Customer object type to find the object for which the value of the name attribute is "Bingley Cycle Hire". This operation corresponds to a **restrict** operation in the object algebra. Once that object has been located, it is then possible to access the objects which represent the sales orders placed by Bingley Cycle Hire and the products ordered, via the orders_placed and ordered relationships which link them to the Customer object.*

2) **Application of operations to objects of interest***fFor each SalesOrder object related to the Bingley Cycle Hire object, it is now necessary to execute the order_value? operation, which calculates the total value of the products ordered, and then to add all of the order values together using a total function. This corresponds to the **fold** operation of the object algebra.*

3) **Return of an object which contains the required information**—*the result of this query is the total of the sales order values computed in the previous step. This is the value of the query and is returned as a single literal.*

## THE OBJECT ALGEBRA

The following sections describe the object algebra in detail. Though the meaning of object algebra expressions are mathematically well defined, the explanations are given in a non–mathematical form. The aim is to provide the reader with an understanding of the range of operations upon object databases that can be expressed in object algebra. (Formal (mathematical) definitions of the algebra can be found in [Leung 93]). Accordingly, we avoid cryptic mathematical notation and instead use plain English, with the aid of examples based upon the sales order processing object database used in previous chapters (see Figure 5.1).

The operators described are applied to objects which conform to the Object Data Model (described in Chapter 3). We describe operations on set– and bag–objects only, since other types of collection–object can be derived from these [Subramanian 95].

### EXPRESSIONS

Expressions in the object algebra are constructed from **variables,** **constants,** and **operators** that are applied to objects represented by the variables and constants. This parallels the situation in "conventional" algebra, where, for example, an expression, such as (x + 12) / sin(y), is constructed from a number (12), variables (x, y) and operations upon them (+, /, sin). Each expression in the object algebra returns an expression value when it is evaluated. This value is always a single object, and the type of the object returned can always be determined by analysing the expression itself. A consequence is that object algebra expressions can be freely constructed from other expressions. This is illustrated by the example object algebra expression,

retail_customers
UNION[Customer]
SET(Customer(customer_no:'C2', name:'Barry'))

This expression is constructed from other expressions, i.e., retail_customers and SET(Customer(customer_no:'C2',name:'Barry')), by applying the operator, UNION[Customer].

The ability to build object algebra expressions from other expressions enables us to model very complex object database manipulations in single expressions. Expressions in the Object Data Model query language, OQL (described in Chapter 6), are constructed in a similar way, i.e., by building expressions from other expressions to provide a powerful language for querying actual object databases.

### OBJECT ALGEBRA OPERATORS
Object algebra operators can be divided into four groups. The first two correspond to the first two general functions identified in the previous section A non–mathematical overview:

1)  **Operations which define objects that are of interest**, i.e., the "pick" and "mix" operators. These are:
    * **restrict**—picks out objects which satisfy a specified condition;
    * **union** (and **additive–union**)—picks out objects from two collections of objects;
    * **intersect**—picks out objects contained in both of two collections;
    * **difference**—picks out objects in one collection, but not the other;
    * **choose**—picks out an object from a collection;

- **duplicate–elimination**—picks out one of each object contained in a collection;
- **group**—picks out groups of equivalent objects from a collection.

Each operation in this first group defines an object or a collection of objects picked out from one or more collections of objects. These operators are used to define collections of "interesting" objects, so that they can be processed.

2) **Operators which apply operations to objects of interest.** These are:
- **apply**—processes a collection of objects;
- **fold**—processes a collection of objects and summarises the resulting information;
- **join**           |
- **tuple–join**       | — combines and processes informatio
                       |     contained in two collections;
- **outer–join**   |
- **least–fixed–point**—repeatedly applies a function to a collection of objects until no further information can be extracted.

The above operators allow us to describe how collections of "interesting" objects are processed.

3) **Control operators.** Many of the operators in the previous two groups operate upon objects only when a specified condition, or predicate, is true. The operators in this third set are used to specify the conditions for such operators. They are:
- **exists**—does any object in a collection satisfy a condition?
- **forall**—do all objects in a collection satisfy a condition?
- **member**—is a specified object a member of a collection?

Each of the operators in this third group tests to see if some condition holds for a collection of objects and returns a Boolean literal, which is true if the condition holds; otherwise false.

4)      **operators for restructuring objects.** There are various types of structured object that can exist within an object database, i.e., structure-, set–, bag–, list– and array–objects. The operators in this

last class are used to convert objects from one structured type into another (here we consider only structures, sets and bags)

- **set**—converts an object into a set–object containing that object;
- **bag**—converts an object into a bag–object containing that object;
- **nest**—creates a nested structure which aggregates together information from a collection of objects;
- **unnest**—removes nested structures;
- **convert** — converts a set–object into a bag–object, or a bag–object into a set–object.

Each of the above operators is described and illustrated in the following sections. The notation used has been modified from that defined for AQUA [Leung 93], so as to better express the natural language meaning of the operators and their arguments. Section 5.3 explains operations on set–objects. Additional complexities of operating upon bag–objects are described in Section 5.4. Operations on other types of collections, i.e., lists and arrays, are not covered, but can be derived from the set and bag operators (those interested should refer to [Subramanian 95] in which operators upon ordered collections, e.g. lists and arrays, are defined within the AQUA object algebra).

## 5.3 OPERATIONS ON SET–OBJECTS

### PICK AND MIX OPERATORS

The first set of operators described are for selecting interesting objects from one or more set–objects.

### RESTRICT

RESTRICT is a unary operator (it operates on just one object). This operator is sometime called select, but here we use the name restrict so as to avoid confusion with the select operation in OQL. This operator is used to define a set–object which contains objects for which some condition is true, as illustrated in Figure 5.2. RESTRICT provides a way of picking the objects which satisfy our requirements.

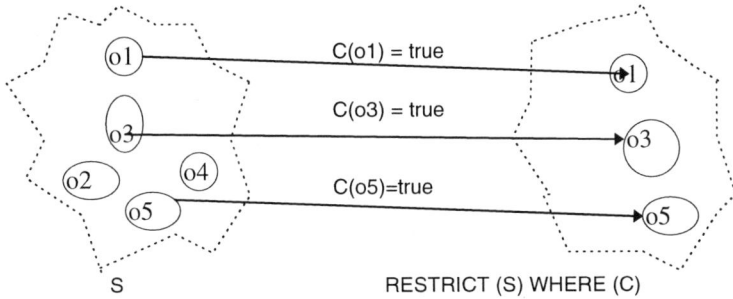

Figure 5.2 RESTRICT

---

*EXAMPLE 5.2*

*The following object algebra expression models the query "retrieve details of black products".*

RESTRICT products WHERE colour = 'black'

*When applied to the database in Figure 5.1, this expression defines the set–objects shown in Figure 5.3.*

---

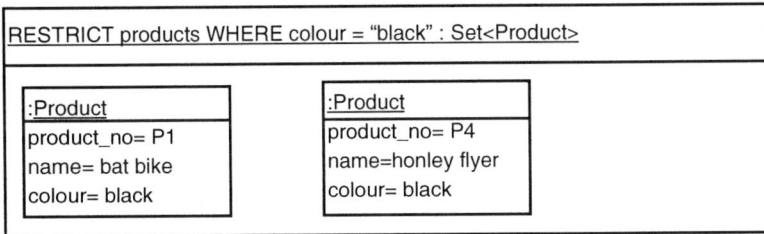

| RESTRICT products WHERE colour = "black" : Set<Product> |
|---|

:Product
product_no= P1
name= bat bike
colour= black

:Product
product_no= P4
name=honley flyer
colour= black

Figure 5.3 The value of the Example 5.2 expression when applied to Figure 5.1

It is clear in Example 5.2 that colour refers to the colour property of objects in products. In cases where there is ambiguity, this is resolved by introducting **bound variables** which refer to objects in specific collection–objects. For instance, the expression,

RESTRICT x IN products WHERE x.colour = 'black'

has the same meaning as the Example 5.2 expression. The difference is that we have introduced the variable x to make explicit the binding between the variable in the condition, colour, with the objects in the operand set–object, products.

A restrict operation which defines a set–object containing those objects contained in the set–object S, for which a condition C is true, is denoted:

RESTRICT S WHERE C

The value of the expression is of the same type as the set–object, S.

The condition C is called the **restrict predicate** and will evaluate to *true* or *false* for each object contained in S. A restrict predicate is used to compare the properties of an object in S with the properties of other objects, and has the following characteristics:

1) A restrict predicate must be an expression in the object algebra which returns a Boolean literal, i.e., true or false.
2) The variables must represent objects in the object database.
3) At least one of the variables must represent (be bound to) objects or properties of objects in the set–object to which the restrict is applied (e.g., colour in Example 5.2).
4) Other variables and constants can represent other objects in the object database, or literals or objects defined by other expressions.
5) The operators used can be any that are defined for the relevant objects and which return a Boolean literal.

The following two examples of restrict expressions provide more complex examples of restrict predicates.

---

*EXAMPLE 5.3*

*The following expression represents the query "retrieve details of products which are not called tricycle, and which are either black, blue or pink".*

RESTRICT products WHERE
            NOT (name='tricycle') AND
            (colour = 'black' OR colour = 'blue' OR colour = 'pink')

*The effect of the above expressions when applied to the Figure 5.1 object database is to retrieve all of the Product objects in products, since the condition is true for each of them.*

The Example 5.3 expression illustrates the use of the logic operators NOT, AND, and OR which are defined for Boolean literals. Their meaning is given in Table 5.1, which shows the values of the expressions applying each of these operators to the Boolean expressions X and Y. For example, the first and third columns show that if expression X has the value true, then NOT X returns the value false, and conversely, if X is false, then NOT X is true. (Evaluation of Boolean expressions is explained in greater detail when OQL is described in Chapter 6.)

Table 5.1 Operators on Boolean literals

| X | Y | NOT X | X AND Y | X OR Y |
|---|---|-------|---------|--------|
| true | true | false | true | true |
| true | false | false | false | true |
| false | true | true | false | true |
| false | false | true | false | false |

The next example illustrates how relationships between objects can be navigated.

*EXAMPLE 5.4*

*The following expression models the query "retrieve details of sales orders placed by Faulties for Road Runner bicycles".*

> RESTRICT sales_orders WHERE
> (placed_by.name = 'Faulties')
> AND (ordered.name = 'Road Runner')

*The expression value when executed against the Figure 5.1 object database will be an object of type Set<SalesOrder>, but with the empty set as its state, since there are no SalesOrder objects for which the restrict predicate is true.*

Note that the restrict predicate in Example 5.4 includes references to placed_by.name and ordered.name. These references are composed of relationship names and the names of properties of the related objects. For instance, placed_by is a relationship from SalesOrder objects to Customer objects, and name is an attribute of Customer objects. The reference `placed_by.name` therefore refers to the value of the name attribute of the Customer object related to the relevant SalesOrder object via the placed_by relationship.

## UNION

UNION is a binary operator (it takes two objects as operands). The UNION of two set–objects, illustrated in Figure 5.4, is a set–object which contains all of the objects contained in one or both of the two operand set–objects.

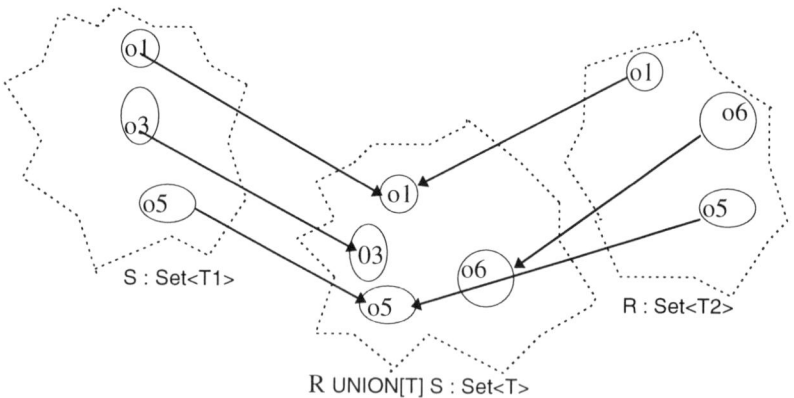

Figure 5.4 UNION

When defining a UNION operation, it is necessary to specify the type of the objects in the resulting set–object. This is because the objects contained in the two argument collections may not always have the same type and may have a number of different supertypes in common.

Consider the UNION of two set–objects, respectively of type Set<ProductionLineOperator> and Set<QualityController>, where ProductionLineOperator and QualityController are subtypes of both FactoryStaff and WagedStaff, as illustrated below.

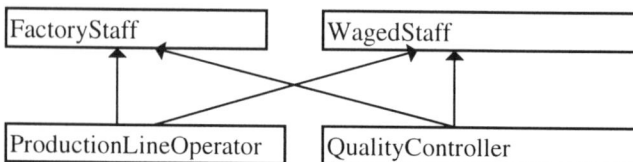

Two possibilities are to define their union as being of type Set<FactoryStaff> or of type Set<WagedStaff>. The choice of type may affect the value of the expression, since object equality can be defined differently for different types. It is therefore necessary to specify the expression type within the union expression.

UNION is used to define a collection of objects taken from more than one collection, for example to represent the insertion of new objects into the object database. The latter is done by constructing a new object from literals, placing it within a set–object, and then forming the union of the new set–object and the existing object type extent.

---

*EXAMPLE 5.5*

*The following expression represents the query "retrieve details of customers who are retail and/or trade customers":*

> retail_customers UNION[Customer]  trade_customers

*The two operand objects, retail_customers and trade_customers, are of type Set<Customer>. The result is an object of type Set<Customer> which contains objects contained in either or both of the operand set–objects. Figure 5.5 shows the result of the above expression when applied to the example instances of retail_customers and trade_customers.*

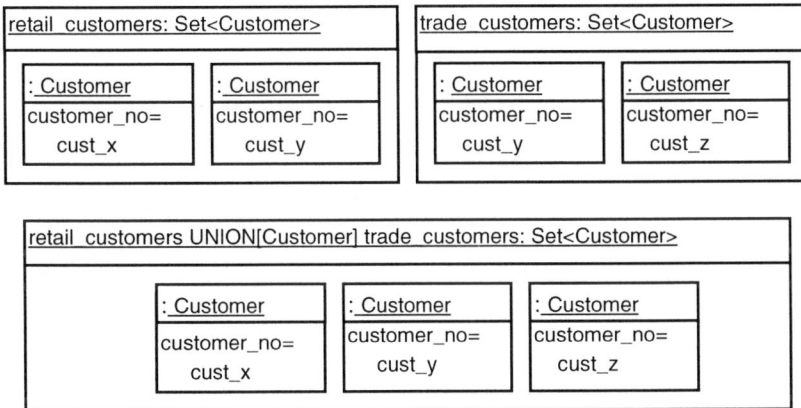

Figure 5.5 The Example 5.5 UNION operation

*Note that in the example we have allowed a customer to be a member of both retail_customers and trade_customers, but this replication is removed in the resulting object—all objects in a set must be distinct.*

A UNION operation on the set–objects, set_of_objects_1 and set_of_objects_2, where the result is an object of type Set<UnionType>, is denoted:

set_of_objects_1 UNION[UnionType] set_of_objects_2

## INTERSECT

INTERSECT, like UNION, operates upon two set–objects. The intersection of two set–objects contains objects which occur in both of them, as illustrated in Figure 5.6.

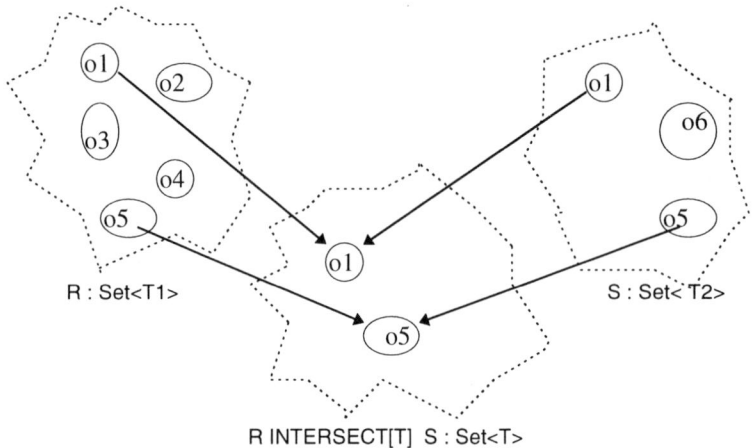

R INTERSECT[T] S : Set<T>

Figure 5.6 INTERSECT

As for the UNION operation, the type of the objects in the intersection must be defined to avoid any ambiguity. INTERSECT is used to retrieve objects which are contained within more than one collection.

## EXAMPLE 5.6

*The query "which customers are classified as both retail and trade?", is modelled by the expression:*

(retail_customers) INTERSECT[Customer] (trade_customers)

*where retail_customers and trade_customers are as described in Example 5.5. The value of this expression is an object of type Set<Customer> which contains all of those objects contained in both of the argument set–objects. Given the instances of trade_customers and retail_customers in Figure 5.5, the value of the above expression is therefore as shown in Figure 5.7.*

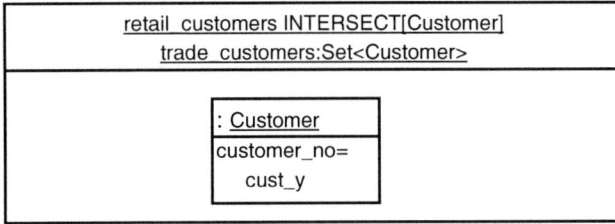

Figure 5.7 The value of the Example 5.6 INTERSECT operation.

The set–object of type Set<T> which is the intersection of two set–objects, R and S, is denoted:

R INTERSECT[T] S

## DIFFERENCE

The difference (MINUS) operator, like UNION and INTERSECT, operates upon two set–objects. DIFFERENCE defines a set–object which contains objects which occur in the first of the operand set–objects, but not in the second, as illustrated in Figure 5.8.

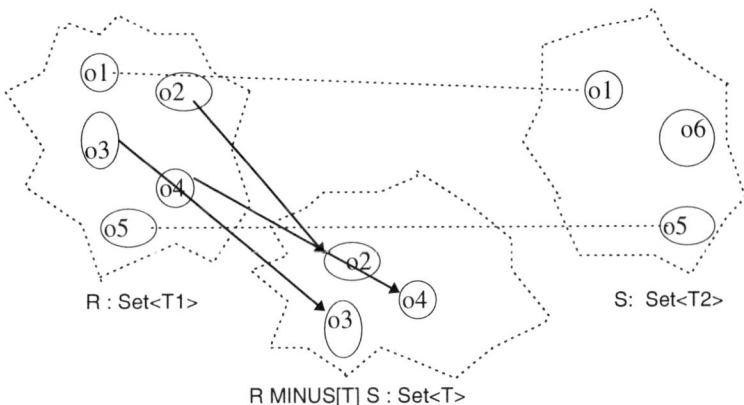

Figure 5.8  DIFFERENCE

The type of the objects in the intersection must be defined to avoid any ambiguity (as explained above for the UNION operator).

DIFFERENCE can be used to represent deletions from an object database and queries which retrieve objects which are in one collection but not in another.

---

### EXAMPLE 5.7

*The query "which customers are classed as retail, but not trade? ", is expressed in the object algebra as:*

retail_customers  MINUS[Customer]   trade_customers

*where retail_customers and trade_customers are as described in Example 5.5. The value of this expression is an object of type Set<Customer> which contains all those objects in retail_customers which are not also in trade_customers. Given the instances of trade_customers and retail_customers in Figure 5.5, the value of the above expression is therefore as shown in Figure 5.9.*

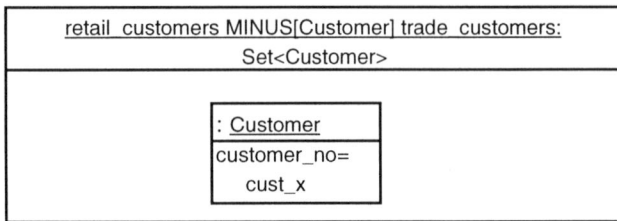

```
┌─────────────────────────────────────────────────────────┐
│   retail_customers MINUS[Customer] trade_customers:       │
│                  Set<Customer>                            │
├─────────────────────────────────────────────────────────┤
│               ┌───────────────────┐                       │
│               │ : Customer         │                      │
│               ├───────────────────┤                      │
│               │ customer_no=       │                      │
│               │     cust_x         │                      │
│               └───────────────────┘                       │
└─────────────────────────────────────────────────────────┘
```

Figure 5.9 The value of the Example 5.7 INTERSECT operation

---

The set–object of type Set<T> which contains the difference of two set–objects, R and S, is denoted:

R MINUS[T] S

### CHOOSE

CHOOSE is a unary operator (it operates on a single operand object) which "picks" a single object (any object) contained in the argument set–object, as illustrated in Figure 5.10. CHOOSE can be used, for example, to model an application which accesses objects contained in a collection–object, one at a time.

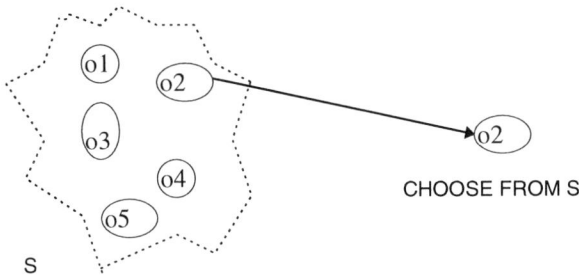

Figure 5.10 CHOOSE

---

## EXAMPLE 5.8

*An application program processes each SalesOrder object contained in a set–object called delivered_orders, so as to generate invoices for them. The following CHOOSE operation represents what the program must do, each time it require another SalesOrder object to process:*

CHOOSE FROM delivered_orders

*CHOOSE makes an arbitrary choice, so the chosen object should be removed from the operand set–object to avoid choosing it again. The object can be removed using the MINUS operator, previously described.*

---

An object chosen from a set–object S is denoted:

CHOOSE FROM S

## GROUP

GROUP, a unary operator, is used to partition the objects contained in a set–object. The result is an object which contains sets of objects which are equivalent in some way. The GROUP operation is more complex than the previous ones, but should become clear with the aid of the example given below.

Consider the following problem. Some customers have outstanding sales orders, and others do not. We wish to process these two groups in different ways and can test which group each customer belongs to by applying a function, *outstanding_orders?*. This function returns true for Customer objects in the first group and false for those in the second. It is convenient for us to place each Customer object in one of two set–objects, depending on whether *outstanding_orders?* returns true or false. We can express this partitioning of Customer objects using the GROUP operator,

GROUP customers BY outstanding_orders?

The result is a set–object which contains two objects, one of which includes objects in customers for which the function *outstanding_orders* returns true, and the other contains objects in customers for which the function returns false. In addition, and so as to be able to distinguish between them, these two objects contain the respective values (true or false in this case) returned by the grouping function, *outstanding_orders*. The value of the above expression when applied to the Figure 5.1 object database is shown in Figure 5.11.

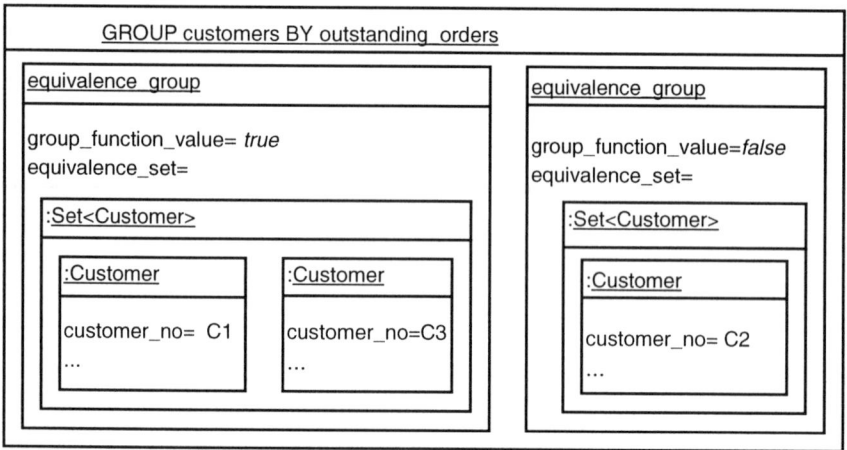

```
┌────────────────────────────────────────────────────────────────────────────┐
│             GROUP customers BY outstanding  orders                           │
│  ┌──────────────────────────────────────┐  ┌──────────────────────────────┐ │
│  │equivalence  group                     │  │equivalence  group            │ │
│  │                                       │  │                              │ │
│  │group_function_value= true             │  │group_function_value=false    │ │
│  │equivalence_set=                       │  │equivalence_set=              │ │
│  │  ┌─────────────────────────────────┐  │  │  ┌────────────────────────┐  │ │
│  │  │:Set<Customer>                   │  │  │  │:Set<Customer>          │  │ │
│  │  │  ┌────────────┐ ┌────────────┐  │  │  │  │  ┌──────────────┐      │  │ │
│  │  │  │:Customer   │ │:Customer   │  │  │  │  │  │:Customer     │      │  │ │
│  │  │  │customer_no=│ │customer_no=│  │  │  │  │  │customer_no=  │      │  │ │
│  │  │  │   C1       │ │   C3       │  │  │  │  │  │   C2         │      │  │ │
│  │  │  │...         │ │...         │  │  │  │  │  │...           │      │  │ │
│  │  │  └────────────┘ └────────────┘  │  │  │  │  └──────────────┘      │  │ │
│  │  └─────────────────────────────────┘  │  │  └────────────────────────┘  │ │
│  └──────────────────────────────────────┘  └──────────────────────────────┘ │
└────────────────────────────────────────────────────────────────────────────┘
```

Figure 5.11 Grouping the Customer objects

The group operator, as defined in AQUA, does not name the attribute which stores the values of the grouping function. However, it has been named group_function_value in Figure 5.11 to make clear its meaning, and to conform to the Object Data Model in which all attributes are named.

The value of a GROUP operation upon a set–object is a set–object which contains one "group" object for each distinct value returned by the grouping function. Each " group" object is a structure which contains the object returned by the grouping function and all of the objects for which the grouping function returns that value, as shown in Figure 5.12.

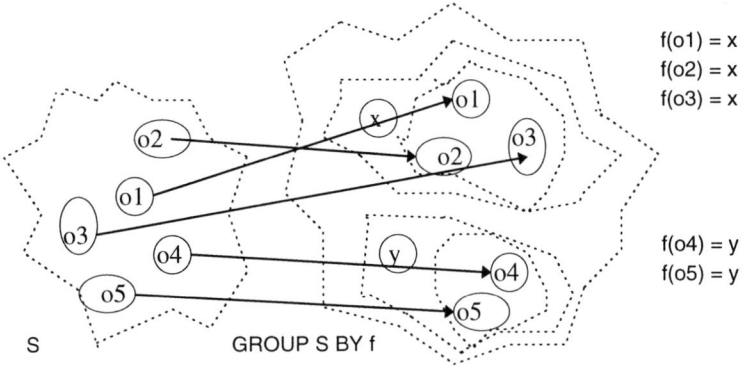

f(o1) = x
f(o2) = x
f(o3) = x

f(o4) = y
f(o5) = y

S                    GROUP S BY f

Figure 5.12 GROUP

The operation for grouping objects in a set–object, S, on the values returned by a grouping function, f, is denoted:

  GROUP S BY f

*ELIMINATE_DUPLICATES*

The last operator in this "pick" and "mix" group is the ELIMINATE_DUPLICATES operator. This operator returns a set–object which contains only one of each of the objects contained in the set–object upon which it operates (see Figure 5.13).

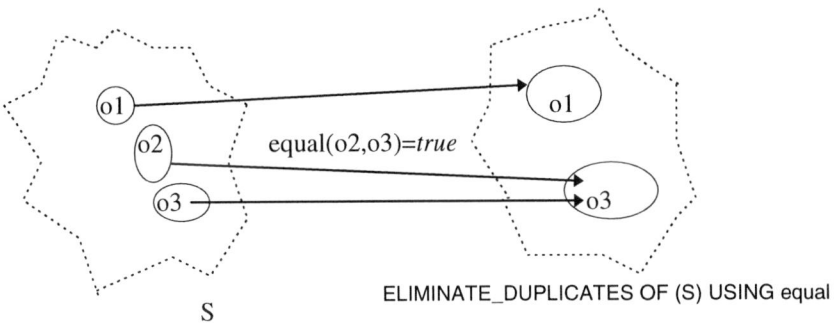

equal(o2,o3)=*true*

S                    ELIMINATE_DUPLICATES OF (S) USING equal

Figure 5.13 ELIMINATE_DUPLICATES

On first reading, this operator may appear to be redundant, since by definition there can be only one of each object within a set. However, the operation exists because there may be many application–specific criteria for considering two objects to be equal. ELIMINATE_DUPLICATES allows us to specify a function for testing object equality.

---

*EXAMPLE 5.9*

*The following expression in the object algebra uses the ELIMINATE_DUPLICATES operator to create a set–object containing only one Product object of each colour.*

ELIMINATE_DUPLICATES OF products
USING colour_equality

*In the above expression we assume that colour_equality is defined elsewhere to return true if two Product objects have the same value for the colour attribute; otherwise false. Where there is more than one equal object, one of them is arbitrarily chosen to be included in the resulting set–object. The result of applying the above expression to the Figure 5.1 object database is shown in Figure 5.14.*

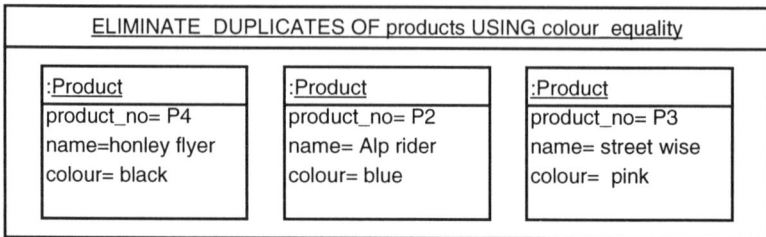

| ELIMINATE_DUPLICATES OF products USING colour_equality | | |
|---|---|---|
| :Product | :Product | :Product |
| product_no= P4 | product_no= P2 | product_no= P3 |
| name=honley flyer | name= Alp rider | name= street wise |
| colour= black | colour= blue | colour= pink |

Figure 5.14 The Example 5.9 query

---

An ELIMINATE_DUPLICATES operation which eliminates duplicate objects from a set–object, S, using the operation equiv to determine equality between objects, is denoted:

ELIMINATE_DUPLICATES FROM S USING equiv

OBJECT PROCESSING OPERATORS

The next set of operators upon set–objects are those which can be used to process objects by applying operations to them. The operations that can be applied can either be application–specific functions or the operations defined for the relevant object types.

## APPLY

The APPLY operator is used to process the objects in a set by applying to each of them a specific operation, as illustrated in Figure 5.15.

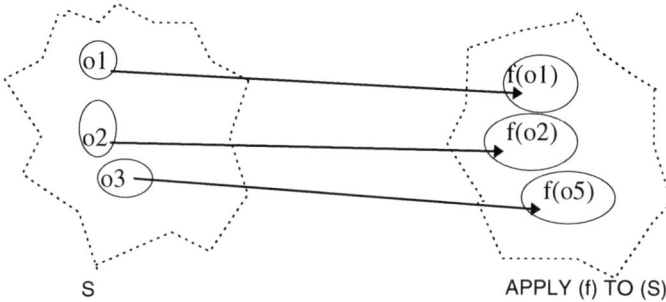

Figure 5.15 APPLY

---

### EXAMPLE 5.10

*The following expression in the object algebra uses the APPLY operator to represent an application which computes the value of sales orders. It does this by applying the operatio, sales_order_value? to each SalesOrder object.*

APPLY sales_order_value? TO sales_orders

*The object returned by this operation is the set–object which contains the set of literals returned by the calculate_order_value? function, each of which represents a value of one of the SalesOrder objects.*

---

The operation which applies the function f to each object in the set–object S is denoted,

APPLY f TO S

## FOLD

The FOLD operator, like APPLY, applies an operation to each object in a set, but also applies a second operation to the resulting objects so as to combine them into a single object, as illustrated in Figure 5.16. In this way FOLD summarises information.

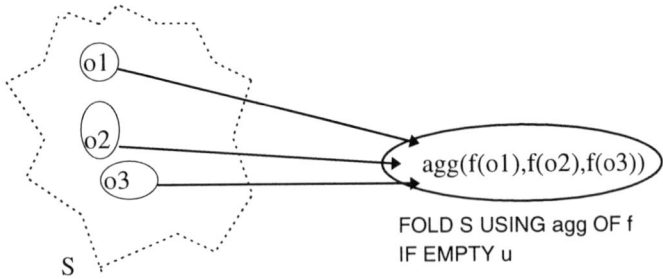

Figure 5.16 FOLD

---

EXAMPLE 5.11

*In order to compute the total value of outstanding sales orders, it is necessary to compute the value of each sales order (using the sales_order_value? operation) and then to total together the computed sales order values (using the sum operation). This can be represented in the object algebra as follows:*

> FOLD salesorders USING
> > sum OF sales_order_value?
> > IF EMPTY 0

*If the values of the three SalesOrder objects in salesorders (see Figure 5.1) (computed by the sales_order_value? operation) are 100, 200, and 200, then the value of the above expression will be the literal 500, returned by the sum operation when applied to the three sales order values. Note that the above expression also includes an IF EMPTY clause which specifies the object to be returned if the set–object to which fold is applied is empty. If there were no objects in salesorders, then the literal 0 would be returned.*

---

The fold of a set–object, S, computed by applying the aggregation operation agg to the values returned by applying an operation f to each object in S, where u is the value returned if S is empty, is denoted:

> FOLD S USING agg OF f
> IF EMPTY u

### JOIN

A JOIN operation matches objects within different sets–objects, and then applies a specified function to each matching pair. This is illustrated in

Figure 5.17. The figure depicts how a join causes pairs of objects, one from S and one from R, are to be joined where they satisfy a specified condition, p. Each pair is joined by applying a function, f. Join is used to bring together related information contained in different collection–objects. It is an important and powerful operation because it allows us to use relationships between objects which exist by virtue of common values within their states, as well as those associations which are explicit in the relationships.

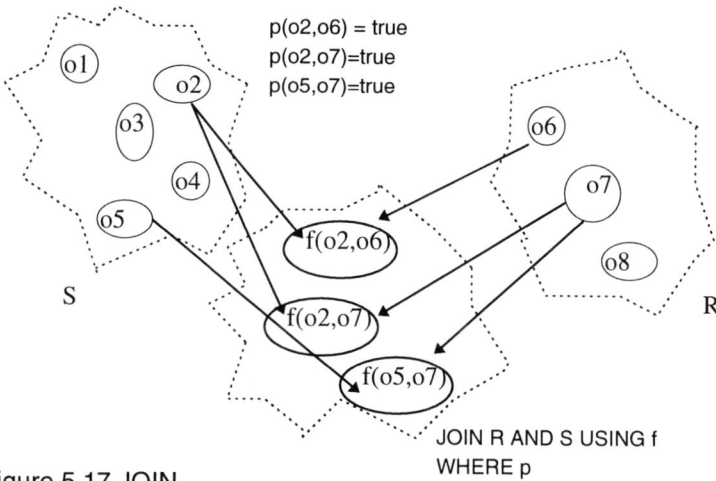

Figure 5.17 JOIN

---

*EXAMPLE 5.12*

*When processing a sales order, it is necessary to combine information about the sales order with information about the relevant customer. This combining of information can be represented by the object algebra join operation,*

> JOIN customers AND salesorders USING concat
> WHERE customers.customer_no =
>      salesorders.placed_by.customer_no

*There are two interesting points to note in this expression.*

1) *The join condition compares an attribute of a Customer object with an attribute of the Customer object related to a SalesOrder object via the placed_by relationship.*

2) *Matching objects are combined using the special operation concat (concatenate). Concat creates a new object with all of the properties of both of the two objects being combined.*

*The result of the above expression when applied to the Figure 5.1. object database is shown in Figure 5.18. Note that the information contained in objects which do not match is lost, and the information contained in matching objects is duplicated for each match.*

| JOIN customers AND salesorders USING concat WHERE customers.customer_no = salesorders.placed_by.customer_no | | |
|---|---|---|
| concat (...) <br> order_no=O6 <br> order_lines= <br>   [< P2, 100>, <br>    < P4, 50>] <br> customer_no= C1 <br> name= Faulties <br> address= <br>   <5 Road, Leeds> <br> telephones= <br> {1234567, 13243} | concat (...) <br> order_no=O4 <br> order_lines= <br>   [< P2, 50>] <br> customer_no= C1 <br> name= Faulties <br> address= <br>   <5 Road, Leeds> <br> telephones= <br> {1234567, 13243} | concat (...) <br> order_no=O9 <br> order_lines= <br>   [<P1, 100> <br>   <P2, 200>] <br> customer_no= C3 <br> name=Graft Ltd <br> address= <br>   <7 Street, Wyke> <br> telephones= <br> {0456132435, <br>   02349854} |

Figure 5.18 The Example 5.12 JOIN

The join of two sets–object, S and R, where objects are combined using the operation f, when they satisfy the condition p, is denoted:

JOIN R AND S USING f WHERE p

The join operation in Example 5.12 is of a common type, where the properties of matched objects are simply combined using the concat operation to form the properties of the resulting object. In the object algebra this type of join operation is called a **tuple_join**.

The tuple_join of two set–objects, R and S, using the matching function p, is denoted:

TUPLE_JOIN R AND S WHERE p

The above tuple_join notation is simply shorthand for

JOIN R AND S USING concat WHERE p

Both the join and tuple_join lose unmatched objects. However, there is another variation of the join operator, called the **outer_join**, for applications which are also interested in unmatched objects. The outer_join operation is used to represent queries which retrieve details of two different types of entity, together with other relevant information which associates them, where appropriate.

The outer_join combines objects taken from two operand set–objects, and uses three functions. The first processes pairs of matching objects, the second processes unmatched objects from the first operand, and the third processes unmatched objects from the second operand (as illustrated in Figure 5.19).

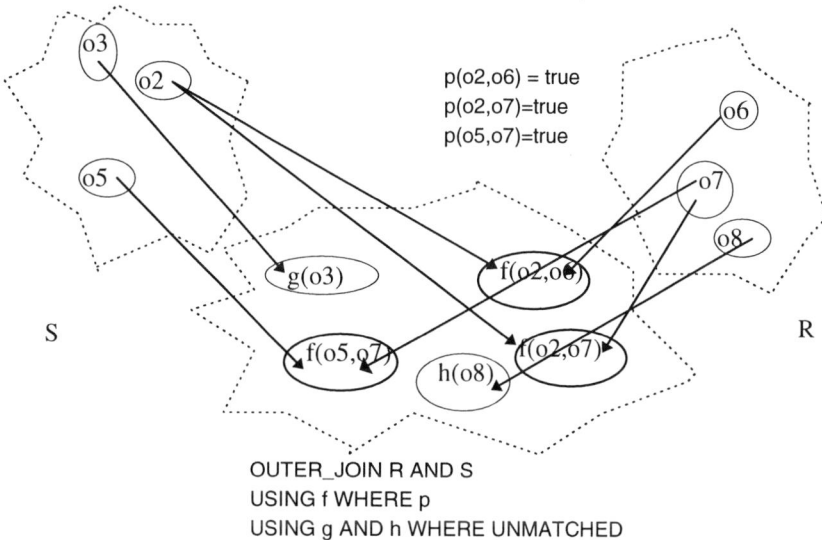

p(o2,o6) = true
p(o2,o7)=true
p(o5,o7)=true

OUTER_JOIN R AND S
USING f WHERE p
USING g AND h WHERE UNMATCHED

Figure 5.19 OUTER_JOIN

*EXAMPLE 5.13*
*The following expression represents the query "retrieve details of customers and sales orders, together with details of associations between them":*

> OUTER_JOIN customers AND salesorders USING concat
> WHERE customers.customer_no =
> salesorders.placed_by.customer_no
> USING pad AND pad WHERE UNMATCHED

*The effect of the above expression it to create a set–object with the following contents:*

1) *For each pair of matching Customer and SalesOrder objects, an object is created by applying the concat operation to them—concat creates an object which combines the properties of the two argument objects.*
2) *For each unmatched Customer object, an object formed by applying the pad operation to it—pad assigns a null value to unspecified properties (i.e., the SalesOrder properties).*
3) *For each unmatched SalesOrder object (though there should not be any), an object is formed by applying the pad operation to it—in this case, pad sets the Customer properties to null.*

*The result of the above when applied to the Figure 5.1 object database is shown in Figure 5.20. Note that, unlike for the join in Example 5.12, the information contained in objects which do not match is not lost.*

The following expression denotes the outer_join which:
- joins two set–objects, R and S;
- uses a function, f, to process matching objects;
- uses a condition, p, to match objects in R and S;
- and uses two functions, r and s respectively, to generate result objects from unmatched objects in R and S.

> OUTER_JOIN R AND S USING f WHERE p
> USING r AND s WHERE UNMATCHED

Join operations are particularly important when querying an object database on the basis of object property values. A join can be used to aggregate together information taken from several associated objects of different types, simply by stating the conditions which must hold for the values of related objects.

```
┌─────────────────────────────────────────────────────────────────────┐
│            OUTER  JOIN customers AND salesorders USING concat         │
│      WHERE customers.customer_no = salesorders.placed_by.customer_no  │
│                 USING pad AND pad WHERE UNMATCHED                      │
│  ┌──────────────────┐  ┌──────────────────┐  ┌──────────────────┐    │
│  │concat (...)      │  │concat (...)      │  │concat (...)      │    │
│  │order_no=O6       │  │order_no=O4       │  │order_no=O9       │    │
│  │order_lines=      │  │order_lines=      │  │order_lines=      │    │
│  │  [< P2, 100>,    │  │  [< P2, 50>]     │  │  [<P1, 100>      │    │
│  │   < P4,  50>]    │  │customer_no= C1   │  │   <P2, 200>]     │    │
│  │customer_no= C1   │  │name= Faulties    │  │customer_no= C3   │    │
│  │name= Faulties    │  │address=          │  │name=Graft Ltd    │    │
│  │address=          │  │  <5 Road, Leeds> │  │address=          │    │
│  │  <5 Road, Leeds> │  │telephones=       │  │<7 Street, Wyke>  │    │
│  │telephones=       │  │{1234567, 13243}  │  │telephones=       │    │
│  │{1234567. 13243}  │  └──────────────────┘  │{0456132435,      │    │
│  └──────────────────┘                        │  02349854}       │    │
│  ┌──────────────────┐                        └──────────────────┘    │
│  │pad(...)          │                                                 │
│  │order_no= nil     │                                                 │
│  │order_lines= nil  │                                                 │
│  │customer_no= C2   │                                                 │
│  │name= Harding Bros│                                                 │
│  │address= <2 Way, Honley> │                                          │
│  │telephones= {1923857}    │                                          │
│  └─────────────────────────┘                                         │
└─────────────────────────────────────────────────────────────────────┘
```

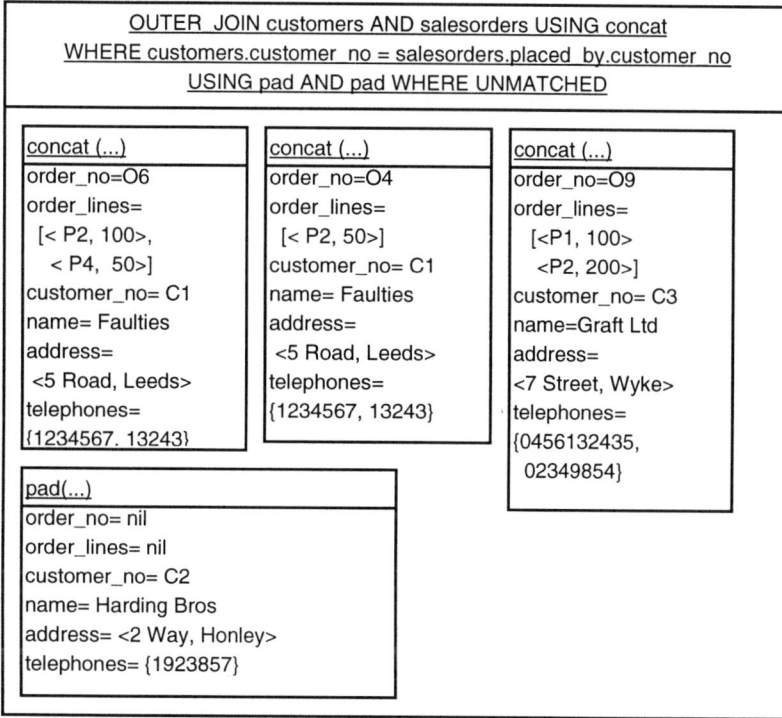

Figure 5.20 The Example 5.13 OUTER_JOIN

*LEAST_FIXED_POINT*

The last operator in this group is LEAST_FIXED_POINT. This operator retrieves information by repeatedly applying a specified function until no further information can be generated. The precise meaning of this operator is more complex than previous ones and so we explain it with the aid of an example.

Consider the situation (known as the bill of materials problem) where we wish to retrieve information about all of the components of a particular manufactured part. Information about parts and their composition can be represented in the object database by relationships which associate Part objects and their component Part objects (see Figure 5.21). Using this representation:

1) Each part is modelled by a Part object which is associated with other Part objects which represent its components via the is_part_of relationship.

2) Each part component is modelled by a Part object which is associated with other Part objects which represent the parts of which it is a component via the is_used_in relationship.

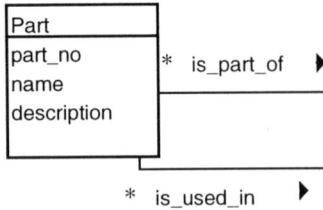

Figure 5.21 A representation of composite parts

An example set of Part objects instances is given in Figure 5.21. In this figure, the direction of the is_part_of relationships is from the top to the bottom of the diagram. The diagram shows that part P1 has two components, P3 and P4; P3 has one component, P6; P4 has two components, P6 and P7; and so on.

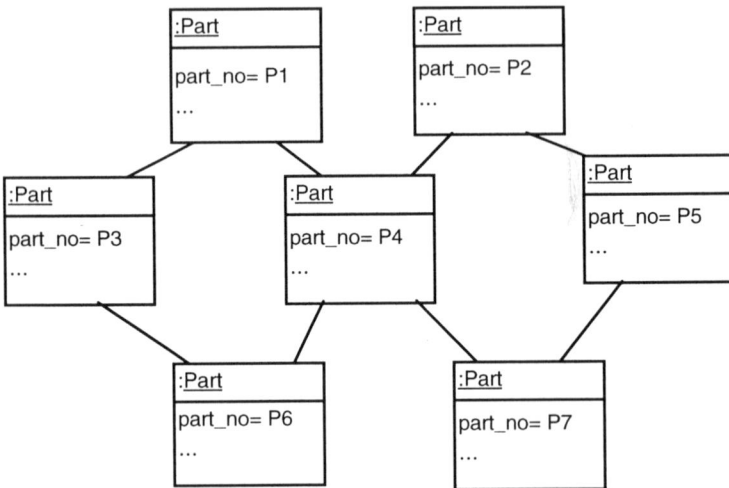

Figure 5.22 Instances of Part objects (defined in Figure 5.21)

In order to satisfy the query "what different parts are used in P1?" we must navigate the is_part_of relationships, starting at the object that represents P1, and collect together details of all the objects that we encounter on the way. We can describe this process more precisely in terms of a function, get_component_parts?, which retrieves objects related to a set of Part objects via the is_part_of relationship.

1) **Apply get_component_parts? zero time**—the result of this step is the empty set.
2) **Apply get_component_parts? once**—the function is applied to the operand object set, which contains the Part object for part P1. This step returns the set containing Part objects for P3 and P4 (these are the two objects related to P1 via the is_part_of relationship).
3) **Apply get_component_parts? a second time**—the function is applied to the result of step 2, and returns the set containing Part objects for P6 and P7 (these are the two objects related to P3 and P4 via the is_part_of relationship).
4) **Return the union of the results of the preceding steps.**

The above process accumulates the set of all objects that can be derived from the initial operand object using the given function. The process of re–applying get_component_parts? could go on for ever, but this is not necessary, since no additional objects will be retrieved after step 3. The point at which no further information can be extracted in this way is called the **least fixed point**. The general problem of retrieving all objects that can be reached via some relationship, called the **transitive closure** problem, is common in database applications. However, a least fixed point operator for solving it is not usually provided in database languages (with the exception of deductive databases (see Chapter 10)).

LEAST_FIXED_POINT expresses queries of the type illustrated above. It returns the union of the sets of objects generated by repeatedly applying some function until no further objects are generated. The above query is represented using this operator as follows:

> LEAST_FIXED_POINT[Set<Part>] OF
> (RESTRICT parts WHERE part_no = 'P1')
> USING   get_component_parts?

Note that in the operand set–object is defined by a restrict expression and that the expression specifies the type of the object returned, Set<Part>.

The least fixed point, of type Set<T>, of a set–object, S, derived using the function f is denoted:

LEAST_FIXED_POINT[T] OF S USING f

The above operation is valid only if the function f satisfies two requirements:

1) The result of the function must be of the same type as that of the operand object—this in necessary if the function is to be re–applied repeatedly. A function, such as who_has_ordered?, which when applied to Part objects returns Customer objects, is not acceptable, since it cannot be re–applied to the returned Customer object.

2) The function should be such that a least fixed point is eventually reached which is a sensible answer to the query. The successor function which returns the next integer (e.g., successor(1) = 2) is not acceptable because the least fixed point will never be reached! The logical NOT function is also unacceptable, because repeated application will always alternate between true and false, causing the LEAST_FIXED_POINT operator to always return {true,false}!

(A formal study of fixed point operators in database theory is given in [Abiteboul 95]).

## BOOLEAN OPERATORS

The final group of operations upon set–objects are to test their properties. The following operators are Boolean, i.e., they return true or false, and can be used within restrict predicates and join conditions.

### EXISTS

The EXISTS operator returns true if there exists within a set–object an object for which a specified Boolean condition evaluates to true; otherwise it returns false (see Figure 5.23).

---

*EXAMPLE 5.14*

*The following expression tests if there exists a sales order which was placed by customer C1:*

EXISTS (ordered_by.customer_no = 'C1') IN salesorders

*When applied to the Figure 5.1 object database the above expression will return the Boolean literal, true. Note the use of the relationship ordered_by to navigate from the SalesOrder objects to the associated Customer objects.*

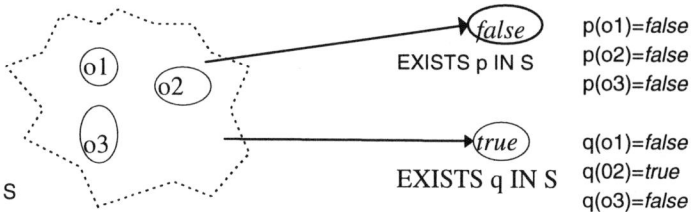

Figure 5.23  EXISTS

The expression for testing if a condition, p, is true for any of the objects contained in a set–object, S, is denoted:

EXISTS p IN S

*FORALL*

The FORALL operator returns true if a specified Boolean expression returns true for **all** objects contained in the operand set–object; otherwise the expression returns false (see Figure 5.24).

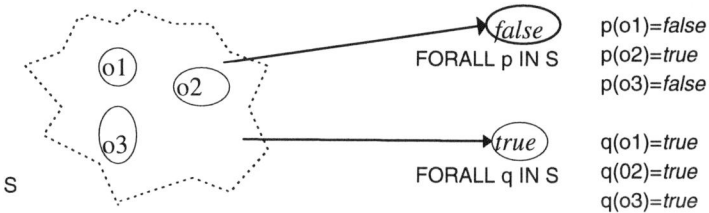

Figure 5.24  FORALL

*EXAMPLE 5.15*

*The following expression returns true if all Product objects are black:*

FORALL colour = 'black'  IN products

*If executed against the Figure 5.1 object database the above expression will return false, since there are also pink and blue products.*

---

An operation which returns true if a specified condition, p, returns true for every object in a set object, S, is denoted:

FORALL p IN S

## MEMBER

The MEMBER operator returns true if a specified object is contained with a set–object; otherwise it returns false (see Figure 5.25).

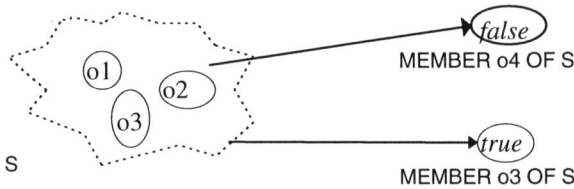

Figure 5.25  MEMBER

---

## EXAMPLE 5.16

*The following expression returns a set–object containing products which are either black or pink. The MEMBER operator is used in the restrict predicate to test if the value of the colour attributes is a member of the literal set–object containing the literals black and pink.*

RESTRICT products WHERE
(colour MEMBER OF {'black','pink'})

*This example illustrates how expressions can freely be used as arguments for other expressions, providing their value is of the expected type. Given the Figure 5.1 object database, the above expression will return a set–object containing the Product objects for products P1, P2, and P4, because the MEMBER operator will return true for each of these.*

---

The expression which returns true if an object, O, is a member of a set–object, S, is denoted:

MEMBER O OF S

## 5.4. OPERATIONS ON OTHER TYPES OF OBJECT COLLECTIONS

The object algebra can represent the manipulation of all of the types supported by the Object Data Model. This section describes the operators for manipulating bag–objects and for conversion between atomic, set– and bag–object types. Operators for manipulating list– and array–objects are not described here, but can be derived from the operators described in this chapter [Subramanian 95].

### OPERATIONS ON BAGS

A bag–object, like a set–object, contains an unordered collection of objects of the same type. However, a bag and a set differ—a bag may contain more than one occurrence of an object, whereas all objects in a set must be distinct. Most of the operators on set–objects can operate in the same way upon bag–objects, the only difference being that the operands and result are bag–objects, not set–objects. The exceptions are the UNION, INTERSECT, and MINUS operators. The definitions of these are adapted to allow for multiple occurrences of an object.

### UNION

UNION can be applied to two bag–objects, in which case the result is also a bag–object. The result contains each distinct object contained in one or both of the operand bags. If a particular object occurs more times in one operand bag–object than the other, then that is the number of times it will occur in the resulting bag–object (see Figure 5.26).

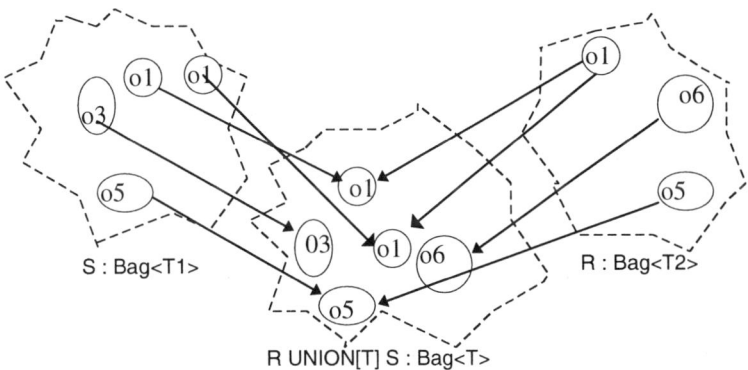

Figure 5.26 BAG UNION

When union is applied it is necessary to specify the type of object contained in the resulting bag–object, since there may be a number of different supertypes that objects contained in the operand bag–objects have in common, as was the case for set union.

---

*EXAMPLE 5.17*

*Two objects, product1_parts and product2_parts, both of type Bag<Part>, respectively contain the Part objects which represent the components of products P1 and P2. These are bag–objects so that multiple occurrences of a component can be represented. The following object algebra represents the query "retrieve details of the products which could be used to construct either product1 or product2". (Figure 5.25 shows the result for a specific bag-objects).*

product1_parts UNION[Product] product2_parts

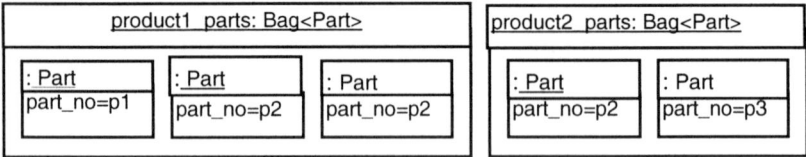

---

| product1_parts: Bag<Part> | | | product2_parts: Bag<Part> | |
|---|---|---|---|---|
| : Part<br>part_no=p1 | : Part<br>part_no=p2 | : Part<br>part_no=p2 | : Part<br>part_no=p2 | : Part<br>part_no=p3 |

(a) Operand bag–objects

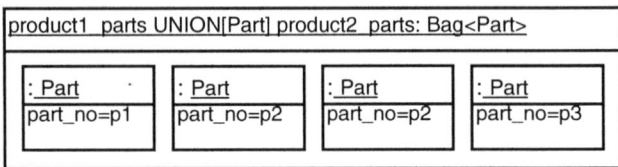

| product1_parts UNION[Part] product2_parts: Bag<Part> | | | |
|---|---|---|---|
| : Part<br>part_no=p1 | : Part<br>part_no=p2 | : Part<br>part_no=p2 | : Part<br>part_no=p3 |

(b) Result bag–object

Figure 5.27 The Example 5.17 UNION operation

An alternative definition is that the union of bag–objects contains all of the objects contained in the two operand bag–objects. This second interpretation is implemented by the ADDITIVE_UNION operator (see Figure 5.28). For example, iff two operand bag–objects respectively contain three and two of object o1, then the bag–objects defined by the UNION and ADDITIVE_UNION operators will respectively contain three and five of object o1.

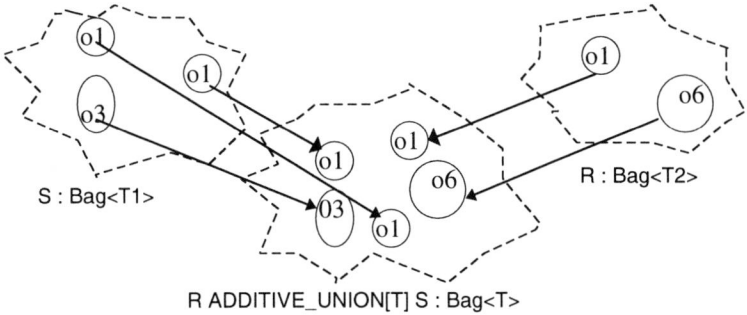

R ADDITIVE_UNION[T] S : Bag<T>

Figure 5.28 ADDITIVE_UNION

---

## EXAMPLE 5.18

*The following object algebra expression represents the query "retrieve details of the products which could be used to construct both product1 and product2", where product1_parts and product2_parts are as defined in Example 5.17.*

product1_parts ADDITIVE_UNION[Part] product2_parts

*Figure 5.29 gives the result when applied to the bag-objects in Figure 5.27(a).*

---

| product1_parts ADDITIVE_UNION[Part] product2_parts: Bag<Part> | | | | |
|---|---|---|---|---|
| : Part | : Part | : Part | : Part | : Part |
| part_no=p1 | part_no=p2 | part_no=p2 | part_no=p3 | part_no=p3 |

Figure 5.29 The Example 5.18 ADDITIVE_UNION operation

The UNION and ADDITIVE_UNION of two bag-objects, R and S, where the result is of type Bag<T> are respectively denoted:

R UNION[T] S
R ADDITIVE_UNION[T] S

## INTERSECT

The INTERSECT operator defines a bag–object which includes objects contained in both of the two argument bag–objects. The number of each object in the result will therefore be the smaller number of that object in one or other of the operand bags–objects. For example, the result of an intersection of two bags which respectively contain five and ten of object o1 will contain five of o1 (see Figure 5.30).

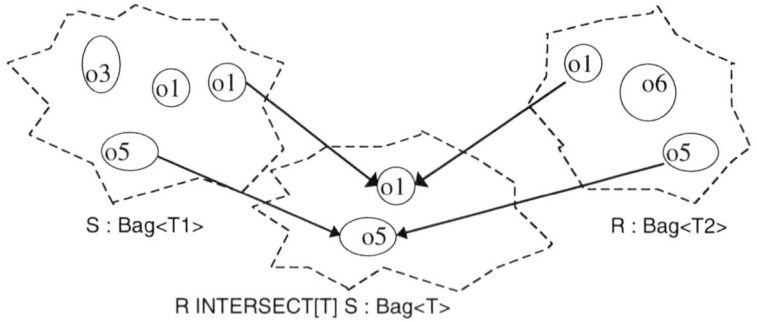

Figure 5.30. INTERSECT

---

*EXAMPLE 5.19*

*The following object algebra expression represents the query "retrieve details of the products which are common to both product1 and product2", where product1_parts and product2_parts are as defined in Example 5.25.*

(product1_parts) INTERSECT[Part] (product2_parts)

*Figure 5.31 gives the result when applied to the bag-objects in Figure 5.27(a).*

---

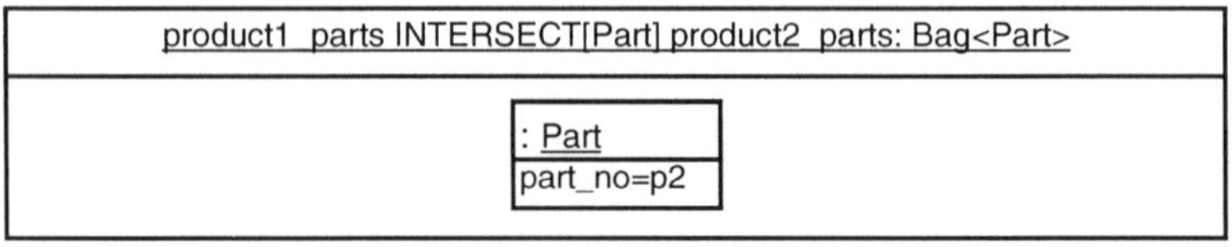

Figure 5.31 The Example 5.19 INTERSECT operation

The intersection of two bag–objects, R and S, which returns an object of type Bag<T> is denoted:

R INTERSECT[T] S

*DIFFERENCE*
The MINUS operator defines a bag–object which contains the difference between two operand bag–objects, i.e., all of the objects in the first, once the objects in the second have been removed (see Figure 5.32).

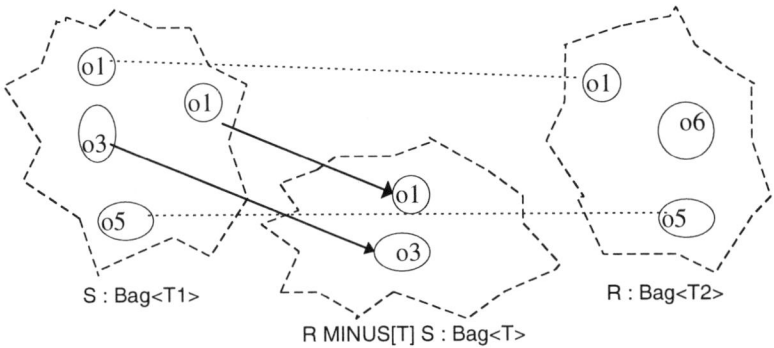

Figure 5.32 DIFFERENCE

---

*EXAMPLE 5.20*

*The following object algebra expression represents the query "given the set of parts needed to construct product1, retrieve details of the parts which remain after removing ones needed to construct product2", where product1_parts and product2_parts are as defined in Example 5.25.*

product1_parts MINUS[Part] product2_parts

*Figure 5.33 gives the result when applied to the bag-objects in Figure 5.27(a).*

---

Figure 5.33 The Example 5.20 MINUS operation

The difference of two bag–objects, R and S, which returns an object of type Bag<T> is denoted:

R MINUS[T] S

## 5.5 TYPE CONVERSION

Finally, we describe operators for converting from one type to another. This is necessary in order to create new objects and to present information in suitable forms. The operators described convert between bag–objects, set–objects, and atomic objects, and modify structure–objects.

## CHOOSE
The CHOOSE operator, previously described as part of the "pick" and "mix" group, can also be viewed as a conversion operator, since it can be used to convert a set–object to the object that is contains.

## BAG, SET, AND CONVERT
The BAG, SET, and CONVERT operators are used to create bag– and set–objects, and to convert objects from one of these types to the another (see Figure 5.34).
- SET creates a set–object which contains a single specified object.
- BAG creates a bag–object which contains a single specified object.
- CONVERT converts a specified bag–object into a set–object (removing any duplicate objects), or a specified set–object into a bag–object.

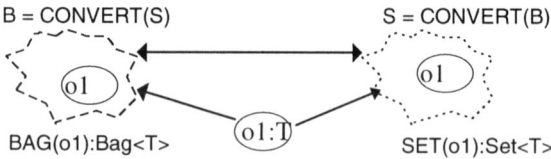

Figure 5.34  BAG, SET, and CONVERT

---

## EXAMPLE 5.21
*The following object algebra expressions represent the conversion between atomic–, set– and bag–object types.*

1)  *This expression defines a set–object which contains two literal objects. These respectively represent the total weight of the parts of product1 and product2. The bag–objects, product1_parts and product2_parts, are as defined in Figure 5.27.*

> (SET(FOLD (product1_parts) USING sum OF weight
> IF EMPTY 0))
> UNION(Float)
> (SET(FOLD (product2_parts) USING sum OF weight
> IF EMPTY 0))

*The two FOLD operators which are applied to the bag–objects respectively return the total weight of product1 and product2 as literals of type Float. The SET operators are applied to these literals to create two set–objects, each of which contains one of the values returned by a FOLD operation. Finally, the UNION operator returns a set–object which contains both of those literals.*

2) *The above is a poor solution, since in certain circumstances it will not produce the desired result. This is because if both products have exactly the same total weight, then one of the duplicate literals will be removed (objects in a set must be distinct). We should therefore use a bag–object, rather than a set-object, so as to always retain both literals, as follows:*

   (BAG(FOLD (product1_parts) USING sum OF weight
   IF EMPTY 0))
   UNION(Float)
   (BAG(FOLD (product2_parts) USING sum OF weight
   IF EMPTY 0))

3) *An alternative way of defining the set–object in (1) is to define the bag–object as in( 2) and then to convert it into a set–object:*

   CONVERT
   (BAG(FOLD(product1_parts) USING sum OF weight
   IF EMPTY 0))
   UNION(Float)
   (BAG(FOLD (product2_parts) USING sum OF weight
   IF EMPTY 0)))

   *Note that conversion from a bag to a set can cause loss of information, since it will lose any duplicate objects.*

---

The creation of a set–object and a bag–object, both of which contain a single object, R, are respectively denoted:

   SET (R)
   BAG (R)

The conversion of bag–object R into a set–object, and of set–object R into a bag–object is denoted:

CONVERT R

*NEST AND UNNEST*
The NEST and UNNEST operators are used to modify the structure of objects contained within a set–objects.

NEST operates upon a set–object and returns a set–object within which the original information has been re–structured into a more concise form. To illustrate this process, consider a set–object which contains objects with two attributes, named department and employee, shown in Figure 5.35 (a). A more concise way of representing the information in the above set–object is for it to contain only one object for each department, with an employee attribute which contains the set of all of a department's employees (as in Figure 5.35 (b)) This removes the need to duplicate a department number for each of its employees. The NEST operator can be used to perform this conversion.

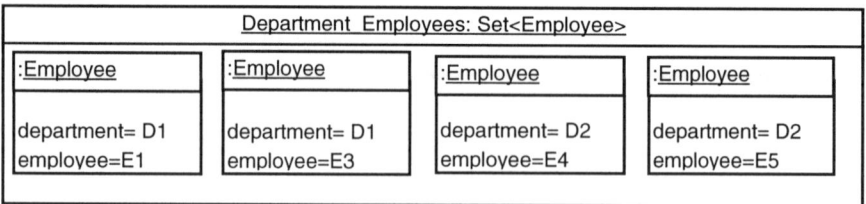

| Department_Employees: Set<Employee> | | | |
|---|---|---|---|
| :Employee | :Employee | :Employee | :Employee |
| department= D1 <br> employee=E1 | department= D1 <br> employee=E3 | department= D2 <br> employee=E4 | department= D2 <br> employee=E5 |

a) A representation of department employee information

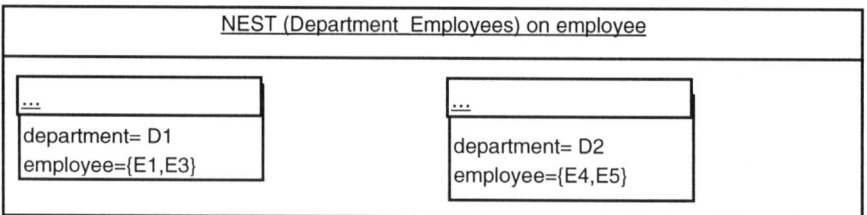

| NEST (Department_Employees) on employee | |
|---|---|
| ... <br> department= D1 <br> employee={E1,E3} | ... <br> department= D2 <br> employee={E4,E5} |

b) A nested representation of department employee information

Figure 5.35 Representations of department information

When we nest a set–object, R, on a property, Y, the following happens (see Figure 5.36):

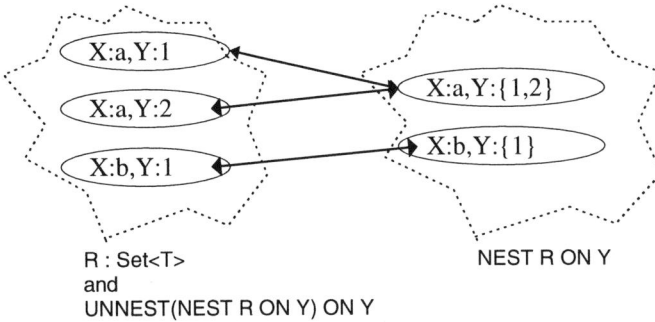

R : Set<T>
and
UNNEST(NEST R ON Y) ON Y

NEST R ON Y

Figure 5.36 NEST AND UNNEST

1)  A new set–object is created in which every set of objects in R for which properties other than Y are equal is replaced by a single object.

2)  Each of the objects in the result have the same property values as the objects that they replace, with the exception of the Y property. The Y property is replaced by a set–valued attribute which contains all of the values of the Y property of the replaced objects.

UNNEST performs the reverse process (for example, UNNEST could be used to convert from the structure in Figure 5.35 (b) back to the structure in Figure 5.35 (a)).

Note, however, that if we take a nested structure, unnest it, and then nest it again, we do not necessarily recreate the original set–objects, since re–nesting cannot always recreate structural information lost by the unnest operation. For example, unnesting {(X:1, Y:{a,b}), (X:1,Y:{c}) on Y creates {(X:1,Y:a), (X:1,Y:b), (X:1,Y:c)}, but if we then nest on Y we create {(X:1, Y:{a,b,c}), not what we started with.

The nest and unnest operations upon a set–object, R, on a property, Y, are respectively denoted:

NEST R ON Y
UNNEST R ON Y

CONSTRUCTION OF NEW OBJECTS USING TYPE NAMES

We can create new objects from the literals which will form their attribute values. This is done using the type name as a constructor operator. To illustrate this we return to the very first example of object algebra given in this chapter, i.e.,

> retail_customers
> UNION[Customer]
> SET(Customer(customer_no:'C2', name:'Barry'))

This expression defines the union of the retail_customer set–object (see Example 5.5) and a newly created Customer object with attribute values 'C2' and 'Barry'. Having defined this new object, the SET operator creates a set–object which contains it, and the UNION operator combines it with the set–object retail_customers. The object type name, Customer, is used here as the operator which returns a new Customer object. Property names and their values are provided as parameters. Properties which are not provided with an initial value are set to the null value.

The construction of a new object of type T with property values v and w for properties V and W is denoted:

> T (V:v, W:w)

## 5.6 SUMMARY

The **manipulative part** of the Object Data Model is the set of things that can be done to an object database. This is defined in a mathematical form called an **object algebra**. The example object algebra described in this chapter, **AQUA**, is one of a number of published object algebras. There is as yet no single object algebra which has wide acceptance. A formal object data model and object algebra provide a precise way of explaining the meaning of object database languages and a theory with which to research associated issues.

Object algebra is to objects, what conventional algebra is to numbers. **expressions** define objects by applying **operators** to other objects represented by **constants** and **variables**. The operators of our object algebra can be used to (i) define objects which are of interest; (ii) apply operations to them; and (iii) create new objects which contain the required information.

Every object algebra expression has an **expression value** which is an object. The type of the expression value can be determined by analysing the expression. Expressions can be constructed from other expressions by applying operatons to them.

The "pick" and "mix" operators upon set–objects are **RESTRICT, UNION, INTERSECT, DIFFERENCE, CHOOSE, GROUP,** and **ELIMINATE_DUPLICATES.**

The operators upon set–objects which apply operations to objects within a collection–object are **APPLY, FOLD, JOIN** (including **TUPLE_JOIN** and **OUTER_JOIN**) and **LEAST_FIXED_POINT.**

The object algebra also includes Boolean operators which are used to test the properties of objects within a collection. These are **EXISTS, FORALL** and **MEMBER.**

The above operators apply to all types of set– and bag–objects, with the exception of **UNION, INTERSECT,** and **DIFFERENCE.** These need to be redefined to operate upon bag–objects to take into account the fact that an object may occur more than once within a bag.

The object algebra also includes operators to change the type of an object. Set– and bag–objects can be created using the **SET** and **BAG** operators. The **CONVERT** operator convert a set–object into a bag–object, and a bag–object into a set–object. **NEST** and **UNNEST** are used to add and remove structures within an object. **Type names** can be used as operators with which to construct new instances.

## EXERCISES:

(5.1)    What does the manipulative part of the Object Data Model define?

(5.2)    What is the difference between an object database language and an object algebra?

(5.3)    In what way is it useful to have an object algebra, in addition to object database languages?

(5.4)    In what ways are object algebra and conventional algebra similar?

(5.5)    What are the components of an object algebra expression?

(5.6)   What is meant by the value of an object algebra expression?

(5.7)   Describe three general functions that the operators of an object algebra must be able to represent in order to model object database queries.

(5.8)   Given the example object database in Figure 5.1 (and assuming that all collection–objects are sets), what is the value of each of the following expressions in object algebra:

(i)     RESTRICT products WHERE name = 'street wise'

(ii)    RESTRICT products WHERE NOT (colour = 'black')

(iii)   RESTRICT products WHERE NOT(colour='pink' AND name='street wise') OR name='street wise'

(iv)    RESTRICT (RESTRICT products WHERE NOT (name = 'bat bike') WHERE colour = 'black'

(v)     RESTRICT salesorders WHERE placed_by.name = 'Faulties'

(vi)    (RESTRICT products WHERE colour='pink') UNION[Product] (RESTRICT products WHERE colour='black')

(vii)   (RESTRICT products WHERE colour='black') INTERSECT[Product] (RESTRICT products WHERE NOT(name='bat bike')

(viii)  (RESTRICT products WHERE colour='black') MINUS[Product] (RESTRICT products WHERE NOT(name='bat bike')

(5.9)   Why was it necessary to specify a type parameter in the UNION, INTERSECT, and MINUS operations in the previous exercise?

(5.10)  What are the three possible values for the following expression:
CHOOSE FROM salesorders

(5.11)  Explain the purpose of the CHOOSE operator.

(5.12)  Given a function, number_of_order_lines?, which counts the number of order lines in a specified SalesOrder object, what is the value of the following expression when applied to Figure 5.1:

GROUP salesorders BY number_of_order_lines?

(5.13)  Given a function, colour_equality?, which returns true if two Product objects have the same colour, false otherwise, what are the two possible values of the following expression (on Figure 5.1):

ELIMINATE_DUPLICATES OF salesorders
USING colour_equality?

(5.14)  Given two functions, number_of_products? and total, which
respectively return the number of products a specific SalesOrder
object is for, and the total value of a collection of integer literals,
what are the values of the following expressions (on Figure 5.1):
   (i)    APPLY number_of_products? TO (RESTRICT
          salesorders WHERE NOT (order_no = 'O9'))
   (ii)   FOLD salesorders USING total OF
          number_of_products?

(5.15)  Associated objects can be retrieved by navigating the
relationships between them. Explain the way in which the JOIN
operator provides an alternative method of retrieving
information from associated objects on the basis of attribute
values.

(5.16)  What are the values returned by the following expressions (on
Figure 5.1):
   (i)    JOIN (s IN salesorders) AND
          (c IN (RESTRICT customers
               WHERE address.city='Leeds'))
           USING CONCAT
          WHERE s.has_been_ordered.name = c.name
   (ii)   JOIN (c1 IN customers) AND (c2 IN customers)
          USING STRUCT (name1:c1.name, name2:c2.name)
          WHERE c1.address = c2.address AND c1 != c2
   (iv)   OUTER_TUPLE_ JOIN (c1 IN customers)
          AND (o2 IN salesorders)
          WHERE c1.name = o2.placed_by.name
          USING pad AND pad WHERE UNMATCHED

(5.17)  Consider a set–object UNDERGROUND which is of the type
Set<Struct<from:String,to:String>>. The two elements of each
structure respectively name two adjacent stations on the London
Underground transport system. Use the LEAST_FIXED_POINT
operator to retrieve all stations that can be reached from
Totteridge Station (on the Northern Line).

(5.18)  What are the values of the following expressions:
   (i)    RESTRICT (s IN salesorders)

         WHERE EXISTS

              (s.order_lines.quantity < 100)  IN order_lines

  (ii)      RESTRICT (s IN salesorders)

         WHERE FORALL  (s.order_lines.quantity > 99) IN

            s.order_lines

  (iii)     RESTRICT (c IN customers)

         WHERE MEMBER '02349854' OF c.telephones

(5.19)    What would the results of (5.8) be if all collection–object types are bags? Also, what would the results be if, in addition, the UNION operation was replaced by ADDITIVE_UNION?

(5.20)    Retrieve a set–object which contains the Customer object for Faulties.

(5.21)    Retrieve a bag–object which contains the Product object for P3.

(5.22)    If the order_lines attribute of SalesOrder objects is a set–object, retrieve a bag–object which contains the order lines for order O9.

(5.23)    If the order_lines attribute of SalesOrder objects is a bag–object, retrieve a set–object which contains the order lines for order O9.

(5.24)    Retrieve the set–object containing all order lines from all sales orders, with duplicates removed (using UNNEST).

(5.25)    Retrieve a set containing the name and address of each customer, and then form a set within one element for each distinct address, containing the address and the set of names at that address (using NEST).

(5.26)    Add a new Product record to products, for a red product P5, called Magdale Rambler.

(5.27)    Write a short report, for a manager of a small manufacturing company, explaining the significance of object algebra.

6

# THE OBJECT QUERY LANGUAGE, OQL

This chapter describes the object database language for querying and manipulating object databases which conform to the Object Data Model. The language described is called **Object Query Language**, or **OQL**, and is defined as part of the ODMG standards.

OQL expressions can be thought of as a user–friendly and executable form of the object algebra (see Chapter 5). Object database systems are built using OQL, in conjunction with the Object Definition Language (ODL) for defining interfaces to object types (see Chapter 4), and other programming languages, such as C++, Smalltalk, and Java, for implementing methods and application programs (see Chapter 7). OQL can also be used as a stand–alone language for making ad hoc queries on an object database.

Sections 6.1 and 6.2 respectively present a preliminary overview of OQL and an extended tutorial which guides readers through OQL features. Finally, Section 6.3 provides a summary. Readers are encouraged to work through the many examples in the Section 6.2 tutorial and the exercises at the end of this chapter using an ODMG–compatible ODBMS if available.

Most of the examples given are based on the Bruddersfield Bikes case study and the example object database used in previous chapters (see Figure 6.1). The OQL syntax is given using extended BNF definitions (as in Chapter 4). The following conventions are used to highlight important features of OQL:

1) OQL keywords are emboldened.
2) Mutable object type names start with upper case letters and variable names with lower case.
3) The meaning of OQL is often explained in terms of the object algebra (in Chapter 5). Object algebra operators are given in upper case to distinguish them from OQL.

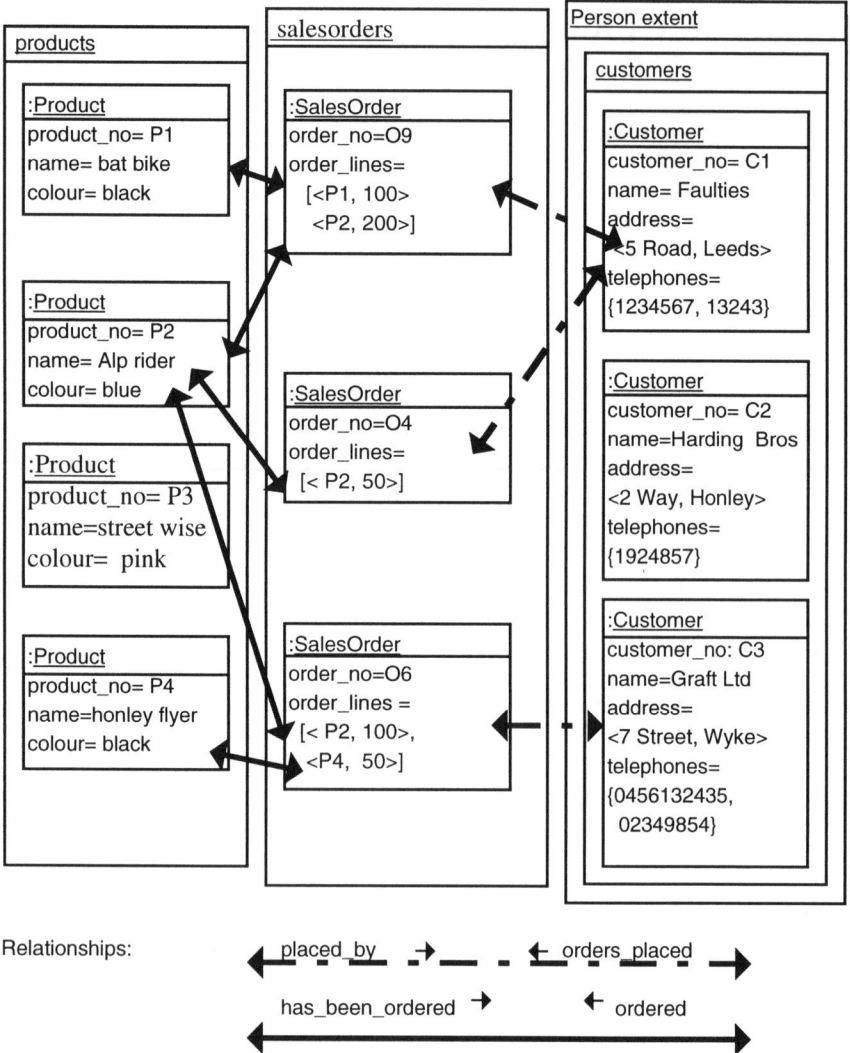

Figure 6.1 An example sales order processing object database (see Chapter 4, Figure 4.4 for the ODL schema)

## 6.1 AN OVERVIEW OF OQL

OQL is an object database query language, and is specified as part of the ODMG standards [Cattell 97]. OQL can also be classified as an **object database sub–language** in that its scope is limited to performing just one aspect of object database applications, i.e., the sort of queries and manipulations that can be expressed in the object algebra. It is a simple query language and does not provide a full programming environment. A particular limitation is that OQL cannot express arbitrarily complex computations, i.e., OQL is not **computationally complete**. It is therefore necessary to use OQL in conjunction with other computer languages:

1)  OQL is used to describe the retrieval and manipulation of objects;
2)  the Object Definition Language (ODL) defines interfaces to object types used by the OQL code (see Chapter 4);
3)  other programming languages, such as C++, Smalltalk and Java, are used to implement object operations, i.e., methods;
4)  other programming languages (C++, Smalltalk ,and Java) are used to implement applications programs, with embedded OQL statements to manipulate the object database (see Chapter 7).

In case 4), OQL is being used as an **embedded query language**. OQL can also be used as a **stand–alone query language**, i.e., the user can express object database manipulations purely in OQL without having to embed OQL in programs written in other programming languages.

Like the object algebra, OQL provides a **declarative** way of describing object database manipulations. By declarative, we mean that expressions in OQL state what is required, but not how it is achieved. This contrasts with **procedural** (or **imperative**) programming languages, such as C, C++, Smalltalk, and Java, where the programs must define the procedures for accomplishing the required results. It is therefore the task of the ODBMS to determine how each OQL statement can be executed in an optimal manner, i.e., query optimisation.

OQL can be used for both **collection–oriented** and **navigational** queries.

1)  A collection–oriented query retrieves a collection of objects—the way in which those objects are located is the responsibility of the ODBMS, rather than the application program.

2) Navigational queries access individual objects and use object relationships to navigate from one object to another—it is the responsibility of the applications program within which the OQL is embedded to specify the navigation procedure for accessing all objects of interest.

The designers of OQL have adopted an evolutionary approach. Rather than designing a completely new language, they have based OQL on SQL [Cattell 97, p 83], the standard language for the previous generation of (relational) databases. Many queries in SQL are also valid in OQL, though sometimes with minor changes, and have a similar meaning. However, OQL also extends SQL to deal with object–oriented notions, such as complex structured objects, object identity, relationships (including subtype/supertype relationships), and operation invocation— none which occur within the relational data model. The design of OQL is functional that is, the results of queries have types which allow them to be queried again, so complex queries can be built up. To allow greater compatibility with SQL, it is also possible, using OQL, to use some ad hoc constructions that are valid SQL.

By integrating features of SQL, OQL builds upon foundations provided by the previous generation of (relational) databases. However, the relationship between SQL and OQL is complicated by the fact that SQL is still evolving (see Section 10.2, Object–relational databases). The ODMG's stated intention is to maintain a degree of compatibility between object database technology and object–relational database technology by integrating features of future versions of SQL within future versions of OQL. However, given the size and complexity of the next generation of SQL (SQL3) apparent in the working draft [ANSI 95], it is hard to see how this compatibility can be maintained. (Similarities between OQL and SQL are illustrated in Example 6.1.)

---

*EXAMPLE 6.1*

*The following SQL represents the query "what are the names of the black products? ", and is also valid in OQL.*

```
select distinct p.name
from     products p
where    colour = "black"
```

The respective meanings of the Example 6.1 expression are as follows.

1) In **SQL**, this statement will query a relational database, i.e., a set of table–like structures (see Section 2.2, Second generation database technology), and return a table, the rows of which are rows of the table called products in which the column called colour has the value "black". If the relational database contains the products table in Figure 6.2 (a), the result of the query will be the Figure 6.2 (b) table.

products

| product_no | name | colour |
|---|---|---|
| P1 | bat bike | black |
| P2 | alp rider | blue |
| P3 | street wise | pink |
| P4 | honley flyer | black |

Figure 6.2 (a) Example relational products table

| name |
|---|
| bat bike |
| honley flyer |

Figure 6.2 (b) Result of Example 6.1 SQL query when applied to Figure 6.2(a)

2) In **OQL** this statement will query an object database and return a collection–object which contains objects contained in the collection–object called products for which the value of the colour attribute is the literal "black". Given the object database in Figure 6.1, this OQL statement will return the object represented in Figure 6.3.

| select p.name from products p where p.colour="black" : Set<String> | |
|---|---|
| **:String** | :String |
| bat bike | honley flyer |

Figure 6.3 Result of Example 6.1 OQL when applied to Figure 6.1.

Example 6.1 illustrates the following differences in meaning between SQL and OQL:

1) That which is interpreted as a table name in SQL, is interpreted as a collection–object name in OQL;
2) That which is interpreted as the name of a column of a table in SQL is interpreted as an object characteristic name (an attribute, relationship, or operation name) in OQL.

Note also that the meaning of the Example 6.1 OQL can be expressed in the object algebra. The OQL expresses a RESTRICT operation on products which defines a collection–object that contains Product objects for black products, and an APPLY operation whic,h when applied to this collection, returns a collection of string literals (the object names), i.e.,

> APPLY (b.name) TO
> (b IN (RESTRICT p IN products WHERE
> p.colour = 'black'))

SQL–like OQL queries (as illustrated in Example 6.1) are extremely versatile, since they can combine all three aspects of querying an object database, i.e., "picking" and "mixing" interesting objects, processing them, and creating a resultant object that represents the required information. This versatility will be illustrated as this chapter progresses.

The Example 6.1 OQL also illustrates another important property of OQL—the ability to construct complex queries from simpler ones. For instance, the condition part of the Example 6.1 OQL, i.e., p.colour = "black", is also an OQL expression. Expressions in OQL are constructed in the same way as expressions in the object algebra (see Chapter 5). An OQL expression is constructed from variables and constants which represent objects, and from operations upon objects. The result returned when an OQL statement is executed is always an object. Also, the type of the resulting object can always be determined by analysing the expression. Like the object algebra, OQL exploits this property by allowing expressions to be constructed freely from other expressions—an expression can occur within another expression wherever the type of the object it returns is expected (a language with this property is said to be **orthogonal**). Example 6.2 further illustrates OQL's orthogonality by incorporating the Example 6.1 OQL as part of a more complex query.

---

*EXAMPLE 6.2*

*This expression retrieves names of black products which are not called honley flyer. It does this by including, as a part of the OQL query, the Example 6.1 OQL. The embedded OQL query retrieves Product objects for black products. The outer query then selects from that collection those Product objects which do not represent honley flyer.*

```
select x.name
from   x in (select distinct p.name
             from    products p
             where colour = "black")
where not (x.name = "honley flyer")
```

---

## 6.2 AN EXTENDED OQL TUTORIAL

This section provides a practical tutorial which guides readers progressively through the features of OQL. The examples are based mainly on the Bruddersfield Bikes sales order processing object database (used in Chapters 4 and 5; see Figure 6.1). Readers are encouraged to execute the tutorial examples and answer the exercises at the end of this chapter using an actual ODMG–compliant ODBMS, if available.

OQL expressions can be thought of as executable representations of object algebra expressions. Accordingly, OQL supports the three functions that were identified when the object algebra was described (see Section 5.2, The object algebra: a non–mathematical overview). These are:

1)      **Definition of the objects that are of interest**—this facility supports a set of "pick" and "mix" operations, whereby new

collections of "interesting" objects are created by "mixing" together objects "picked" from existing collections.

2)   **Application of operations to objects of interest**—this is necessary in order to modify the states of objects, or to extract interesting information about the objects. OQL does not include special operators for modifying the states of objects, but can do this by executing object instance operations.

3)   **Return of an object which contains the required information**— the result of an OQL expression is always an object, typically a collection–object that contains the objects which satisfy the query. OQL queries can return literals or mutable objects, which may be existing or newly created objects.

The following subsections use these three facilities as a framework within which to describe and illustrate the features of OQL. Many of the OQL features are introduced in terms of the object algebra operations that they express—this is for explanatory purposes and to establish the relationship between OQL and the algebra. However, the aim of this section is to provide the reader with an understanding of how ideas can be expressed in OQL, such that OQL expressions can be formulated intuitively without having first to think in terms of the object algebra.

## PICK AND MIX OPERATIONS

The first set of OQL features we shall describe are for accessing objects of interest. These features correspond to the "pick" and "mix" operations of the object algebra, such as RESTRICT and UNION (see Section 5.3, Pick and mix operators).

### ACCESSING LITERALS AND NAMED OBJECTS

The simplest form of OQL query is an object name—object names are used as entry points into an object database. In the case of a literal, the literal value can be used as the object name. An object name returns the identified object.

---

### EXAMPLE 6.3

*This example illustrates the use of object names and literal values as queries.*

1) *The following OQL query returns the integer literal: 21.*

```
21
```

2) *The next OQL query returns the string literal: "Barry Eaglestone".*

```
"Barry Eaglestone"
```

3) *If the Product object for product P1 in the Figure 6.1 object database has the object nam, best_seller, it will be returned by the OQL, query:*

```
best_seller
```

4) *Given the Figure 6.1 object database, this next OQL query returns the extent of the Product object type:*

```
products
```

---

The syntax of this simplest form of OQL query is:

```
<query>  ::= <object name> | <literal value>
```

A literal value may be of any of the literal types supported, i.e.,
- integer (e.g., 25, -27);
- floating point number (e.g., 1.54, 198., 3.14e-2);
- Boolean (true, false);
- character (e.g., 'B','a','r');
- string (e.g.,"Barry", "Mick");
- **nil**, i.e., the null value which represents absence of any value at all.

### ACCESSING OBJECT VALUES

The OQL expressions illustrated in the previous subsection access either a literal (as in Example 6.3, (1) and (2)) or a mutable object (as in Example 6.3, (3) and (4)). When accessing a mutable object, OQL also allows us to access the value (or state) of that object. To do this, the query must be preceded by an asterisk, "*". This process is called **dereferencing**.

---

## EXAMPLE 6.4

*The mutable object typ, Diary_entr, has a single attribute, called entry, which is of type string. Two Diary_entry objects have respectively been assigned the object names project_start and project_end. The values of these objects are both "Equinox team meeting".*

1) *The following OQL will return false, because project_start and project_end are the names of different objects:*

```
project_start = project_end
```

2) *The following query will return true because \*project_start and \*project_end will return the_values of the respective named objects, and these are the same literal, "Equinox team meeting":*

```
*project_start = *project_end
```

---

The syntax of a query which returns the value of a mutable object is:

```
<query> ::= *<query>
```

## ACCESSING CHARACTERISTICS OF OBJECTS

An object name can be used, in conjunction with the names of object characteristics (attributes, relationships, and operations), to access the individual characteristics of the named object or of others related to it.

Object and characteristic names can be put together to form a **path** from a named object to the object or characteristic that we wish to access. The steps in the path are separated by dots, ".", or alternatively by arrows, "->". Dots and arrows are interchangeable in OQL, but we use the convention that a dot denotes the path from an object to its characteristic and an arrow denotes the path from an object to another object, via a relationship.

The next example illustrates access to objects via paths constructed from object names and characteristic names.

---

## EXAMPLE 6.5

*The following queries assume that the Product object for product P1 in the
Figure 6.1 object database is named best_seller and the SalesOrder object for
order number O9 is named biggest_order.*

1)  *The value returned by the OQL query*

```
best_seller.name
```

   *is the literal "bat bike", since this is the value of the name attribute of the
   Product object named best_seller.*

2)  *The value returned by the OQL query*

```
best_seller.has_been_ordered
```

   *is a set–object containing the SalesOrder objects associated with the P1
   Product object via the has_been_ordered relationship. In this case the
   collection will contain just the one SalesOrder object for order number O9.*

3 ) *The value returned by the OQL query*

```
biggest_order.ordered->name
```

   *is the string literal, "Faulties", since this is the value of the name attribute
   of the Customer object related to the SaleOrder object named biggest_order,
   via the ordered_by relationship. Note that in this last example we follow the
   convention of using a dot to separate an object and its property, and an
   arrow to separate the relationship and that to which it refers.*

---

The orthogonality of OQL means that any OQL query which returns an
object of an appropriate type can be used in place of a name (this feature
will become clearer as this chapter progresses). The syntax for OQL
queries which access objects' characteristics via a path is therefore as
follows:

```
<query> ::= <query> <dot or arrow> <attribute name>
         | <query> <dot or arrow> <relationship name>
```

Note that the components of a path are queries. The objects returned by these queries provide the "stepping stones" by which we eventually reach the required object, attribute, or relationship.

## SELECTING OBJECTS FROM A COLLECTION

Often we will require objects which have some common property to be picked from a collection–object, e.g., all customers in a particular sales area, or all sales orders for a particular product. In the object algebra we describe this sort of operation using the RESTRICT operator. In OQL we can implement RESTRICT operations using SQL-like queries, as illustrated in Examples 6.1 and 6.2.

The general form of this type of OQL query is

```
select <variable>
from <collection-object> <variable>
where <restrict-predicate>
```

In the above syntax

1) <collection–object> can be an object name, or another OQL query which returns the required collection–object;
2) <variable> is an **iterator variable** which is used to range over the objects in the collection object. The variable name can be used throughout the query as a means of addressing an individual object's characteristic for testing and display;
3) <restrict–predicate> is an OQL query which returns a Boolean value, i.e., true or false, when evaluated against an object contained in <collection–object>.

The meaning of this form of OQL query is: "retrieve objects from <collection–object> where <restrict–predicate> is true". Accordingly, the object algebra expressed by the OQL is:

```
RESTRICT (<variable> in <collection–object>)
WHERE <restrict–predicate>
```

---

### EXAMPLE 6.6
*The following OQL retrieves details of the customer called Faulties.*

```
select   c
from   customers c
where  c.name = "Faulties";
```

*The object returned is the collection–object (in fact the result is a bag–object because we have not included the keyword **distinct** to remove duplicates (unlike in Example 6.1)) The result contains every object, c, in the collection-object customers for which the condition c.name = "Faulties" is true. The OQL therefore represents the object algebra expression:*

RESTRICT (c IN customers) WHERE (c.name = 'Faulties')

*The result of applying the above OQL to the Figure 6.1 object database is given in Figure 6.4.*

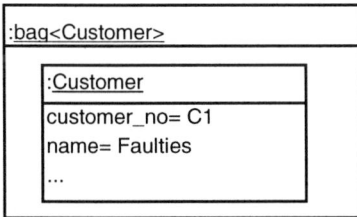

---

```
:bag<Customer>
   ┌─────────────────────┐
   │ :Customer           │
   ├─────────────────────┤
   │ customer_no= C1     │
   │ name= Faulties      │
   │ ...                 │
   └─────────────────────┘
```

Figure 6.4  The result of the Example 6.6 OQL

The restrict–predicate in the above form of OQL query is a Boolean expression and is used to test which objects should be "picked" from a collection. Objects may be selected on a variety of criteria, such as numerical values, names, and descriptions. For example, Bruddersfield Bikes may wish to retrieve Customer objects for customers in the Manchester sales area who have unpaid bills with a value of over £2,000 and where the goods were delivered over two months ago. The following subsections describe OQL features for expressing different selection criteria as an OQL Boolean expression.

## COMPLEX TESTS ON OBJECTS

It is often necessary to select objects on the basis of combinations of selection criteria. We can do this in OQL by constructing complex Boolean expressions from simpler ones which represent each of the selection criteria. The simple expressions can be combined using the built–in logical operators—**and, or,** and **not.** These are applied to objects represented by object names, values, or other queries, and return a Boolean value (true or false).

The meaning of the logical operators is shown in Table 6.1—rows of this truth table show values of the Boolean expressions X, Y, X **and** Y, X **or** Y, and **not** X. For instance, the first row shows that when X and Y are both true, then X **and** Y and X **or** Y are also true, but **not** X is false.

The rules for evaluating a Boolean expression constructed using **and, or,** and **not,** are:
- an expression is evaluated from left to right;
- sub–expressions in brackets are evaluated first;
- **not**s are evaluated before **and**s and **or**s.

Table 6.1 Truth table for the logical operators

| X | Y | X and Y | X or Y | not X |
|---|---|---------|--------|-------|
| true | true | true | true | false |
| true | false | false | true | false |
| true | nil | nil | true | false |
| false | true | false | true | true |
| false | false | false | false | true |
| false | nil | false | nil | true |
| nil | true | nil | true | nil |
| nil | false | false | nil | nil |
| nil | nil | nil | nil | nil |

---

EXAMPLE 6.7

*The following OQL query illustrates the use of the built–in logical operators to form a restrict predicate. Note also the use of brackets to establish the way in which the predicate must be evaluated.*

```
select p
from products p
where not (p.colour = "black") and
      (p.name = "bat bike" or
       p.name = "street wise");
```

*The effect of this OQL is to select all the Product objects contained in products which describe either bat bike or street wise, but excluding those which are black.*

*Given the Figure 6.1 object database, execution of the OQL statement will produce the bag–object in Figure 6.5.*

*To illustrate the way in which the restrict predicate in the OQL query is evaluated, we now evaluate it for the following Product object,*

```
:Product
product_no= P1
name:=bat bike
colour=black
```

*The evaluation proceeds in the following manner:*

1) *The expressions in brackets are evaluated first (left to right):*
   `(colour = "black")`          *returns true*
   *To evaluate the sub-expression*
   `(name = "bat bike" **or** name = "street wise")`
   *we first evaluate the terms.*
   `name = "bat bike"`          *returns true*
   `name = "street wise"`       *returns false*
   *This sub–expression therefore becomes*
   `(false   **or**   true)`
   *which has the value true (see line 2 of the above truth table).*
2) *Having evaluated the expressions in brackets the condition*
   **not** `(colour = "black")` **and**
   `(name = "bat bike" **or** name = "street wise")`
   *becomes*
   **not** `true` **and** `true`
3) *The **not**s are evaluated before **and**s and **or**s.*
   **not** `true`
   *has the value false (see line 1,2, or 3 of the truth table above).*
   *The condition*
   **not** `true`   **and** `true`
   *therefore becomes*
   `false` **and** `true`
   *which returns the value false (see line 4 of the decision table above).*
   *Thus the condition returns the value false and the object is not retrieved.*

```
: bag<Product>

  :Product
  product_no=P3
  name= street wise
  colour= pink
```

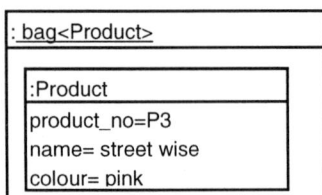

Figure 6.5 The result of the Example 6.7 OQL

In general, the meanings of the logical operators **and, or,** and **not** are similar to their meanings in the English language. However, care should be taken in their use. A person may say "tell me about red and green products" meaning that she requires details of products which are red and products which are green. However, this request is ambiguous. Another interpretation is "retrieve details of products which are both red and green". Though there is no such ambiguity in logic, it is common for users who are new to OQL to use "**and**" in the same ambiguous way that they use it in speech. It would not be unusual for a novice user to express the above query using the following OQL:

```
select p
from product p
where (colour = "red" and
       colour = "green");
```

This does not correctly express the intended query, and will always retrieve an empty bag–object, since there cannot be an object where the colour attribute has two values—"red" and "green". The correct OQL is

```
select p
from product p
where (colour = "red" or
       colour = "green");
```

The syntax for OQL queries which are Boolean expressions constructed using the logical operators is:

```
<query> ::= not <query>
        | query> and <query>
        | <query> or <query>
```

## ARITHMETIC COMPARISONS

OQL Boolean expressions can test numerical properties of objects by applying arithmetic comparison operators to queries which return numeric values. The built–in numerical comparison operators are the conventional ones, i.e., = (equals), != (not equal to), > (greater than), >= (greater than or equal to), < (less than), <= (less than or equal to).

---

### EXAMPLE 6.8

*An Employee type has an extent called employees, and the instance attributes include salary and years_of_service. The following OQL query will return a bag–object which contains details of employees who have twenty-five or more years service and are earning less than 20,000 a year:*

```
select x
from employees x
where (x.years_of_service >= 25) and
      (x.salary < 20000)
```

---

Once again, Example 6.8 illustrates how OQL expressions can be constructed from other expressions—**and** is used to construct the restrict predicate (following the **where** keyword) from the expressions (x.years_of_service >= 25) and (x.salary < 20000)). These two expressions, in turn, are constructed from four other expressions, i.e., 25, x.years_of_service, x.salary, and 20000, using the mathematical comparison operators, >= and <.

The syntax for queries which include the arithmetical operators is:

```
<query> ::= <query>  = <query>
        | <query> != <query>
        | <query> <  <query>
        | <query> <= <query>
        | <query> >  <query>
        | <query> >= <query>
```

## TESTS ON COLLECTIONS

OQL Boolean expressions can test the membership of collection–objects, as in the object algebra (see Section 5.3, Operations on set-objects: Boolean operators). The following comparisons can be made.

1) **for all**—this comparison operator tests if a condition is true for all objects contained in a collection–object. (This operator is called the universal quantifier in predicate logic.)

2) **exists**—this operator tests if there exists an object within a collection–object for which the specified condition is true. (This operator is called the existential quantifier in predicate logic.)

3) **unique**—this operator tests to see if there is one and only one object within a collection–object returned by a specified query.

4) **in**—this tests if a specified object is contained within a collection–object. (One particular use of **in**, described in the following subsection, is for testing for characters in a string literal.)

5) **some, any,** and **all**—these are comparison operator quantifiers, and are used to specify if the comparison is with at least one (**some** or **any**) or all (**all**) of the objects in a collection–object. Any of the built–in comparison operators (e.g., !=, <, >, <=, >=) can be qualified in this way.

6) **set inclusion**—the comparison operators <, <= , >, and >=, when applied to collection–objects, test if one collection is included in the other.

---

*EXAMPLE 6.9*

*1)* *The following OQL query returns true if all products are red:*

```
for all x in products: x.name = "red";
```

*2)* *The next OQL query returns true if at least one of the products is red:*

```
exists x in products: x.name = "red";
```

*3)* *An alternative way of expressing the query in (2) is:*

```
exists (select x
        from products x
        where x.name="red");
```

*In its second form **exists** returns true if the collection–object returned by the query is not empty.*

*4)* *If we wish to test if there is one, and only one, red product, we can use the unique **operator**, as follows*

```
unique (select x
        from products x
        where x.name="red");
```

5) *The OQL queries in (1) and (2) can also be expressed by qualifying the equals ('=') comparison operator, as in the following two OQL queries:*

```
"red" = all (select x.colour from products x)
"red" = any (select x.colour from products x)
```

6) *This OQL query returns true if the Product object named best_seller is contained in products:*

```
best_seller in products;
```

7) *The first two of the next four queries return true if the set–object customers includes all of the Customer objects contained in retail–customers. The third and fourth return true if customers contains all, but not only the objects in retail_customers:*

```
retail_customers <= customers
customers >= retail_customers
retail_customers <customers
customers > retail_customers
```

---

The syntax for queries which use **for all, exists,** and **in** is:

```
<query> ::=for all <query> in <query> : <query>
         | exists<identifier> in <query> : <query>
         | exists ( <query> )
         | unique ( <query> )
         | <query> in <query>
         | <query> <comparison_operator>
               [ some | any | all ] <query>
         | <query> [ < | <= | > | >= ] <query>
```

## STRING MATCHING

String matching can be used to select objects on the basis of textual properties, such as names or descriptions.

We can test if a character is contained in a string using the comparison operator **in**, described in the previous subsection—c **in** s tests whether a string s contains a character c. For example, the expression 'a' **in** "name" will return *true*, but 'c' in "name" will return *false*.

The comparison operator **like** is used for "fuzzy" matching of character strings, i.e., matching strings which are similar but not necessarily identical. The **like** operator compares an expression of type string with a string literal. The string literal can include the following special **wildcard characters** to describe a set of similar strings:

1) ? or _—these represent any character. For example, "Barry" **like** "Barr?" returns true.
2) * or %—these represent any string of characters. For example, "Barry" **like** "Bar*" returns true.

---

### EXAMPLE 6.10

*The following OQL query retrieves details of customers whose names start with the letters "Fa" and include the letter, 't':*

```
select c
from Customer c
where c.name like "Fa*" and 't' in c.name;
```

*When executed on the Figure 6.1 object database, this query will retrieve the bag–object containing the Customer object for Faulties Ltd. Note that the string 'Fa*' includes an asterisk to denote any string, and therefore represents the letters 'F' and 'a' followed by anything. The above condition would therefore return true for "Fantasies" or "Fatalities", but false for "Follies" or "Banjo".*

---

This syntax of queries which apply the **like** operator is:

```
<query>::=   <query> like <string literal>
```

### ACCESSING OBJECTS IN A LIST OR AN ARRAY

OQL allows us to access objects contained in ordered collection–objects, i.e., list– and array–objects, by specifying their positions within the collections. This is done in the following ways:

1) **first, last**—as their names suggest, these operations respectively return the first and the last object contained in a list– or array–object.

2) **access by index**—each object contained in a list– or array–object is indexed by a number which indicates the object's positions (the first element is indexed with 0, the next with 1, and so on). OQL queries can access objects contained in a list– or array–object by specifying their index numbers.

3) **list (or array) addition**—two or more lists (or arrays) can be combined such that the second becomes a continuation of the first using the conventional addition operator, "+".

---

*EXAMPLE 6.11*

*The objec, product_list, of type list<Product>, contains Product objects in ascending price order.*

1) *The following two OQL queries, respectively, return the Product object for the cheapest and the most expensive products:*

```
first (product_list)
last (product_list)
```

2) *This query returns the Product object for the second cheapest product:*

```
product_list [1]
```

*Note that the index number for the second object in the list is 1, because the numbering is from 0 upwards.*

3) *This query returns an object of type list<Product> which contains the Product objects for the five cheapest products, in ascending price sequence:*

```
product_list [0:4]
```

4) *A second list–object, luxury_products, contains a list of product in the luxury range. The following query will return the list–object which contains the objects in product_list and also the objects in luxury_products as a continuation:*

```
product_list + luxury_products
```

---

The syntax of the above OQL queries on list- or array-object is:

```
<query> ::= <query> [ <query> ]
        | <query> [<query> : <query>]
        | first (<query> )
        | last ( <query> )
        | <query> + <query>
```

## SELECTING OBJECTS FROM MORE THAN ONE COLLECTION

The next group of "pick" and "mix" queries are those which select objects contained in two or more set- or bag-objects. The OQL operators are implementations of the object algebra UNION, INTERSECT, and DIFFERENCE operators.

1) **union**—the union of two set-objects is a set-object which contains objects which occur in one or other of the operands set-objects. The union of two bags is the additive-union (described in Section 5.4, UNION). Additive-union returns the bag-object which contains all of the objects in the first operand bag-object and also all of the objects in the second operand bag-object.

2) **intersect**—the intersections of set- and of bag-objects, are respectively, the set-object and bag-object containing objects which occur in both operands.

3) **except**—the **except** operator implements the difference operator of the object algebra. The exceptions of two set- and of two bag-objects, ar,e respectively, the set- and bag-object containing objects in the first operand but not in the second.

The use of the above three OQL set- and bag-object operators is illustrated in the following example.

---

### EXAMPLE 6.12

*Two collection-objects, retail_customers and trade_customers, are of type Set<Customer>. Example instances are given in Figure 6.6 (a).*

1) *The following OQL query retrieves details of customers who are retail and/or trade customers. The result is given in Figure 6.6 (b).*

```
retail_customers union trade_customers
```

*Note that we have allowed a customer to be a member of both retail_customers and trade_customers, but this replication is removed in the resulting object—all objects contained in a set–object must be distinct.*

2) *The next query retrieves details of customers classified as retail and trade:*

```
retail_customers intersect trade_customers
```

*The object returned is of type Set<Customer> and contains all of those objects contained in both of the argument set–objects (see Figure 6.6 (c)).*

3) *The next OQL query retrieves details of customers who are classed as retail, but not trade:*

```
retail_customers except trade_customers
```

*The value of this expression is an object of type Set<Customer> which contains all those objects in retail_customers which are not also in trade_customers (see Figure 6.6 (d)).*

Figure 6.6  union, intersect, and except operations

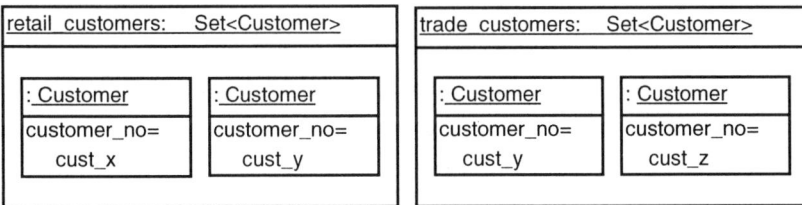

Figure 6.6 (a) Example instances of the Example 6.12 collection–objects

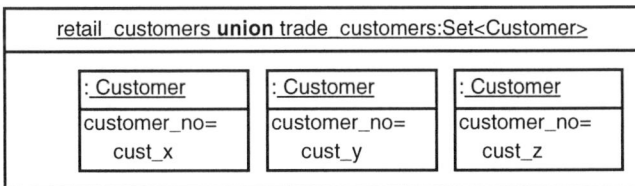

Figure 6.6 (b) Result of the Example 6.12 (1) query

Figure 6.6 union, intersect, and except operations—continued

```
┌─────────────────────────────────────────────────────────┐
│ retail_customers intersect trade_customers: Set<Customer> │
│        ┌──────────────────────┐                           │
│        │ : Customer           │                           │
│        ├──────────────────────┤                           │
│        │ customer_no=         │                           │
│        │      cust_y          │                           │
│        └──────────────────────┘                           │
└─────────────────────────────────────────────────────────┘
```

Figure 6.6 (c) Result of the Example 6.12 (2) query

```
┌─────────────────────────────────────────────────────────┐
│ retail_customers except trade_customer: Set<Customer>    │
│        ┌──────────────────────┐                           │
│        │ : Customer           │                           │
│        ├──────────────────────┤                           │
│        │ customer_no=         │                           │
│        │      cust_x          │                           │
│        └──────────────────────┘                           │
└─────────────────────────────────────────────────────────┘
```

Figure 6.6 (d) Result of the Example 6.12 (3) query

Figure 6.6 union, intersect, and except operations

OQL operations upon sets are generally a direct implementation of the equivalent formula in set theory, with more or less the same syntax and meaning. The syntax is as follows:

```
<query> ::=  <query> union <query>
          |  <query> intersect <query>
          |  <query> except <query>
```

## GROUPING OBJECTS

The last of the "pick" and "mix" OQL facilities groups together similar objects contained in a collection–object. This OQL feature implements the GROUP operator of the object algebra. This facility is provided in OQL by appending a **group by** clause, which states the grouping criterion, to the **select, from,** and **where** clauses.

---

*EXAMPLE 6.13*

*The following OQL returns groups of Product objects with the same colour.*

```
select *
from products p
group by colour: p.colour
```

*The object returned will be a set–object containing structures. Each structure contains the property by which the objects are grouped (the partition attribute) and a bag–object (the partition) containing the group of objects (see Figure 6.7). Note that the OQL expresses the object algebra expression,*

GROUP (p IN products) BY p.colour

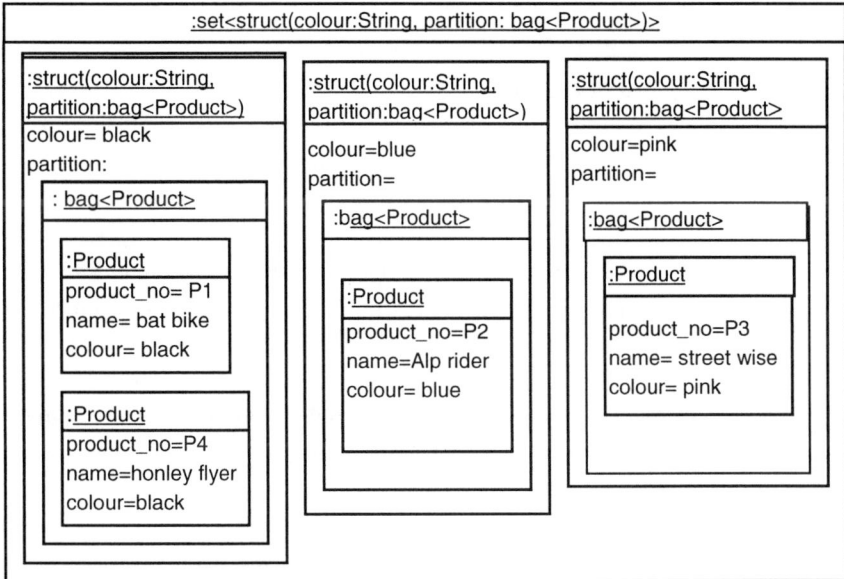

Figure 6.7 The value of Example 6.13 when applied to the Figure 6.1 object database

Example 6.13 illustrates the simplest form of **group by** operation, which groups objects according to the value of a single partition attribute. Example 6.14 illustrates how more complex grouping criteria can be specified,

1) by using queries to compute the values for multiple partition attributes;

2) by adding a "filter" condition so that only those objects for which the condition returns true are grouped.

## EXAMPLE 6.14

*An Employee object type includes location and salary attributes. The following OQL will partition Employee objects in the extent employees such that there are four partitions, respectively containing:*

- *employees located in Manchester earning over 40,000;*
- *employees in Manchester earning 40,000 or less;*
- *employees not in Manchester earning over 40,000;*
- *employees not in Manchester earning 40,000 or less.*

```
select *
from employees e
group by
        which_city? :
                e.location = "Manchester" ,
        overpaid?: e.salary > 40000;
```

*The OQL specifies two partition attributes (which_city? and overpaid?), which are defined on partitioning functions (e.location = "Manchester", and e.salary > 40000). The partition attributes which_city? and overpaid? are of the types of the value returned by their respective partition functions, i.e., they are both Boolean. The objects which are grouped are Employee objects contained in the type's extent, employees. The type of the result is therefore*

```
set<struct(which_city?:Boolean,
        overpaid?:Boolean, bag<Employee>)>
```

*The following OQL is equivalent to the previous one, apart from the addition of a "filter" condition (e.salary > 1000 and not (e.location = "Slough")) which excludes from the groups all objects for which this condition does not return true, i.e., employees located in Slough earning 1000 or less will be ignored:*

```
select e
from employees e
group by
```

```
which_city?
        :e.location = "Manchester" ,
    overpaid?: e.salary > 40000
having (e.salary > 1000 and
    not(e.location = "Slough"));
```

*The result will be an object of the same type as the result of the previous OQL, but there may be fewer objects in the partitions.*

The OQL query which groups objects from a collection, C, on the basis of the partitioning attributes P1, P2, ... , Pn respectively defined on the grouping functions E1, E2, ... , En, but excluding those objects for which the condition F is *false*, has the form:

```
select *
from C
group by P1 : E1, P2 : E2, ... , Pn : En
having F;
```

The syntax is:

```
<query> ::= <select...from...where query>
        [ group by <partition_attributes>]
        [having <query>]
```

where each partition attribute declaration has the following syntax:

```
<partition attribute> ::=
        <identifier> : <query>
        | <query> as <identifier>
        | <query>
```

## PROCESSING THE SELECTED OBJECTS

This section describes how OQL is used to process objects once they have been selected using the features described in the previous section. Objects are processed in order to extract information or to change their states. The two ways in which objects can be manipulated are described, i.e., using instance operations on mutable objects, and using built–in operations on literals.

## PROCESSING MUTABLE OBJECTS

Mutable objects are manipulated by executing the operations defined for the respective object types. In fact, this is the only way to change the state of an existing object—OQL does not include any built–in facilities for updating an object database (unlike SQL, which has special update, insert, and delete instructions).

The OQL facilities for executing instance operations illustrate one of the less satisfactory features of object database technology. The Object Data Model does not distinguish between retrieval and update operations, and so there is the risk of **side effects** when an operation is executed simply to access its value—the side effect of retrieving a value can be a change to the object's state. Also, the designer of an ODBMS must take into account and devise strategies for avoiding the problem of inappropriate and multiple executions of an operation upon an object when executing a query. This latter point complicates the problem of optimising the execution of OQL queries.

An instance operation is accessed and executed via a **path** in the same way that other object characteristics (i.e., attributes and relationships) are accessed. This is done using the dot notation previously described. The only difference is that it is often necessary to provide operations with parameter values—if required, parameter values are appended to the path in brackets.

---

### EXAMPLE 6.15

1) *The following OQL query executes the quantity_on_order_to? operation (declared in the schema in Figure 4.4) with the parameter "Faulties" on the Product object named best_seller:*

```
best_seller.quantity_on_order_to? ("Faulties")
```

*Note that the parameter required by the operation is provided in brackets after the operation name, as when executing a procedure in a conventional programming language, such as Pascal, C, or C++. The above query will return a literal of type Long, i.e., the value of the operation.*

2) *The following query returns a set–object containing the values returned by executing the quantity_on_order_to? operation with the parameter "Faulties." on all Product objects in the exten, products.*

```
select distinct
        p.quantity_on_order_to? ("Faulties")
from p in products
```

*Note the use of distinct to remove duplicates from the resulting collection–object. If omitted, the returned object would be a bag, rather than a set. Note also that the **where** clause has been omitted. This is because there is no restrict predicate—we are interested in all objects contained in products.*

*The above query implements the object algebra expression:*

APPLY p.quantity_on_order_to? ('Faulties')
TO (p  IN products)

The syntax of a query which executes an object operation is:

```
<query> ::= <query> < .|-> > <operation name>
        [ ( [<query> [,<query> ]* ) ]
```

## PROCESSING A COLLECTION OF MANY TYPES OF OBJECT

An added complexity can occur when executing operations on a collection–object which contains objects of many types. In such situations, there may be multiple implementations of the operation. It is therefore necessary to determine, for each object, which implementation to use. OQL supports two different ways of resolving this problem.

1)  **Late binding**—this mechanism allow general queries to be specialised for each object when the query is executed.
2)  **class indicators**—class indicators override late binding to ensure that only objects of a specified type are accessed.

## EXAMPLE 6.16

*A Customer type has two subtypes, TradeCustomer and RetailCustomer, and there are three implementations of the create_invoice operation, one for each of the three types. The following OQL exploits late binding in order to execute the most appropriate implementation of create_invoice for each Customer object in a collection–object, customers:*

```
select c.create_invoice from customers c
```

*The late binding mechanism ensures that when the OQL is executed, each object in the collection is considered separately and the most specific implementation of create_invoice for that object is applied. For instance, the RetailCustomer implementation of create_invoice will be executed for a Customer object which is also of type RetailCustomer.*

Late binding is a useful mechanism, since it allows operations to be invoked at the most general level but then executed at the most specific. This simplifies applications programs, since they do not have to take into account differences between subtypes. Late binding also insulates applications programs from many changes to the object database. By adding a new specialisation of Customer, Employee_Customer, and providing a fourth implementation of create_invoice for the new subtype, for instance, the OQL in Example 6.16 will still be valid, and will operate correctly on collections which also include Employee_Customer objects.

Sometimes we may wish to override late binding, and ensure that we process only specific types of object within a collection. This is done using **class indicators**, as in the following example.

*EXAMPLE 6.17*

*The following OQL will access the discount attribute, but only for Customer objects contained in customers which are also of the subtype RetailCustomer:*

```
select ((RetailCustomer)c).discount
from customers c
```

OQL which utilises late binding has no special syntax, because late binding automatically takes place by default. The syntax for specifying class indicators to override late binding is:

```
<query> ::= (<class_name>) <query>
```

*COMPUTATIONS ON ARITHMETIC AND STRING LITERALS*

In addition to the user–defined operations on objects, OQL includes a number of built-in operations upon literals. These can be used to construct queries which perform arithmetic computations on numeric literals and which derive new character strings from existing character and string literals.

The built–in arithmetic operators are the conventional ones, as illustrated in the following example.

---

### EXAMPLE 6.18

*The following OQL computes a floating point literal, -8, by applying the arithmetic operators "+" , "/", and "-" to the three integer literals 5, 11, and 2:*

```
-((5 + 11)/2)
```

---

As can be seen from Example 6.18, arithmetic computations are expressed in a natural way, using conventional arithmetic operators and notation. In general, OQL queries of this type are direct implementations of arithmetic formulas, with the same notation and meaning. The syntax of arithmetic queries is as follows:

&lt;query&gt; ::=    &lt;query&gt; **+** &lt;query&gt;
      | &lt;query&gt; **-** &lt;query&gt;
      | &lt;query&gt; **/** &lt;query&gt;
      | &lt;query&gt; **\*** &lt;query&gt;
      | **-** &lt;query&gt;
      | &lt;query&gt; **mod** &lt;query&gt;
      | **abs** (&lt;query&gt;)

Of the above arithmetic operators, "+" (addition), "-" (subtraction), "/" (division), and "*" (multiplication) will be familiar. The meaning of the other two operators:

    x **mod** y        denotes x modulus y. The value is the remainder when x is divided by y, e.g.,

```
12 mod 5 = 2
```

    **abs** (x)        denotes the absolute value of x, e.g.,

```
abs(-12) = 12
```

OQL also includes a number of built–in **aggregating functions** for deriving a single value from a collection of values. These can be used to implement object algebra FOLD operations—FOLD applies an aggregating function to the values returned by an APPLY operation. The aggregation functions supported are the same as those supported by SQL, i.e., **sum, min, max, avg,** and **count.**

The functions **sum, min, max,** and **avg** are defined for collection–objects which contain numeric literals, and respectively return the sum of the objects, the object with the minimum value, that with the maximum value, and the average object value. The function **count** is defined for any collection–object and returns the number of objects that it contains.

---

*EXAMPLE 6.19*

1) *The following query returns the total value of the quantities of the sales orders. It does this by applying the sum function to the bag–object which contains the values returned by executing the value_of_order? operation on each SalesOrder object in the extent, salesorders:*

> **sum (select** x.value_of_order?
>   **from** salesorders x)

*Note that the result of the nested select expression is a bag–object because we have not specified **distinct** to remove duplicate values.*

*The OQL defines the collection–object which contains the values of the specified function when applied to each object contained in products, and implements the following object algebra expression:*

> FOLD (s IN salesorders) USING sum OF s.value_of_order?
> IF EMPTY 0

2) *The next query returns the number of sales orders placed by Faulties*

> **count (select distinct** x
>   **from** salesorders x
>   **where** x.ordered_by.name = "Faulties")

*The **count** function is a built–in function which, when applied to a collection–object, returns the number of objects it contains.*

---

The syntax for queries which apply **count, sum, min, max,** or **avg** is:

```
<query> ::= count ( <query> )
        | sum ( <query> )
        | min ( <query> )
        | max ( <query> )
        | avg( <query> )
```

OQL also includes built–in operators with which to manipulate character strings. These are used to combine strings and extract parts of a string.

1) Strings are combined using "+" or alternatively, "||". For example, the expression "Bar" + "ry" (or alternatively "Bar" || "ry") will return the string literal "Barry".
2) If s is an expression of type string and i an expression of type integer, then s[i] will return the $i+1^{th}$ character in the string (the first character is s[0]). For example, if name has the value "Barry", then name[4] will return the value 'y'.
3) If s is an expression of type string, and low and high are of type integer, then s[low:high] will return the substring starting at the $low+1^{th}$ character of s up to the $high+1^{th}$ character. For example, name[1:3] will return "arr".

---

*EXAMPLE 6.20*
*The following OQL returns a string literal which comprises the first five letters of the name attribute, followed by the first three letters of the town attribute of the address of each Employee.*

```
select distinct e.name[0:4] +
         e.address.town[0:2]
from employees e;
```

*The result of the OQL will be a literal set–object containing string literals. Note that literals of type character are denoted by single quotes (strings have double quotes). Also, note that the elements of a string (or list or array) are numbered from zero upwards.*

---

The syntax for the above OQL character string operations is:

```
<query>  ::= <query>  +  <query>
        | <query> || <query>
        | <query> [ <query> ]
        | <query> [ <query> : <query> ]
```

## PROCESSING INFORMATION FROM MORE THAN ONE COLLECTION

Often the information that is required for a particular application is distributed across a number of objects contained in different collection–objects. For example, when processing a sales order, Bruddersfield Bikes require information from the relevant Customer, SalesOrders and Product objects. Information contained in different objects can be brought together and processed using the **select…from…where** form of OQL query—the collection–objects to be accessed are listed after the **from** keyword.

---

### EXAMPLE 6.21

*The following OQL retrieves the attributes customer_no and order_no from the Figure 6.1 object database, in cases where the customer is Faulties and the order_no is for a sales order placed by Faulties:*

```
select distinct c.customer_no, o.order_no
from   customers c,  salesorders o
where  c.customer_no = o.placed_by.customer_no
       and c.name = "Faulties";
```

*The iterator variables c and o respectively refer to objects in customers and salesorders. The result of this query is a set–object containing literal structures, each containing values of customer_no and of order_no (see Figure 6.8).*

---

The meaning of the above type of query can be explained in terms of the object algebra **JOIN** operator. JOIN returns information contained in more than one collection–object. Pairs of objects from the collection–objects, one from each collection, are selected in cases when a specified Boolean expression (the matching function) returns *true*. The object pairs are then combined by applying a specified function (the join function).

```
:set<struct( customer_no:String, order_no:String)>

    :struct(String,String)          :struct(String,String)
    customer_no= C1                 customer_no= C1
    order_no= O9                    order_no= O4
```

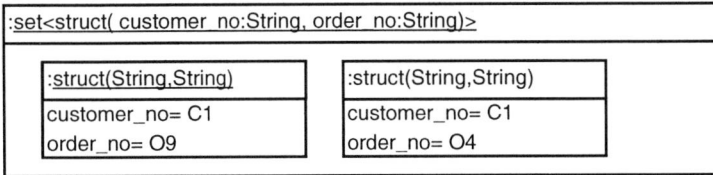

Figure 6.8 The value of Example 6.21 when applied to the Figure 6.1 object database

A join operation is specified in OQL by:

```
select <join function>
from   <collection-object₁>, <collection-object₂>
where <matching function>
```

This is equivalent to the object algebra expression:

```
JOIN <collection-object₁> AND
        <collection-object₂>
WHERE <matching function>
USING <join function>
```

---

*EXAMPLE 6.22*

*Two set–objects, customers, of type set<Customer> (as in Figure 6.1), and employees, of type set<Employee>, respectively represent customers and employees of Bruddersfield Bikes. Employee attributes are employee_number, name, address, value of purchases to date, etc. The following OQL joins customers and employees to return a set–object which contains the employee number, customer number, and value of purchases to date, for each customer who is also an employee:*

```
select distinct
        e.employee_number, c.customer_number,
        e.purchases_to_date
from employees e, customers c
where e.name = c.name;
```

*The above OQL expresses the following object algebra:*

```
JOIN (e IN employees) AND (c IN customers)
WHERE e.name = c.name
USING struct(e.employee_number,
        c.customer_number, e.purchase_to_date)
```

The simplest form of join, the **tuple–join**, combines matching objects using the **concat** operator which simply combines them into a single object with the attributes of both. OQL expresses the tuple–join operation by listing all the attributes of the objects in the operand collection–objects after the **select** keyword.

---

*EXAMPLE 6.23*

*The following OQL tuple–joins customers and salesorders in the Figure 6.1 object database:*

```
select distinct c.customer_no, c.name,
        c.address, c.telephones,
        s.order_no, s.order_lines
from    customer c, salesorders s
where   c.customer_no = s.ordered_by.product_no
```

*The OQL returns a set–object containing structure literals for each matching pair of objects, one from customers and one from salesorders. Objects match when the where–clause condition is true, i.e., the customer_no attribute values in the SalesOrder object and the customer_no in the Customer object related via the ordered_by relationship are equal. Each structure literal in the result contains all of the attributes of the matching Customer and SalesOrder objects.*

---

The above example's OQL join operations return only information about matching objects, i.e., pairs of objects for which the matching function returns *true*. If information about all objects, matched and unmatched, is required, the query can be expressed in object algebra using the **outer–join** operation. A special case is the **outer–tuple–join,** which is an information preserving extension of the tuple–join—unmatched objects are included in the result, but with null values for the missing attributes.

The outer–join can be expressed in OQL as the union of three select queries.

- One of the select queries will join the collection–objects (as in the previous examples).
- The other two select queries will respectively select unmatched objects from the first and second argument collection–objects and apply appropriate functions, for example, to set the missing attributes to null.

---

*EXAMPLE 6.24*

*The following OQL outer–tuple–joins customers and salesorders in the Figure 6.1 object database:*

```
(select distinct c.customer_no,
        c.name, c.address, c.telephones,
        s.order_no, s.order_lines
 from   customer c, salesorders s
 where  c.customer_no = s.ordered_by.customer_no)
union (select distinct c.customer_no, c.name,
        c.address, c.telephones, nil, nil,
        nil, nil
       from   customer c, salesorders s
       where not exists x in salesorders :
        c.customer_no = x.ordered_by.customer_no)
union (select distinct nil, nil, nil, nil,
        s.order_no, s.order_lines,
        s.order_no, s.order_lines
       from   customer c, salesorders s
       where not exists y in customers :
        y.customer_no = s.ordered_by.customer_no)
```

---

In the join examples so far, the **join function** has simply been to construct a structure which contains attributes from the matching objects. This has been specified by listing, after the **select distinct** keywords, the attributes to be included in the resulting structures. In cases where all of the attributes of the matching objects are required we can use an asterisk, "*", as shorthand for listing all of the attribute names (as in SQL). This is also true for a select query from one collection-object. For instance, the following two OQL queries are equivalent:

```
select *                    select product_no, name, colour
from products;              from products;
```

More complex join functions can be specified by defining the elements of the result structures on expressions—the expressions operate upon matching objects and return values for the respective structure elements. This feature is illustrated in Example 6.25, which also illustrates the use of **paths** and **iteration variables**. These contribute significantly to the versatility and expressiveness of **select..from...where** OQL queries by allowing collections to be joinedeither with themselves or with related objects.

---

### EXAMPLE 6.25

*A Person type includes the attributes, name and address. Person also has two relationships. The husband_of relationship and its inverse relationship, wife_of, associate Person objects for a married couple. The children relationship, and its inverse relationship, parents, associate Person objects which represent parents and their children.*

1) *The following OQL query returns the names of husbands and wives, by using the husband relationship to join husband and wife Person objects:*

```
select distinct wife:w.name, husband:h.name
from persons w, persons h
where w.husband = h;
```

   *The result is a set–object of type set<struct(wife:string, husband:string)>. The two elements of the structure, wife and husband, are respectively defined upon the expressions w.name and h.name. The values are taken from the name attributes of a pair of Person objects for which the join condition is true. Note that the two iterator variables are both defined for the same collection–object, persons, so that pairs of objects can be created from within persons.*

2) *This OQL query operates on the persons extent of the Person type and returns the addresses of persons who live in Magdale and have two or more children at least one of whom lives in a different city to their parents:*

```
select p.address
from persons p,
```

```
            p.children c
where   p.address.street = "Magdale" and
        count(p.children) >= 2 and
        c.address.city != p.address.city
```

*Note the use of iterator variables in this example. Two iterator variables are defined in the from–clause, p and c. The first, p, is defined to access objects in persons. The second, c, is defined to access objects in the collection related to the object in persons addressed by p, via the children relationship. In this way, the query considers each parent, represented in persons, and for that parent, each of their children, also represented as objects in persons.*

OQL can, of course, join more than two collection objects in a query. A join of the collection objects $C_1$, $C_2$, ..., $C_n$, where the join condition P is true, using the join function f is expressed in OQL as:

```
select   f
from  C₁,  C₂,  ...,  Cₙ
where  P
```

The join function f may simply be expressed as a list of the names of properties of objects in the operand collections to be included in the result, or alternatively it may be defined on expressions which are executed on matching objects taken from the operand collections.

## CREATING OBJECTS
This section describes OQL features for specifying the form in which the results of a query is returned.

### RETRIEVING EXISTING OBJECTS
Many of the OQL examples in the previous sections return existing mutable objects and literals, rather than creating new ones.

### EXAMPLE 6.26
1)  *This OQL query returns the existing Product object with the object name, best_seller (see Example 6.2):*

```
best_seller
```

2) *This OQL will return a string literal, which is the value of the name attribute of the Product object called best_seller:*

```
best_seller.name
```

3) *This OQL query will return a collection–object which contains the existing mutable Product object for the bat bike product:*

```
select p
from products p
where p.name = "bat bike";
```

4) *This OQL returns a literal collection–object containing string literals which are the values of the colour attribute of mutable Product objects:*

```
select p.colour
from products p
```

An existing object returned by an OQL query may be a mutable or literal object, atomic or structured. OQL also allows us to retrieve information in new forms. The following subsections describe OQL features for creating new objects.

### CREATING STRUCTURED LITERALS

Structured–literals (i.e., set-, bag-, list-, array-, and structure-literals) can be created using the object constructor operators, **struct, set, bag, list**, and **array**, as illustrated in the following example.

### EXAMPLE 6.27

1) *The following OQL returns a bag-literal containing the characters, 'b' , 'a', 'r', ',r', and 'y', (note that an element can occur many times in a bag, but all elements must be of the same type):*

   **bag** ('b', 'a', 'r', 'r', 'y')

2) *The following OQL returns a set-literal, containing the integer literals, 2, 4, 8, and 16 (note that elements must be distinct in a set, and must be of the same type).*

```
set (2, 4, 8, 16)
```

3)  *The following OQL returns a structure-literal, with elements called initials, name, and children. Their respective values are the list–literal, {'M','J'}, the string–literal "Ridley", and the integer–literal 2 (note that elements of a structure are named, and may be of different types):*

```
struct(initials: list('M','J'), name: "Ridley",
       children: 2)
```

The third OQL query in Example 6.27 also illustrates the way in which queries can be freely constructed from others—the queries includes the query `list('M','J')`, which, in turn, includes the queries `'M'` and `'J'`.

The syntax for queries which use constructors to create structured–literals is as follows:

```
<query> ::= struct ([<identifier> : <query>
            [, <identifier> : <query>]*] ) |
            set ( [ <query> [,<query>]*] ) |
            bag ( [<query> [, <query> ]*] ) |
            list ( [<query> [, <query> ]* ]) |
            array ( [<query> [, <query> ]* ])
```

Note that there is currently no facility in OQL [Cattell 97, p 117] for constructing a dictionary type (see Section 3.3, Reprsentation of composite entities: Collection object types).

## CREATING MUTABLE OBJECTS

**Type names** are used as constructor operators to create new mutable objects of the specified type.

### EXAMPLE 6.28
*The following OQL creates a new Product object:*

```
Product (product_no: "P10", name: "land hopper")
```

*The parameters provide initial values for the properties of the new Customer objects. Properiesy that are not initialised, colour in this case, are assigned the null value, nil.*

Example 6.28 illustrates how it is possible to create an object by specifying its attribute values. We can also build a new object from existing objects. This is done by including queries on the object database as parameters for the constructor operator, as in the next example.

*EXAMPLE 6.29*

*In this example we assume that the following types have been declared:*

```
type product_colour
attributes
        product_no: integer
        colour: string
end_type;
type product_colours set<product_colour>;
```

*The following OQL will create a mutable object of type product_colours:*

```
product_colours (select distinct
        p.product_no, colour
        from products);
```

*Note the use of the type name, product_colours, as an object constructor operator. Note that the value is retrieved from existing Product objects. The value returned by the parameter query is a literal collection–object, the elements of which are structures containing a product_no value and a colour value from a Product object. This literal is then assigned as the value of a new mutable object of type product_colours.*

Mutable object creation queries have the following structure:

```
<query> ::= <type name> ( [query] )  |
            <type name> ( <identifier>: <query>
            [ ,<identifier.:<query> ]*)
```

## CREATING COLLECTION–OBJECTS USING SELECT... FROM... WHERE QUERIES

The **select...from...where** form of OQL has a number of variations which can be used to return different types of collection object.

1)  The general form of a **select...from...where** query is

```
[ select <target list>
[ from <collection list> ]
[ where <condition> ]
```

The result will always be a **bag–object**.

2)  The **distinct** keyword can be used to remove duplicates from the result, in which case the result is a **set–object**:

```
select distinct <target list>
[ from <collection list> ]
[ where <condition> ]
```

3)  The **group by** clause constructs a collection–object of structures within which objects are grouped according to some specified criteria (see Grouping objects). Each structure contains the grouping attributes and the group of objects with the same value, excluding any which return false for the filter condition:

```
select distinct <target list>
[ from <collection list> ]
[ where <condition> ]
group by <grouping attributes>
[ having <filter condition> ]
```

4)  An **order by** clause can be used (as described below) to specify the order in which objects occur in the resulting collection–object, in which case the result will be a **list–object**:

```
select <target list>
[ from <collection list> ]
[ where <condition> ]
order by <sort keys>
```

The **order by** clause is used to specify **sort keys** which determine the ordering of objects in the resulting collection–object, as illustrated in Example 6.30. The first example query is a simple illustration, with a single ascending sort key. The second has multiple sort keys, both ascending and descending.

*EXAMPLE 6.30*
1) *The following OQL,*

```
select e
from employees e
order by e.purchases_to_date;
```

*will retrieve a list–object which contains the objects in employees in ascending numerical order of the values of the purchases_to_date attribute.*
2) *The following OQL,*

```
select  p
from products p
order by p.colour asc, p.product_no desc;
```

*will retrieve a list–object containing objects in products, in descending product_no order, within ascending colour order.*

In general, the object returned by an OQL query is a collection–object which contains structures. The form of the structure is specified after the **select distinct** keywords, i.e.,

```
<query> ::= select [ distinct ]
       <structure elements> ...
```

The structure elements may be defined in various ways, producing different results.

1) If <structure elements> defines a single element, then the result is a collection–object which contains the values of that element, e.g.,

```
select colour from products;
```

This OQL returns an object of type bag<string>, the values of which are the values of the colour attributes of the Product objects.

2) <structure elements> may be a list of the characteristics of the operand objects to be included as elements of the returned structures (or "*" if all attributes are required), e.g.,

```
select name, colour
from products;
```

The above OQL returns an object of type bag<struct(name:string, colour:string)>. The element names, types, and values are those of the named attributes.

3) A structure element may be defined on an expression, in which case an element has the type of the value returned by the relevant expressions. For example,

```
select product_code: name + colour
from products;
```

will return an object of type bag<struct(product_code:string)>. The values of the product_code elements will be the values returned by the expression, name + colour, which will be of type string.

4) A structure element may be a query, in which case the values and the type of the corresponding element in the result collection are those of the objects returned by the query, e.g.,

```
select sum(select ol.quantity
        from o.order_lines ol)
from salesorders o
where o.order_no = O9;
```

The above OQL returns an object of type bag<integer>. Note the use of the iterator variables, o and ol. o is used to access objects in salesorders, and ol to query the contents of the order_lines attribute of each of those object.

Structure element specifications in the list following the **select distinct** keywords can therefore have the following syntax:

```
<structure elements> ::= * |
    <structure element [, <structure element> ]*
```

where <structure element> has the following syntax:

```
<structure element> ::=   <query> |
        <identifier : <query> |
        <query> as <identifier>
```

## CONVERSION OF AN OBJECT FROM ONE TYPE TO ANOTHER

OQL includes a number of operators for converting an object from one type into another. These include:

1) **listtoset**—as the name suggests, this operator converts a list-object into a set–object which contains the same object, after any duplicates have been removed, e.g., **listtoset**(list(1,2,3,3,4) )= **set**(1,2,3,4).

2) **distinct**—this operator also removes duplicate objects from a collection–object. However, if the collection is a list (or array), the object returned is also a list (or array), with the same relative ordering of the remaining elements. If **distinct** is applied to a bag it returns a set. For example, **distinct** (list(1,2,2,3,2,5)) = **list**(1,2,3,5); **distinct** (**bag** (1,2,3,3)) = **set**(1,2,3).

3) **element**—when applied to a collection-object containing one object, **element** will return the contained object, e.g., **element**(set(5)) = 5.

4) **flatten**—this operator implements the unnest operator of the object algebra (see Section 5.5, Type conversion: nest and unnest), e.g., **flatten** (list (set(1,2), set(2,3), set(4,5)) = **list**(1,2,2,3,4,5).

---

*EXAMPLE 6.31*

*1)   Assume, the list–objec, products_ordered that contains Product objects, for products ordered during the day. The elements of products–ordered are in chronological order. The following will return the corresponding set–object:*

**listtoset** (products_ordered)

*The respective types of products_ordered and the object returned by the OQL are list<Product> and set<Product>. The other difference is that duplicate objects will have been removed in the returned object and its elements will have no ordering.*

2) *The following OQL returns a list–object which contains the same objects as products_ordered, but with duplicate objects removed. The relative ordering of the remaining elements is preserved:*

    **distinct** (products_ordered);

3) *The next OQL illustrates how distinct is used to convert a bag into a set, in a manner similar to the use of listtoset to convert lists to sets. customers_today is a bag–object which contains Customer objects for customers who have made inquiries during the day. The following OQL returns a set–object containing the same Customer objects, but with duplicates removed:*

    **distinct** (customers_today);

4) *This next OQL example uses element to retrieve a single object from a collection, rather than a collection–object containing that object:*

    **element**(**select distinct** p
        **from** products
        **where** p.name = "bat bike");

*The object returned by the embedded select query is of type set<Product> and the element operator returns the one Product object contained in it.*

5) *This final example uses flatten to return a bag–object of Product objects:*

    **flatten** (**select** s.ordered
        **from** salesorders s)

*The embedded select query returns an object of type bag<set<Product>>. The set–objects it contains are the sets of Product objects related to each SalesOrder object in salesorders. The flatten operator then flattens out the sets, and returns an object of type bag<Product> containing Product objects in the sets.*

The syntax for queries which include the operators described in this subsection is:

```
<query> ::= listtoset ( <query> )
          | element ( <query> )
          | distinct ( <query> )
          | flatten ( <query> )
```

## OPERATOR COMPOSITION

OQL's language orthogonality makes it possible to compose expressions from other simpler expressions as long as the types are consistent. In practice this makes it possible to construct and test a complex query in stages. OQL includes a query naming facility to support this mode of working.

A query is named using a **define** statement, e.g.,

```
define Customers as
       select distinct (Customer)c
       from customers c
       where exists(c.ordered);
```

The above OQL includes a select statement which returns a set–object containing Customer objects for customers who have placed sales orders. The OQL does not execute this query but assigns it a name, Customers, that can be used in subsequent OQL statements instead of the text of the query.

By naming a query, we simplify other queries within which the named query is embedded. For instance, the above definition simplifies the following query which groups customers with orders by city:

```
define Customer_Areas as
       select ca
       from Customers ca
       group by area:c.address.city;
```

Once again the above does not execute, but simply defines and names, a query for future use. Having defined the above two queries, we can now use them, for example, to retrieve a list of customers with outstanding sales orders, grouped and sorted alphabetically by city name, as follows:

```
select sca
from   Customer_Areas sca
ordered by sca.area;
```

The above could have been expressed as a single but much more complex OQL query, as follows:

```
select sca
from   (select ca
        from (select distinct (Customer)c
              from customers c
              where exists(c.ordered)) ca
        group by area:c.address.city) sca
ordered by sca.area;
```

There are obvious advantages in keeping things simple when using a computer, and the above series of subquery definitions have enabled us to do this and avoid the complexity evident in the single query version.

The syntax of a query definition is:

```
<define query> ::=
        define <identifier> as <query>
```

A set of query definitions and a query can be put together to form a **query program,** which has the syntax:

```
<query> ::=[ <define query>
        [ , <define query> ]* ; ] <query>
```

## COMPLETENESS

The **completeness** of a database language is a measure of how much it can do with respect to some underlying model. For example, relational database query languages are said to be relationally complete if they have the expressiveness of the relational data model's algebra. There is currently no widely accepted concept of completeness for object database languages. This is because there is as yet no standard algebra for object databases with respect to which completeness can be defined.

Furthermore, the semantics of most object database languages, have not yet been formally (i.e., mathematically) defined.

There are a number of proposals in the literature for formal object data models and algebras, and these are now converging on some consensus as to what an object algebra should include. One such proposal, the AQUA Data Model and Algebra, has been described in Chapter 5, and is referred to in this book as the object algebra. It is clear from the preceding sections that much of the semantics of OQL can be defined using the object algebra. However, there are also parts of the object algebra which cannot be implemented in OQL—for instance, there currently is no OQL equivalent to the LEAST_FIXED_POINT operator.

The current disparity between what can be represented in object algebra and what can be represented in OQL reflects a compromise between expressiveness, language complexity, and the needs for query optimisation. In general, the current lack of understanding with respect to the exact semantics of object database languages and object data models reflects the immaturity of object database technology.

## 6.3 SUMMARY

**OQL** is an **object database sublanguage** for querying and manipulating object databases which conform to the Object Data Model. Its scope is limited to performing the sort of queries that can be expressed in object algebra. OQL is not **computationally complete** and must be used in conjunction with ODL and other programming languages. OQL can be used, **embedded** within other programming languages, or as a **stand-alone query language** for ad hoc querying. It is a **declarative** language and can be used for both **collection-oriented** and **navigational** queries.

The syntax of OQL is based upon **SQL,** but includes extensions to deal with object-oriented notions. The **orthogonality** of OQL allows complex queries to be constructed from these by applying operators to simpler queries. All expressions in OQL return an object and the type of that object can be determined by analysing the query. Queries can be freely combined using the operators to form more complex expressions, provided the query types are compatible.

OQL can define objects of interest using object names and literal values as entry points into an object database. The simplest form of OQL query is a **name** or a **literal value**. **Paths** are used to access object characteristics and related objects. Queries can access objects. Alternatively, by preceding a query with an asterisk, it can access object values.

Objects are **selected** from a collection using the SQL–like **select...from...where** form of query. The **from–clause** specifies which collection is to be searched, and the **where-clause** specifies the condition for selecting an object. **Iterator variables** are used to refer to each individual object in a collection–object.

OQL expressions can perform complex tests using the logical operators **and, or,** and **not** to combine individual tests. Tests can be on the basis of numerical or textual properties and can be ranged over collection objects. Objects can be selected from multiple collections using the conventional set operators, **union, intersection,** and **except.** It is also possible to select objects into groups using the **group by** and **having clauses.**

Mutable objects can be processed by executing **instance operations.** These are accessed using paths. When this is done, there is a danger of **side–effects.** When a collection contains many types of object, the correct implementation of an operation is chosen using **late binding.** This can be overridden with **class indicators.**

OQL also includes **built–in operators** for performing arithmetic and character string manipulations. Information from more than one collection can be processed by implementing a **join operation,** using the select...from...where form of query. The collections to be joined, the matching condition and the join function are respectively specified in the from–clause, where–clause and the select–clause.

OQL can retrieve existing objects and can also create new ones. New objects can be created using the constructors, **set, bag, list, array,** and **struct. New mutable objects** are created using the type name as the constructor. The select...from...where form of query can create **bag–objects, set–objects** using the **distinct** keyword and **list–objects** using **order by.** In general, this form of query creates a collection–object which contains the structures specified in the select clause. OQL also includes operators for changing the type of an object (**listtoset, distinct, element,** and **flatten**).

Queries can be constructed incrementally as **query programs**, using the **define query** facility to define and name queries.

There is as yet no widely accepted concept of **completeness** for an object database language. Before this can be achieved, it is necessary to agree upon a formal object data model and establish formal semantics for object database languages.

## EXERCISES:

(6.1)   OQL is a database sub–language. What does this mean?

(6.2)   What is the relationship between the object algebra, described in Chapter 5, and OQL.

(6.3)   What is meant by computationally complete and relationally complete? How would you test the "completeness" of OQL?

(6.4)   How and why must OQL be used in conjunction with other computer languages? Which languages must be used, and for what purpose?

(6.5)   OQL can be used either as an embedded query language or as a stand–alone query language. Explain the meaning of that statement.

(6.6)   In what way can OQL be said to be a declarative language, and not procedural or imperative?

(6.7)   Explain what is meant by collection–oriented and navigational OQL queries. Give examples of each.

(6.8)   What is the relationship between OQL and SQL?

(6.9)   The following query is valid in both SQL and OQL. Explain its respective meanings.

```
select distinct *
from products p
where p.product_no = "P1";
```

(6.10)  Express the OQL query in( 6.9) in object algebra.

(6.11)  OQL is an orthogonal language. Explain and illustrate, using an example OQL query, what this statement means.

(6.12)  Three general facilities which must be provided by an object algebra were identified in the previous chapter (see Section 5.2 A Non–Mathematical Overview). Explain what there are, and how they are provided by the select...from...where OQL statements.

(6.13)  What is the simplest form of OQL query? Give examples.

The following are practical exercises in formulating queries on the object database in Figure 6.1. In addition to the objects shown, assume the following:

- Product objects for P2 and P3 are respectively named best_seller and worst_seller.
- Customer object, C1, is named main_customer.
- The SalesOrder object for order O9 is named biggest_order.

Write the OQL to express the following queries.

(6.14)  Retrieve the object for product P2.

(6.15)  Retrieve the string "This is trivial". (A string is a type of literal what other literal types does OQL support?)

(6.16)  Test if the Product objects named best_seller and worst_seller are in fact the same object.

(6.17)  Test if the Product objects named best_seller and worst_seller contain the same values.

(6.18)  Retrieve the name of the main customer.

(6.19)  Retrieve the set of orders placed by the main customer.

(6.20)  What is the name of the customer who placed the biggest order?

(6.21)  What is the result of the query

```
select p
from    products p
where   p.address.city = "Leeds";
```

(6.22)  In the OQL in( 6.21), explain the use of the variable p.

(6.23)  Express the (6.21) OQL in object algebra.

(6.24)  Which are the products which are not pink, have a name which starts with 'h' or 'b', and are not called honley flyer.

(6.25)  Explain, in detail, how your solution OQL for (6.24) will be evaluated for the Product object for P4.

(6.26)  Assume Person operations age? and number_of_orders? which retrieve the age and the cumulative number of orders for a customer. Which customers are between 21 and 30 years old and have placed over 200 orders with Bruddersfiled Bikes?

(6.27)   Which sales orders are for only blue products?

(6.28)   Which sales orders are for at least one blue product?

(6.29)   Which sales orders are for one and only one blue product?

(6.30)   Can any of the customers be reached using the telephone number 02349854?

(6.31)   Write three OQL queries, which, respectively, retrieve customers who share some of the same telephone numbers, none of the same telephone numbers, and all of the same telephone numbers as other customers.

(6.32)   Is there a customer whose name starts with 'G' and ends with 'd', with an 'a' as the third character?

(6.33)   Assume that the telephones attribute of Customer is of type List<Telephone>:

   (i )   Retrieve the first, last and second telephone numbers by which Faulties can be contacted.

   (ii)   Retrieve a list of telephone numbers that can be used to contact Faulties or Harding Bros.

(6.34)   Assume that the telephones attribute of Customer is of type Set<Telephones>:

   (i)   Retrieve the set containing telephone numbers for all customers.

   (ii)   Retrieve the telephone numbers that Faulties and Harding Bros both use.

   (iii)   Retrieve telephone numbers used by Faulties, but not Harding Bros.

(6.35)   Retrieve details of customers, grouped by city.

(6.36)   Retrieve details of customers, other than those in Leeds, grouped by city.

(6.37)   Retrieve customer details grouped by the first letter of their name and city, for example, customers with names starting with an 'h' and located in Huddersfield will be one of the groups.

(6.38)   Assume a SalesOrder operation, create_invoice, which returns an invoice object. Execute this for each sales order, and return the resulting set of invoice objects.

(6.39)   Assume a SalesOrder operation, add_order_line (new_product: Pcode, quantity:Short). Execute this for order O6, to add an additional order line for 200 of product P3.

(6.40)  Why must care be taken when executing operations to return values computed from object states?

(6.41)  Assume that there are two subtypes of SalesOrder InternalSalesOrder and ExternalSalesOrder with different implementation of create_invoice. Explain late binding, with respect to your (6.38) OQL solution.

(6.42)  Modify your (6.41) solution, using a class indicator to ensure that invoices are generated only for external sales orders.

(6.43)  Using the age? and number_of_orders? operations in (6.21), compute the average number of orders for each year of the life of each customer.

(6.44)  Retrieve the first five letters of each customer name, prefixed with the first two letters of their city of location.

(6.45)  Compute the number of customers in Leeds, and their minimum, average, and maximum age.

(6.46)  Assume an Employee subtype of the Person type, which has name and address attributes, as in Customer.

    (i)      Retrieve details of employees who are also customers (where the names and addresses are the same).

    (ii)     Retrieve details of employees who are not customers.

    (iii)    Retrieve details of customers who are not employees.

    (iv)    Use OQL to perform an outer–tuple–join on employees and customers, where names and addresses match.

(6.47)  Retrieve the names of pairs of customers who have the same address.

(6.48)  Retrieve details of sales orders where there is an orderline for 100 of some product.

(6.49)  Create a set, a bag, a list, and an array, each of which contains the names of customers.

(6.50)  Create a list of structures, each of which contains the name and address of a customer.

(6.51)  Create a new customer object, called "Big Bikes", with the same telephone numbers as Faulties, and the same address as Graft Ltd.

(6.52)  Use the select...from...where form of OQL query to create a list of customer names and addresses, in name within address sequence (using the ORDER BY clause).

(6.53)  Assume the telephone_directory is a list of structures, each containing a name, address, and extension number:

(i)     Convert telephone_directory into a mutable set–object, called telephone_directory_set.

(ii)    Remove duplicates from telephone_directory, but retain it as a list.

(ii)    Retrieve the structure–object in telephone_directory which gives details of Dr Brown, Room 5, Extension 26.

(6.54)  What is the result of the OQL,

```
flatten(set(1,2,3), set(3,4,5),set(6,7,))
```

(6.55)  Demonstrate how, using the define query facility, a query which returns the details of customers who have placed orders for quantities in excess of 200 of black products can be put together and tested in stages.

# 7

# BUILDING OBJECT DATABASE APPLICATIONS

This chapter describes ways in which object database languages are used, in conjunction with other programming languages, to build object database applications. The techniques described are illustrated by examining, in detail, a binding for C++ and the Object Data Model, called C++ ODL/OML [Cattell 97] (ODL and OML respectively stand for Object Definition Language and Object Manipulation Lineage). C++ ODL/OML extends the C++ programming language for building applications for object databases which conform to the Object Data Model.

The use of object database programming environment is illustrated by a case study object database application implementation. The example application is based upon the Bruddersfield Bikes case study used in previous chapters, and is developed using the $O_2$ ODMBS. $O_2$ is one of a number of ODMG–compliant OBBMSs and is used as illustrative of object database applications development environments in general.

Note that this chapter is not intended as a reference manual for object database programmers. Instead, it provides the general conceptual and technical background that will provide a basis for learning and exploiting specific object database programming environments.

Section 7.1 gives an overview of OML/OQL programming language binding. The C++ ODL/OML binding is described in Section 7.2. A case study implementation using the $O_2$ ODBMS is in Section 7.3. Finally, a summary is provided in Section 7.4.

## 7.1 PROGRAMMING LANGUAGES FOR OBJECT DATABASE APPLICATIONS

The **Object Query Language, OQL** (see Chapter 6), and **Object Definition Language, ODL** (see Chapter 4), respectively can describe object database queries and the interfaces to object types. However, these languages have limited expressiveness. For example, OQL and ODL are not computationally complete, i.e., they cannot express arbitrarily complex computations. Also, OQL can modify the state of an object or delete it only by executing operations written in other languages. These limitations mean that OQL and ODL must be used in conjunction with other programming languages in order to build object database systems. The additional languages are needed, for example, to implement object types and to implement computations performed by the applications. The relationship between these languages is represented in Figure 7.1.

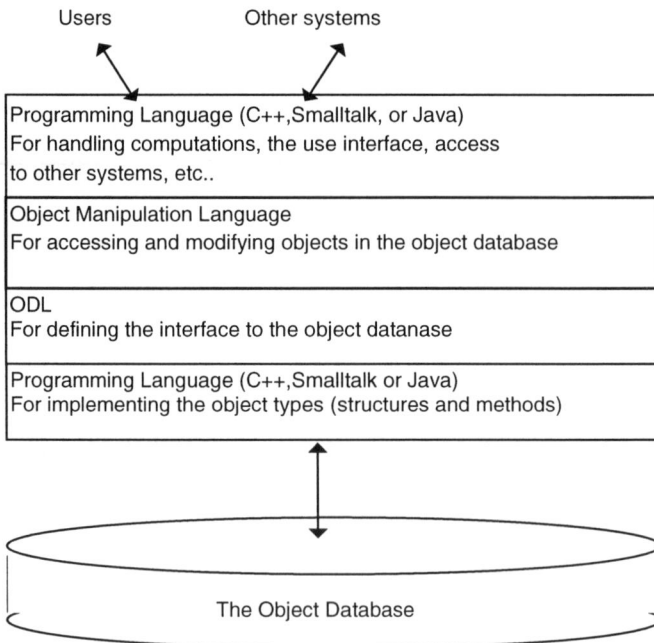

Users          Other systems

| Programming Language (C++,Smalltalk, or Java) |
| --- |
| For handling computations, the use interface, access to other systems, etc.. |
| Object Manipulation Language |
| For accessing and modifying objects in the object database |
| ODL |
| For defining the interface to the object datanase |
| Programming Language (C++,Smalltalk or Java) |
| For implementing the object types (structures and methods) |

The Object Database

Figure 7.1 Object database systems languages

The following subsections overview approaches to combining the object database functionality (provided in OQL and ODL) with the computational capabilities of programming languages.

## PROGRAMMING LANGUAGE ODL/OML BINDING

A **binding** of a program element is its association with one of a number of possible characteristics or properties. Bindings can take place at various times in the life of a programming language and the programs written in it. They may occur when a program is compiled or executed, for example to associate variables with particular storage locations, and when a language is defined and implemented. Here we are concerned with bindings that are made when the programming language is designed. The bindings associate the programming language's elements with characteristics and properties of the Object Data Model. The aim of these bindings is to extend a programming language such that it can also define and manipulate object databases, and can therefore be used to construct object database applications.

In Section 7.2, we illustrate programming languages bindings with the Object Data Model by examining the **C++ ODL/OML** binding specified in the ODMG standard [Cattell 97] (ODMG have also specified standards for Smalltalk and Java bindings).

1) ODL stands for **Object Definition Language** and is the language used for implementing the concepts of the Object Data Model. ODL is used to define object database schemas which describe to a program, the object types and classes that may be accessed.
2) OML stands for **Object Manipulation Language** and is the language used for accessing and modifying objects in an object database.

A programming language ODL/OML binding extends the programming language such that it can be used to implement object database applications. The extensions include the ODL features for definition, and OML features for manipulation, of objects within an object database.

A binding may tightly or loosely couple the programming language and the Object Data Model.

1) A **tightly coupled** binding is achieved by integrating the object database languages into the programming language syntax, e.g., by providing a mechanism for **embedding the object database language** statements within programs.

2) A **loosely coupled** binding, on the other hand, does not include the object database languages within the programming language syntax. Instead, database language expressions are handled as character strings to be processed by appropriate procedures when the program is executed.

C++ ODL/OML has features of both tight and loose coupling. For example, OQL queries are handled as character strings (loose coupling), but ODL facilities are included within the C++ syntax itself (tight coupling).

An aim of a programming language OML/ODL binding is to create, for the programmer, a **seamless environment** within which to work with a single language. This is to avoid the situation where the programmer has to utilise different languages brought together in an arbitrary way. This aim can be achieved if the binding has the following features:

1)  A single type system is shared by both the programming language and the integrated database languages. Instances of types should therefore be either persistent or transient. Persistent instances continue to exist even after the process that created them terminates, until they are explicitly deleted and are contained in the object database. Transient instances are destroyed when the program that created them terminates and are used as the program variables.
2)  The binding retains the characteristics of the programming language. The programming language with the binding should not be a significantly different language to that without it.
3)  There are few extensions to the programming language and these do not duplicate functions already provided by the programming language.
4)  The expressions in the database languages and the programming language can be freely combined to form complex expressions.

Object–oriented programming languages are generally amenable to this form of seamless integration. This is because the correspondences that exist between features of the object model upon which an object–oriented language is based and  features of the Object Data Model can be exploited. In general, types within the Object Data Model will be implemented as classes within the programming language, the programming language's inheritance mechanism will be used to model the inheritance subtype/supertype relationships of the Object Data Model, and so on. Also, object–oriented programming languages provide an extensible type system, whereby new features can be integrated by defining new classes, which are possibly subclasses of existing ones— new facilities can therefore be added within the programming language, rather than by having to extend it.

Problems can occur where there are differences in the underlying object models. For example, definition of the Java binding requires some way of reconciling the fact that Java allows a type to have only one supertype but the Object Data Model allows multiple supertypes. These differences can either restrict the ODBMS features that are made available through a programming language binding (for instance, the C++ ODL/OML environment described below does not support Object Data Model keys or exceptions because these are not part of C++) or can complicate the resulting programming environment.

The technology described in this book is at an early stage and is evolving rapidly. There are still many gaps within the ODMG and other proposed standards. In particular, in addition to the above Object Data Model bindings with object–oriented programming languages, standard bindings are needed for non–object–oriented technologies. This is necessary to allow existing systems to interact with object database systems. Bindings are required, for instance, to allow interoperability between relational and object database systems, and to allow object database programs to be implemented with non-object–oriented programming languages, such as C and Prolog.

## SYSTEM INTERFACING

System interfacing is the very weakest form of programming language/ database system binding. A system interface supports an Application Program Interface (API) which allows applications programs to pass instructions to the DBMS and receive responses. Here the programming language is not extended, but can use special procedures, classes, or system calls to communicate with a separate DBMS. An example of this approach, used for binding programming languages and relational databases, is JDBC (Java DataBase Connectivity).

## PERSISTENT PROGRAMMING LANGUAGES

Persistent programming languages represent the very tightest form of programming language/database system binding. In this approach, persistent data storage facilities are integrated into the programming language. The difference between programming language ODL/OML binding (previously described), and this approach is that the former maps the programming language elements into the object data model of an ODBMS, whereas a persistent programming language extends its own underlying object model to enable all objects to be persistent or transient. The aim is for programs to be able to define and manipulate objects, be they persistent or transient, in the same way. An example of this approach is Persistent Java (PJava) [Spence 97].

## 7.2 C++ ODL/OML BINDING

We now describe a specific programming language/Object Data Model binding [Cattell 97], the ODMG C++ ODL/OML binding, in some detail.

C++ [Stroustrup 92] is an object–oriented extension to the programming language C. Though the detail of C++ may appear cryptic and obscure to non–C++ and non–C programmers, the concepts of the object model upon which it is based will be familiar, having studied the Object Data Model (see Chapter 2).

Both C++ and the Object Data Model are object–oriented and therefore have underlying object models. This simplifies the process of defining a binding between them, since all object models are based upon a common set of core principles. The task of defining a seamless binding is also made easier by strong syntactical similarities between declarations in C++ and the Object Data Model ODL. In fact, the OMG's IDL upon which ODL is based is itself C++ based.

### C++ ODL

C++ ODL is the extension to C++ for declaring persistent object types, and thus implements the binding between C++ and the structural part of the Object Data Model (see Chapter 3). This binding exploits the strong similarities between the ODL and C++ syntax for declaring types. Accordingly, C++ ODL is a subset of C++, but with added built–in types which provide an interface to the Object Data Model. The names of these built–in types are prefixed with "d_" to distinguish them from other C++ names.

---

*EXAMPLE 7.1*

*The following code gives equivalent definitions of a Customer object type/class in C++ OML/ODL and in the Object Data Model ODL.*

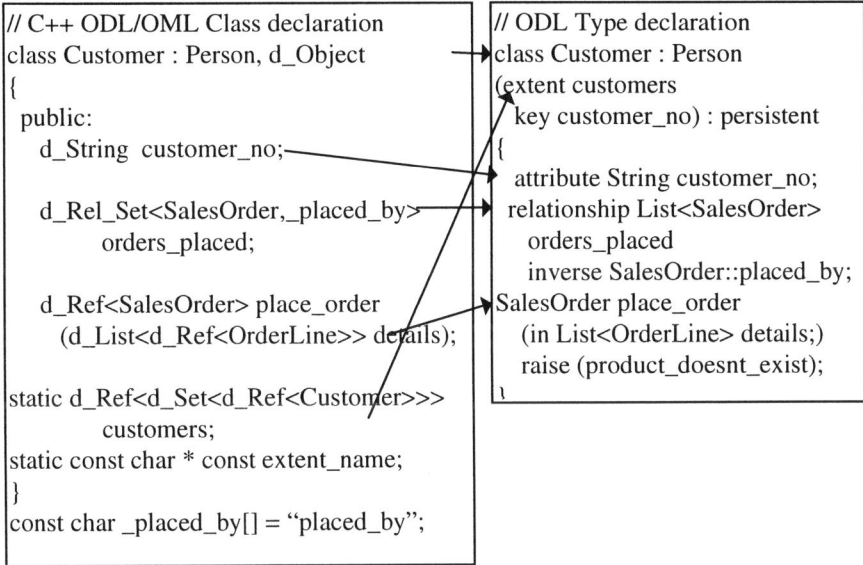

```
// C++ ODL/OML Class declaration
class Customer : Person, d_Object
{
  public:
    d_String  customer_no;

    d_Rel_Set<SalesOrder,_placed_by>
        orders_placed;

    d_Ref<SalesOrder> place_order
      (d_List<d_Ref<OrderLine>> details);

static d_Ref<d_Set<d_Ref<Customer>>>
        customers;
static const char * const extent_name;
}
const char _placed_by[] = "placed_by";
```

```
// ODL Type declaration
class Customer : Person
(extent customers
  key customer_no) : persistent
{
    attribute String customer_no;
    relationship List<SalesOrder>
        orders_placed
        inverse SalesOrder::placed_by;
SalesOrder place_order
    (in List<OrderLine> details;)
    raise (product_doesnt_exist);
}
```

---

Example 7.1 has been contrived to highlight similarities between C++ and ODL, and deliberately avoids complexities of the C++ language. Points to note are:

1) Both the ODL and C++ ODL/OML are concerned with the Customer object type.

2) The ODL code declares the Customer object type interface (see Chapter 4). This declaration specifies the type properties (supertypes, keys, and extents) and the instance characteristics (attributes, relationships, and operations).

3) The C++ ODL/OML code declares a Customer class, which is an implementation of the Customer type. The definition (like the ODL) declares the supertypes from which characteristics are inherited. The instance characteristics are called members in C++. Members are used to define both state properties (attributes and relationships) and operations (called member functions).

4) The final two entries in the C++ OML/ODL class definition (which declare customers and extent_name) are included to create an extent for the Customer class.

5) C++ OML/ODL features which implement the interface to the Object Data Model are prefixed with "d_". Examples are d_List and d_Set. As their names suggest, these implement the corresponding Object Data Model elements, List and Set.

These similarities between the ODL and C++ language elements provide a natural basis for the C++ ODL/OML binding and C++, and are discussed below.

## OBJECT TYPES

Like the Object Data Model, C++ represents information as objects, each of which has a type and is a member of a class (in C++ the term class refers to an implementation object class, i.e., a class is an object type together with an implementation). C++ ODL/OML therefore maps each Object Data Model object type to a C++ class.

```
C++                          Object Data Model
Class        ◄───────────►   Object Type
```

A C++ program not only defines the interfaces to classes (in a similar manner to the ODL interface declarations (see Chapter 4)), but also defines their implementation. However, note that there is currently no distinction in the C++ ODL between interfaces and classes (as there is in the Object Data Model (see Chapter 3)).

1) In C++, object characteristics (attributes, types, and operations) are called **members**. Members provide the interface to a class, but can also be used for "internal" class implementation purposes. In the latter case, members are made non–accessible to users of a class (by declaring them as **protected** or **private**, rather than **public**).

2) In addition, a C++ program must define procedures which implement each of a class's member functions (the operations).

## OBJECTS

Each Object Data Model object (an instance of a type) maps into a C++ object (an instance of a class).

```
┌─────────────┐                          ┌──────────────────┐
│C++          │◄────────────────────────►│Object Data Model │
│Object       │                          │Object            │
└─────────────┘                          └──────────────────┘
```

C++ does not support **persistent objects**, i.e., objects which continue to exist after the process that created them has terminated. Objects created within a C++ program are destroyed when the program terminates. C++ ODL/OML therefore introduces an additional mechanism for creating and referring to objects in the object database, but without having to subsequently create them differently from "conventional" C++ objects. To this end C++ ODL/OML includes three special classes:

1) **d_Object**—this is an abstract class for all persistent objects. An object defined on a class which is a subclass of d_Object can be either persistent or transient. For instance, the declaration,

```
class Customer : public d_Object {...}
```

declares that the class called Customer is a subclass of d_Object, and its instances can therefore be persistent (object database objects) or transient.

2) **d_Ref<T>**—C++ includes variables that can take an object as their value, and pointer variables which can take the address of an object as their value. However, pointer variables cannot directly reference persistent objects, so C++ ODL/OML includes a new class, instances of which serve this purpose. For each class, T, there is an ancillary class, d_Ref<T>, instances of which are used to reference persistent or transient objects of type T (these are called smart pointers).

3) **d_Database**—an instance of this class represents an object database within which persistent objects can be retained. Its operations are used to open and close an object database, to name objects in it, and to access objects by name (d_Database class operations are described later when the C++ OML is explained).

*SUBTYPE/SUPERTYPE RELATIONSHIPS*

Subtype/supertype relationships of the Object Data Model are directly implemented in C++ by the subclass/superclass relationship, and with a syntax which is almost identical to that in the ODL.

---

*EXAMPLE 7.2*

*The C++ class declaration,*

```
class Customer: Person {...}
```

*declares that Customer is a subclass of Person in the same way that this fact would be declared in ODL.*

---

Note that currently C++ ODL does not distinguish between subtype/ supertype and EXTENDS relationships (see Chapter 3), but includes a built–in meta class called d_Inheritance which can potentially describe different types of inheritance relationship between classes.

### EXTENTS

C++ ODL/OML includes a built–in class called d_Extent<T> to support extents. In addition, the programmer must define the C++ variables which will store the extent and the extent's name.

---

*EXAMPLE 7.3*

*The C++ OML/ODL code in Example 7.1 illustrates how a class extent can be created. The penultimate delaration, i.e.,*

```
static d_Ref<d_Set<d_Ref<Customer>>> customers;
```

*explicitly creates a set–object, customers, to contains instances of the Customer type. The last declaration, i.e.,*

```
static const char * const extent_name;
```

*creates a character string, extent_name, within which to store the name of the extent. Note the use of the C++ keyword static, which indicates that these two data members are stored only once for the class, not for each instance of Customer.*

---

### KEYS

C++ does not support object keys, and there is currently no C++ ODL/OML facility for supporting them.

## OBJECT NAMES

The Object Data Model allows an object to be assigned one or more object names by which that object can be accessed. This facility is also supported in C++ ODL/OML. (Object names are assigned and used to access objects using operations on the d_Database class—instances of d_Database represent object databases. This facility is described later when the C++ OML is described.)

## OBJECT CHARACTERISTICS

An Object Data Model object has characteristics, i.e., attributes, relationships, and operations. In C++ the characteristics of an object are called members. C++ class members can be data members, which are used to define data contained in the objects (i.e., the state of the object), or member functions, which are the operations on them. Each Object Data Model object characteristic maps into a C++ member—attributes and relationships map into data members, and operators map into member functions.

| C++ Class Member | ←———————→ | Object Data Model Object Characteristic |
|---|---|---|

## MUTABLE OBJECTS AND LITERALS

Unlike the Object Data Model, C++ does not have a uniform treatment of values and objects. There is no C++ concept of mutable and literal objects, and so the binding must exploit some feature of C++ which has, or can simulate, this concept.

C++ objects which are embedded as class members are used in C++ ODL/OML to represent literals. This is because, when C++ embeds an object as a member of another, it is inserting a copy of the embedded object within the containing object (rather than inserting a reference to the embedded object). A consequence is that the embedded object (the copy) does not have an identity which is independent of its value, and can therefore be treated as a literal.

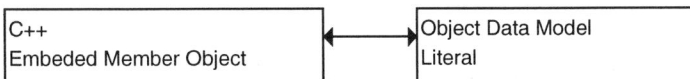

| C++ Embeded Member Object | ←———————→ | Object Data Model Literal |
|---|---|---|

## ATTRIBUTES

The attributes of an Object Data Model object are represented by data members defined on built–in or user–defined types and classes. The values of these are contained in the C++ object and are therefore treated as literals, as prescribed in the Object Data Model (all attribute values must be literals).

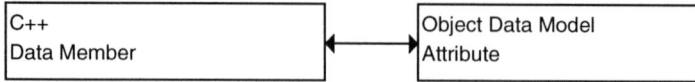

```
┌──────────────────────────┐      ┌──────────────────────────┐
│ C++                      │◄────►│ Object Data Model        │
│ Data Member              │      │ Attribute                │
└──────────────────────────┘      └──────────────────────────┘
```

## EXAMPLE 7.4

*An example attribute declaration is given in Example 7.1, i.e.,*

```
d_String   customer_no;
```

*The above C++ ODL is equivalent to the ODL declaration,*

```
Attribute String customer_no;
```

*Note the use of the prefix d_ in the C++ ODL code to denote that d_String provides an interface to String in the Object Data Model. All of the other standard built–in Object Data Model literal types are supported in a similar way.*

## RELATIONSHIPS

C++ does not include the notion of relationships. The C++ ODL/OML therefore represents a relationship's traversal path as a data member, in the same way that attributes are represented.

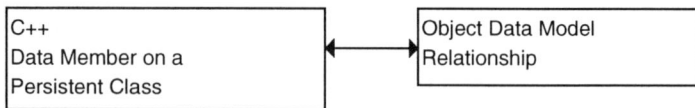

```
┌──────────────────────────┐      ┌──────────────────────────┐
│ C++                      │◄────►│ Object Data Model        │
│ Data Member on a         │      │ Relationship             │
│ Persistent Class         │      │                          │
└──────────────────────────┘      └──────────────────────────┘
```

However, "relationshp" data members must use special types so that the integrity of the relationships can be maintained. A data member which represents a relationship path, called "path" (where the inverse path is called "inverse_path"), and which associates objects of type "Related_objects" must be defined in one of the following ways, depending on the cardinality of the relationship:

```
d_Rel_Ref <Related_objects, _inverse_path>
       path;
d_Rel_Set <Related_objects, _inverse_path>
       path;
d_Rel_List <Related_objects, _inverse_path>
       path;

const char _inverse_path [] = "inverse_path";
```

These respectively represent paths to a single object, a set of objects or a list of objects.

---

### EXAMPLE 7.5

*The relationship property placed_by (the inverse relation is orders_placed), of the SalesOrder type, which associates a SalesOrder object with the relevant Customer object, can be declared within a C++ ODL SalesOrder class declaration as:*

```
d_Rel_Ref<Customer, _orders_placed> placed_by;

const   char _orders_placed[] = "orders_placed"
```

*The above  C++ ODL is equivalent to the ODL declaration,*

```
relationship Customer placed_by
        inverse Customer::orders_placed;
```

*The inverse relationship path will be defined in the Customer class by the following data member:*

```
d_Rel_List<SaleOrder,_placed_by>
        orders_placed

const char _place_by[] = "placed_by"
```

*Note that the inverse relationship relates a Customer instance to a list of SalesOrder instances. The relationship between SalesOrder and Customer is therefore a many–to–one relationship.*

---

## OPERATIONS

Operations in the Object Data Model correspond to member functions in C++, and have similar syntax in both C++ and ODL. Function members therefore map into Object Data Model type operations.

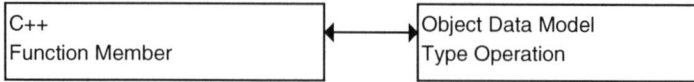

```
┌──────────────────────────┐        ┌──────────────────────────┐
│ C++                      │◄──────►│ Object Data Model        │
│ Function Member          │        │ Type Operation           │
└──────────────────────────┘        └──────────────────────────┘
```

---

### EXAMPLE 7.6

*An example C++ ODL/OML operation declaration is given in Figure 7.2.*

```
d_Ref<SalesOrder> place_order
        (d_List<d_Ref<OrderLine>> details);
```

*This is equivalent to the ODL declaration,*

```
SalesOrder Place_order
        (in List<OrderLine> details)
```

---

Exceptions are handled by the standard C++ exception handler, which is called **exception**. When an error is detected, an instance of a class d_Error is created using this mechanism.

### COLLECTION–OBJECT TYPES

The collection object types (sets, bags, lists, and arrays) of the Object Data Model are also supported by C++. C++ template classes serve the same purpose as the ODMG type generators. For example, in C++ we can create a Set type generator as follows:

```
template<class T> class d_Set:  d_Collection<T>
{...};
```

The above C++ template class definition declares a class generator called d_Set. Its code provides a template within which to include specific class names—when used, e.g., d_Set<Customer>, the parameter T is replaced wherever it occurs in the declaration by the relevant class name, Customer. The above definition declares that the superclass of d_Set<T> is d_Collection<T>, as in the Object Data Model.

The collection–object type generator is used in conjunction with the d_Ref class to declare persistent collection–object types, e.g.,

```
d_Set<d_Ref<Customer>> retail_customers;
```

## STRUCTURE–OBJECT TYPES

C++ allows structure types to be constructed from other types using a constructor, struct. Also, classes can be structured by defining data members on other classes. C++ ODL/OML uses these two C++ features to implement structure–object.

---

### EXAMPLE 7.7

*Consider the structure–object type defined in the ODL attribute declaration,*

```
attribute Struct Address
  {Unsigned Short number,
   String street,
   String city_name} address;
```

*Here we have a structure–object valued attribute called address, of type Address. Address has three elements called number, street, and city_name, respectively of types Unsigned Short, String and String. An equivalent declaration in C++ ODL is:*

```
struct Address
  {d_UShort number;
   d_String street;
   d_String city_name;} address;
```

---

A data member defined on a class also defines a structure–object type, since the data members of the class are embedded within the containing class.

## C++ OML

The elements of the C++ OML map into the manipulative part of the Object Data Model (see Chapters 5 and 6). C++ OML provides features for accessing and manipulating the contents of an object database. This is done mostly in such a way that the C++ ODL creates, deletes, and manipulates persistent objects in the same way that C++ does for "conventional" transient objects.

## CREATING AND DELETING OBJECTS

Object database objects are created in C++ OML using the **new** operator, which is used in C++ to create transient objects. The function of this operator is extended in C++ OML by overloading it. Operator overloading is the technique whereby we provide multiple definitions of a single operator, each distinguished by different types of parameters. The parameters of the additional definitions of the new operator are used to specify whether the new object is persistent or transient and in which object database it is to be stored. If the additional parameters are not provided when new is invoked, then the "conventional" C++ definition of new is invoked to create a transient object. For instance,

```
d_Ref<Customer>    new_customer = new Customer
```

creates a transient instance of Customer. This is because new has not been provided with parameters, and so its conventional C++ implementation is executed. The following C++ OML invokes one of the additional definitions of new:

```
d_Ref<Customer> new_customer =
         new(SOPdatabase) Customer
```

The effect of this second expression is to creates a new persistent instance of Customer in the object database, SOPdatabase.

Other parameters for the new operator in C++ OML may be used, for example, to pass the new object type as a parameter, and to specify where it is to be placed within the object database.

## MODIFICATION OF OBJECTS

The state of an object (transient or persistent) is changed by either updating its properties or executing operations on it. For example, if we have a variable, new_customer, as follows,

```
d_Ref<Customer>        new_customer;
```

and assign to it a reference to a persistent Customer object, we can then modify the state of that object by assigning a new value, next_customer_number, to its customer_no attribute,

```
new_customer->customer_no
       = next_customer_number;
```

Alternatively, we can update the state of the Customer object by executing one of its operations upon it,

```
new_customer->take_order(new_order_details);
```

In both cases, standard C++ is used.

Persistent objects are deleted using an operation of the d_Ref class, implemented as the delete_object member function,

```
new_object->delete_object();
```

It is also necessary to communicate to the ODBMS the fact that the state of the object has been changed or that the object has been deleted, so that the ODBMS can process the changes in the object database itself. This is done using an operation upon the d_Ref class, implemented as the mark_modified member function,

```
new_customer->mark_modified();
```

## MANIPULATING RELATIONSHIPS

Relationships are implemented in C++ OML/ODL as data members defined on Ref classes. The value of a relationship data member can therefore comprise one or more references to persistent (or transient) objects. The standard C++ features for assigning values to data members can therefore be used to create, modify, or remove relationships, and to navigate them from one object to another. Also, where a relationship is to a collection of objects, the special operators for manipulating collections can be used to modify the relationship.

---

## EXAMPLE 7.8

*Consider, for instance, the following relationship declarations, respectively in the SalesOrder and Customer class definitions:*

```
class SalesOrder  {

    . . .

 d_Rel_Ref<Customer,_orders_placed>  placed_by;

    . . .

};


class Customer  {

        . . .

        d_Rel_Set<SalesOrder,_placed_by>
                orders_placed

        . . .

};
```

*These declare a many–to–one relationship—many SalesOrder objects can be related to one Customer object, where the navigation paths are placed_by (from SalesOrder to Customer) and orders_placed (from Customer to SalesOrder).*

*Each SalesOrder is related to just one customer, so we can create or modify the relationship for a specific SalesOrder object by assigning to its placed_by relationship a reference to the associated Customer object,*

```
SalesOrder   new_sales_order;
Customer     existing_customer;
. . .
new_sales_order.placed_by = &existing_customer;
. . .
```

*Note the use of the & symbol—in C++ this means the address of the object that is the value of the variable that it precedes. The effect is therefore to assign the address of the Customer object assigned to existing_customer to the placed_by relationship data member of the SalesOrder object assigned to existing_sales_order. The inverse relationship is then automatically created by the ODBMS.*

C++ OML includes a clear operation upon relationships that removes an association between objects,

```
new_sales_order.placed_by.clear();
```

We can modify a relationship to many objects using the appropriate collection operations. For example, given the above example relationship, we can use set–object operators (insert_element, remove_element, etc.) to modify the relationship between a Customer object and the associated set of SalesOrder objects, e.g.,

```
existing_customer.orders_placed.insert_element
    (&new_sales_order);
...
existing_customer.orders_place.remove_element
    (&new_sales_order);
```

For instance, the persistent class, Customer, has an ancillary reference class called d_Ref<Customer>. We can therefore define a variable which can be assigned references to Customer objects,

```
d_Ref<Customer> new_customer
```

This variable can be assigned a reference to a Customer object, and can then be used to access and manipulate the referenced object as though it were a conventional transient C++ object. For example, the Customer operation, place_order, is executed for that object by the C++ statement,

```
new_customer->place_order (order_details);
```

Note the use of the arrow, ->, to indicate access to a member of the object referenced by the preceding variable. If a dot, ., is used, this indicates access to a member of the object assigned to the preceding variable. This contrasts with OQL, in which dot and arrow mean the same thing and are interchangeable.

## MANIPULATING NAMED OBJECTS

The C++ ODL/OML allows us to name individual objects and use the object names to retrieve the named objects. The object names provide access points into an object database. In C++ ODL/OML, the naming and retrieval by name operations are implemented as member functions of the d_Database class. In effect, we have to talk to the object database itself in order to assign or utilise object names.

If the variable database contains the address of an instance of type d_Database, then the following C++ will respectively open and close an object database called SOPDB:

```
database->open("SOPDB");
database->close();
```

If the variable ref_customer is of type d_Ref<Customer> and has been assigned a reference to a persistent Customer object, then the following C++ will respectively name the object "Customer X", rename it "Customer Y", and retrieve the name of an object:

```
database->set_object_name
        (d_Ref_customer, "Customer X");
database->rename_object
        ("CustomerX", "Customer Y");
obj_name = database->get_object_name
        (d_Ref_customer);
```

Having named an object, there is also a d_Database operation which allows us to retrieve it by name:

```
customer_y = database->lookup_object
        ("Customer Y");
```

## OQL QUERIES

OQL queries can be executed from within C++ OML/ODL programs in two ways either by using the query operation on collection–objects or by using the d_OQL_Query interface.

The d_Collection class is an abstract class (it does not have instances), and is the superclass for the different types of collection–object types (sets–, bag–, list–, and array–object types). The **query** operation takes as its parameters the collection–object to which the result of the query will be assigned, and an OQL Boolean expression to act as a predicate. The result is the collection of objects for which the predicate returns true. For example, we can retrieve the set–object containing black products, using the query operation, as follows:

```
d_Set<d_Ref<Product>>     black_products;
products->query(black_products,
        "colour = "black"");
```

Note that the query operation provides only a subset of the facilities of OQL, corresponding to that which can be expressed using the restrict operator of the object algebra.

The **d_OQL_Query** type provides an interface to the full OQL functionality described in Chapter 6. The method by which an OQL query is executed using this facility is as follows:

1) An object of type d_OQL_Query must be created. This object will be the container of the OQL query to be executed. For example,

```
d_OQL_Query q("select so.placed_by
              from salesorders so
              where so.date > $1");
```

creates an object, q, to contain the OQL which will retrieve the Customer objects for sales orders placed after a specified date.
2) Values must be provided for each of the query parameters. In the example there is only one, denoted $1.

```
q << earliest_order_date;
```

The above C++ copies the parameter value held in the variable earliest_order_date to the query object q.
3) The query is then ready for execution, using

```
d_oql_execute (q, result);
```

The above executes the query using the d_oql_execute operation, and returns the result in a variable called result.

## C++ ODL/OML APPLICATIONS
Figure 7.2 (based on [Cattell 97,p. 124]) shows how the different parts of a C++ ODL/OML application fit together. The program source code comprises the ODL schema and the C++ with OML program. The

preprocessor is used to convert the source code into standard C++, which can then be compiled, linked, and executed in the usual way.

## C++ ODL/OML—SOME GENERAL POINTS

C++ ODL/OML illustrates features which are general to object–oriented programming language/object database bindings.

1) An object–oriented programming language ODL/OML binding can exploit the similarities between the underlying object models of the programming language and object databases.

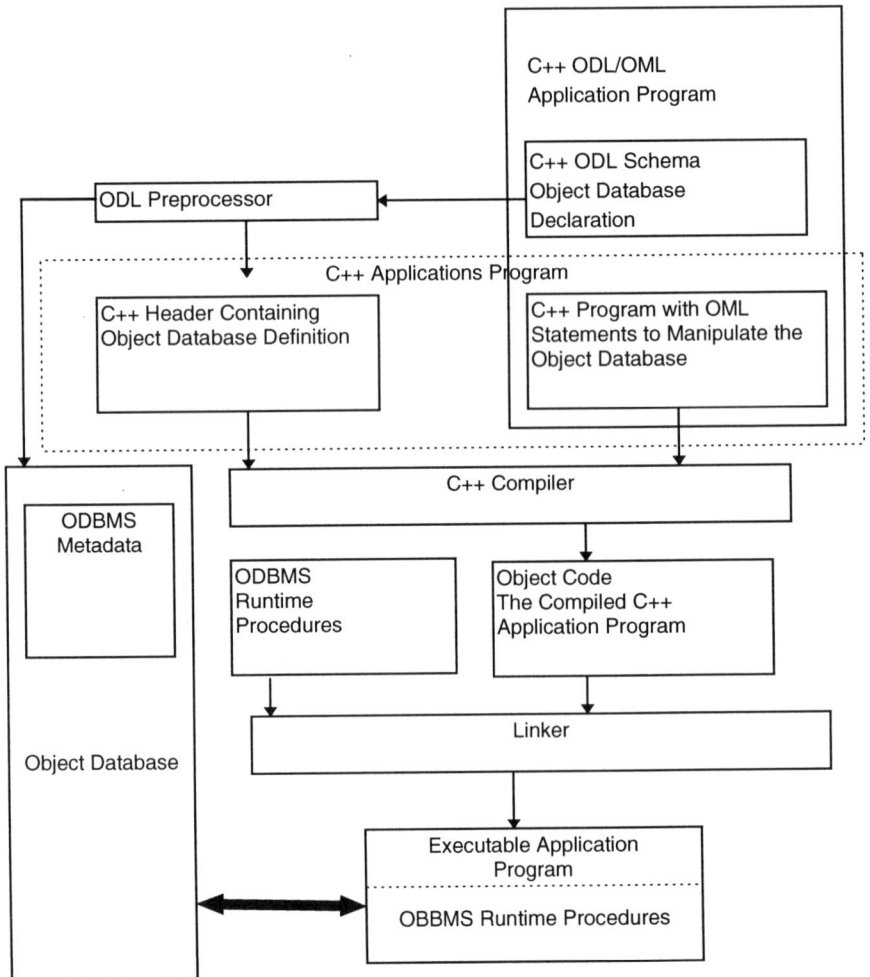

Figure 7.2 Compiling and linking a C++ ODL/OML application

2) An object–oriented programming language provides an extensible type system—programmers can use the language to build new types to support specific applications. This feature can be used to create new types and classes which implement features of the Object Data Model. The importance of this is that the binding is defined within the programming language, rather than by extending it.

3) Subtype/supertype relationships can be used to specialise "conventional" classes such that they also apply to the Object Data Model.

4) Operation overloading can be used to provide additional definitions of "conventional" operators such that they can also apply to Object Data Model elements.

5) Access to the Object Data Model languages can be provided through operations which take language expressions as parameters and return the results of executing those expressions. This is an example of loose binding, in that though the object database languages are made usable, they do not become part of the syntax of the extended programming language. An alternative approach is a tight binding, whereby the object database language statements can be embedded within programs, in which case the object database language syntax is included within the extended programming language.

6) Binding non–object–oriented programming languages is more difficult, since there is less similarity between the underlying models. In such cases, a loosely coupled binding is appropriate.

## 7.3 AN EXAMPLE APPLICATION IN $O_2$

The C++ OML/ODL binding described in the previous sections has been implemented to various degrees of completeness by member companies of the ODMG to produce "ODMG compliant" ODBMSs. The example object database application described in this section has been developed on one such ODBMS, $O_2$ ,and is included to illustrate and bring together the individual element bindings described.

The aim of this section it to illustrate the general appearance and features of current ODBMSs, rather than to provide detailed technical information about a specific database. Accordingly, the database language code used in the example is not explained in detail (even though it differs significantly from the ODL, OML, and C++ ODL/OML languages previously described). Instead, we highlight the ways the general power of the Object Data Model is utilised to support incremental object database development, and reuse of existing solutions, through built–in classes and class libraries.

## THE SCHEMA

The example application implements part of the Bruddersfield Sales Order Processing schema based on the Figure 4.4 ODL schema. The application schema, in which class definitions for Person, Customer, SalesOrder, OrderLine, and Product are given, is shown in Figure 7.3.

Points to note in this schema, are:

1) The schema should be generally understandable to readers, having studied the Object Data Model and ODL, but note that the $O_2C$ language used is different in detail from ODL and C++ ODL/OML. This reflects the current state of ODBMSs. Standards are emerging, but existing systems have yet to conform to them, and still have their own idiosyncrasies.

2) The schema illustrates the use of inheritance to provide generalised operations for many classes—all the classes are defined as subtypes of a class, MyObject, which is itself a specialisation of the built–in (persistent) class Object (similar to d_Object in the C++ ODL/OML binding). This is to allow a more standardised behaviour of all the classes, since they inherit a number of operations, for example, related to displaying objects on a screen.

3) The schema also illustrates the reuse of existing classes to provide standard ready–made solutions to common problems—the class definitions include reference to a class, Date. This is a class imported from $O_2$Kit, a "toolbox" of predefined classes which is a library of classes that are likely to be of use in a number of applications and are supplied with the system, rather than each programmer having to "reinvent the wheel" for common classes.

4) The extents for the classes are defined using name People:set(Person); etc. The name keyword is used in $O_2C$ to specify object names.

```
class Person inherit MyObject
public type tuple (name: string,
          address: tuple(street:string,
                            town:string,
                            district:string,
                            country:string,
                            postcode:string),
          telephones: list(string))
end;
name People:set(Person);

class Customer inherit Person
public type tuple (customer_no:string,
             orders_placed:list(SalesOrder))
end;
name customers:set(Customer);

class OrderLine inherit MyObject
public type tuple(product_no:string,
                  quantity:integer)
end;

class SalesOrder inherit MyObject
public type tuple(order_no:string,
                  order_date:Date,
                  order_lines:list(OrderLine),
                  placed_by:Customer,
                  ordered:set(Product))
end;
name salesorders:set(SalesOrder);

class Product inherit MyObject
public type tuple(product_no:string,
                  name:string,
                  colour:string,
                  has_been_ordered:set(SalesOrder))
end;
name products:set(Product);
```

Figure 7.3 Class definitions for the Bruddersfield system

## ADDING METHODS

The Figure 7.3 class definitions do not include any operation declarations (method signatures), although they could have been present there. Using $O_2$ it is possible to add new methods as the design progresses, and that was the course taken. This allows the designer to develop an object database as a progression of prototypes, each providing more detail.

Figure 7.4 shows a sample method signature and method body which were loaded into the system at a later stage.

```
/* title method */
method public title:string in class Person

method body title:string in class Person
{
        return self->name;
}
```
**Figure 7.4 Sample method signature and body the for Bruddersfield system**

The method in Figure 7.4 further illustrates the potential for reuse of existing classes within an object–oriented system:

The method title, redefines a built–in method from the O₂Look library. This is a library of methods and functions for use with the O₂Look graphic user interface. Each class has a title method used when that class is displayed on screen. The default behaviour is to use the name of the class. The title method shown modifies this so that the name of the object is used instead. This method is defined on the Person class and applies to specialisations of that class as well as the class itself. This can be seen in Figure 7.5 where the members of the Customer class are shown. In this figure, and the subsequent screen shots, the default appearance of O₂ under X Windows is used. The visual appearance can be modified in a number of ways, including through the use of a resource file.

INPUTTING DATA INTO THE OBJECT DATABASE
Figure 7.5 shows two customers represented in the object database.

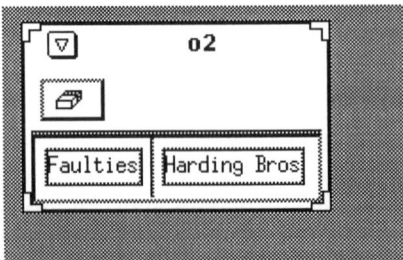

Figure 7.5 Screen shot of customers (showing use of title method)

The data to populate the classes can be added in a number of ways. Figure 7.6 shows the code used to add Faulties—this can be run from a file and demonstrates the way the object database could be populated when first set up. The code shows the creation of a new Customer object, c, and the assignment of values to its attributes. The object c is then added to the customers extent.

```
run body
{
        o2 Customer c = new Customer;
        c->name = "Faulties"
        c->address.street = "5 Road"
        c->address.town = "Leeds";
        c->address.district = "W.Yorks";
        c->address.country ="UK";
        c->address.postcode = "LSI 1QQ";
        c->telephones =list("0113 274123","0113 274124");
        c->customer_no = "C1";
        customers +=set(c);
}
```

Figure 7.6 Code to create "Faulties" Customer object

An alternative way to enter new data is shown in Figure 7.7.

```
run body
{
        o2 Customer c = new Customer;
        c->edit;
        customers +=set(c);
}
```

Figure 7.7 Code to create a new Customer object

The Figure 7.8 code fragment calls the built-in method, edit, to bring up a data entry form into which the values for a new Customer object can be entered. As before, the new object is then added to the extent.

## DISPLAYING DATA

There are a number of other built–in methods that are used in developing an application. One is the display method. This was used, as shown in Figure 7.8, to produce the customers display originally shown in Figure 7.5. This is the equivalent of the OQL queries customers, or, select c from c in customers.

```
run body
{
        display (customers);
}
```

Figure 7.8 Code to display customers

Figure 7.9 shows the display seen when the display method on an individual Customer object is chosen. This is available from a pull-down list of methods when Faulties is selected from the Figure 7.5 screen. Figures 7.10 and 7.11 show respectively, the blank screen brought up by the Figure 7.7 code, ready for the entry of the Graft Ltd data, and the screen with data partly entered. When the data entry is complete, clicking on the pencil icon writes this into the object database. The eraser icon cancels the operation. These figures also show how the complex structure of an object is represented on screen. The parts of the address appear individually named within the address block, and telephones is shown as a list of phone numbers.

Code which is the counterpart to that in Figure 7.8 can be written for all the extents in the database. An example of the output from this is shown in Figure 7.12, where all the Products are shown. These appear simply as boxes labelled "Product" because no alternative title method has been supplied for this class. (A method that titled each product with its number and name could be written, on the lines of the title method for Person previously shown in Figure 7.4.) Figure 7.13 shows the result of choosing the display method for an individual Product, in this case P4, in the same way that Faulties is shown in Figure 7.9.

APPLICATION–SPECIFIC OPERATIONS

In the preceding sections ways of adding a new Customer or Product have been shown using new to create a new object, and then assignment of attributes from a file or with a simple use of the built–in edit method. This section gives an outline of a place_order method for the Customer class. Figure 7.14 shows the method signature and method body for a place_order method. As can be seen from the signature, the method has an input parameter of an order number and returns a SalesOrder object.

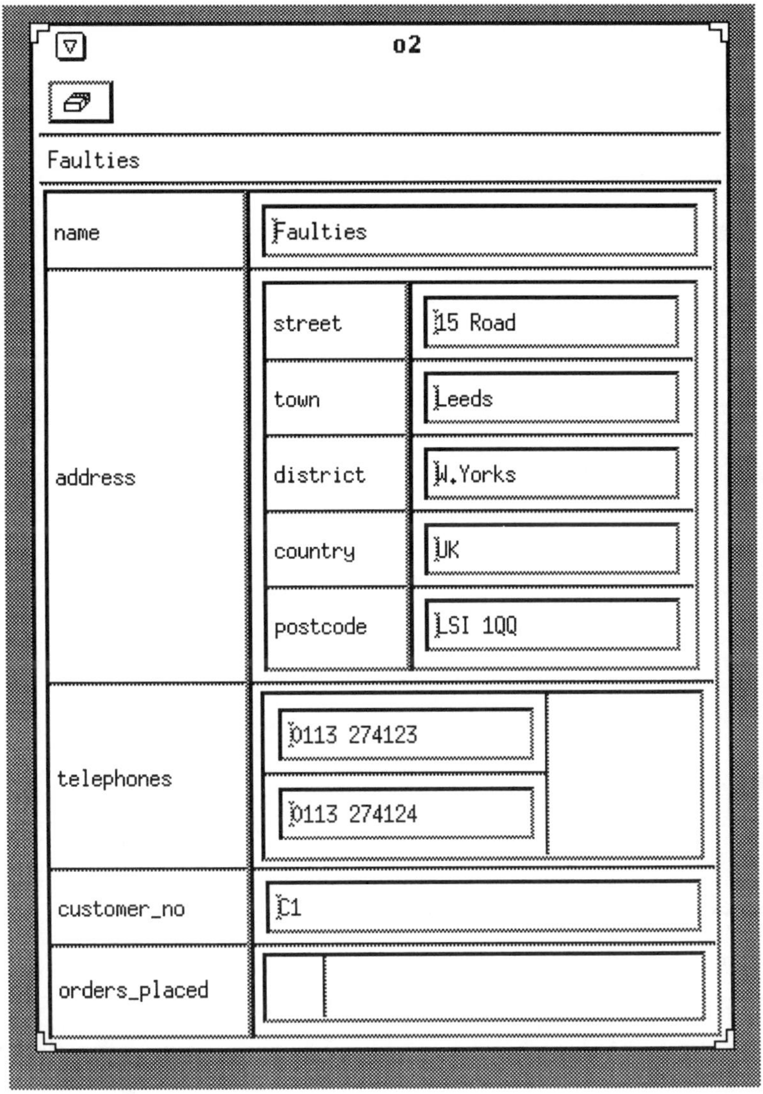

Figure 7.9 Screen showing display of Faulties Customer object

The Figure 7.14 method code creates a new object, so, of the SalesOrder class. The order_no is assigned to the input order_no parameter. The order_date, which was an object of the built-in Date class (see Figure 7.3), is created and initialised to the current date with new Date(0,0,0); placed_by, which is an attribute of class Customer (see Figure 7.3), is assigned to self. Since this is a method in the Customer class although it creates a SalesOrder object, it starts from and therefore has a reference to the Customer object that initiated the method. The placed_by attribute is therefore set to the Customer object that called the method. Other details of the SalesOrder are then entered using the standard `edit` method. The newly created SalesOrder object is then added to the salesorder extent.

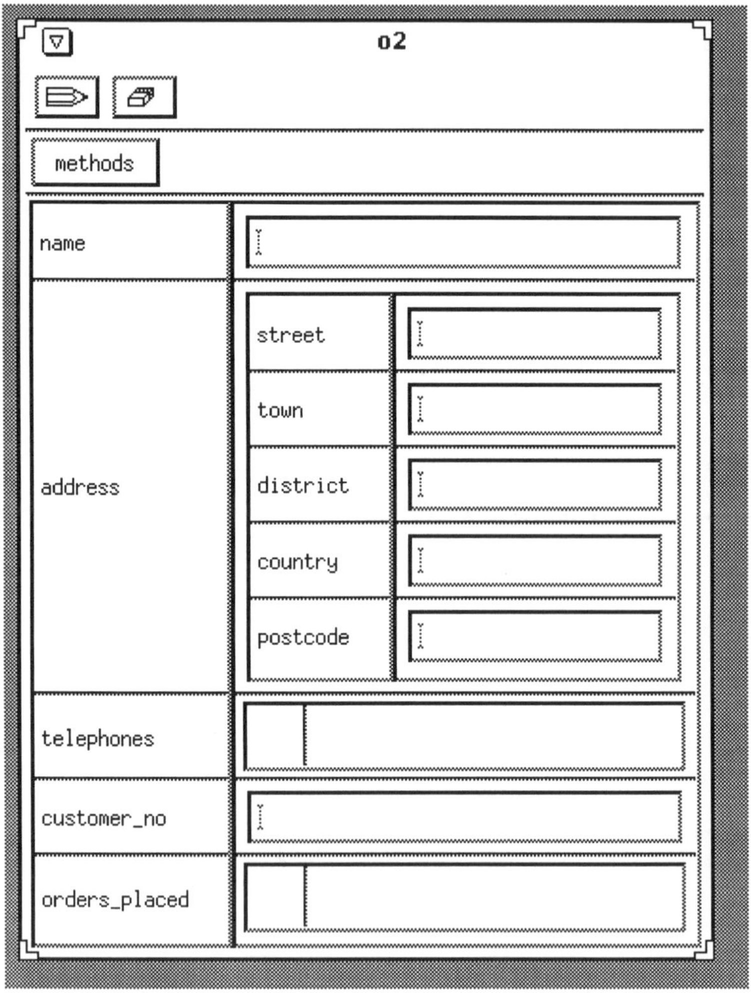

Figure 7.10 Screen showing blank form for data entry

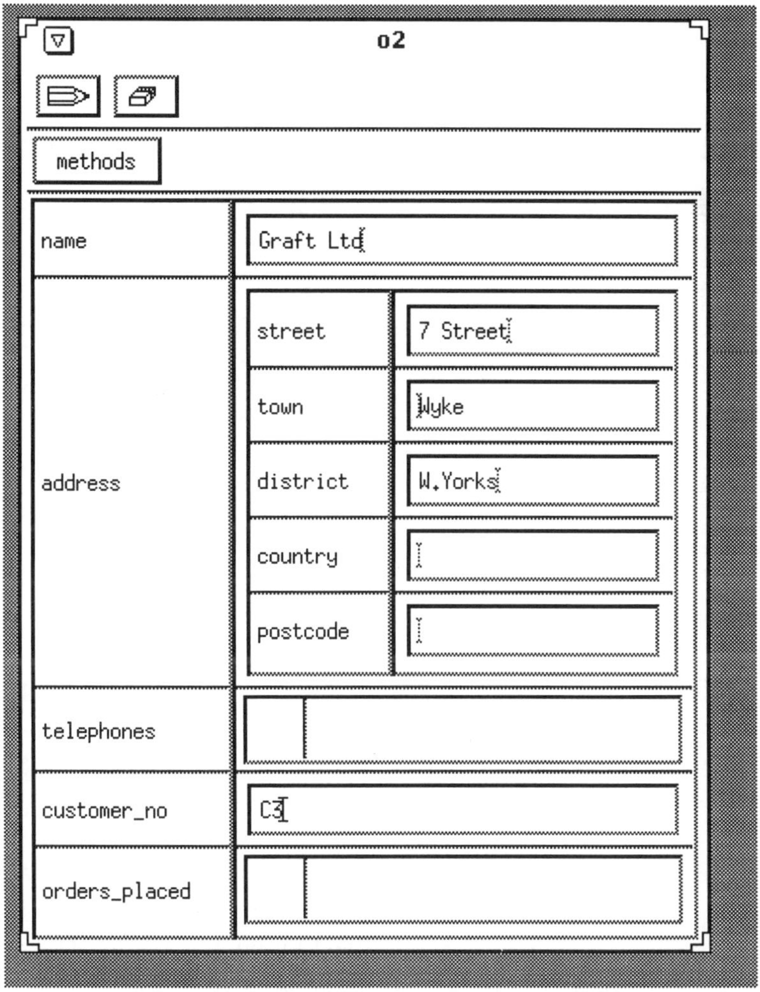

Figure 7.11 Screen showing addition of data for Graft Ltd

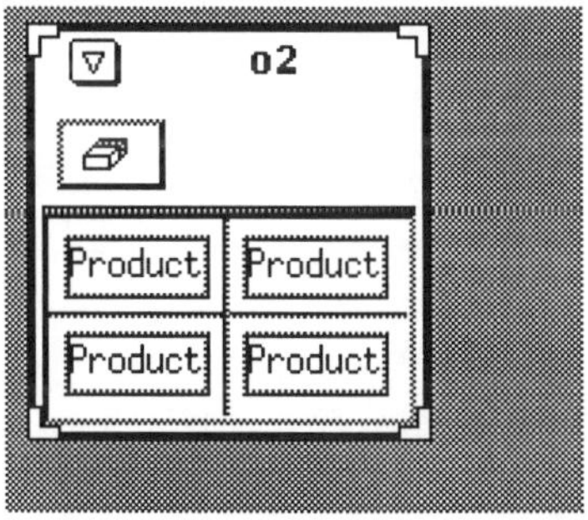

Figure 7.12 Screen shot of Products (showing default titling)

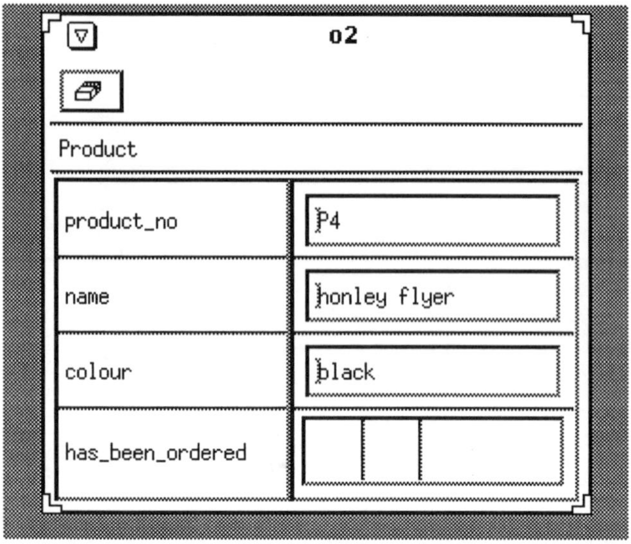

Figure 7.13 Screen shot of an individual Product, P4

Figures 7.15–7.18 show the place_order method in operation. In Figure 7.15 the screen shown is what can be seen after choosing the place_order method from the pulldown menu for Faulties. This pop-up prompts for the order_no to be created. Completing this leads to the screen shown in Figure 7.16 where the standard screen for creating a SalesOrder is on display—this corresponds to the `so->edit;` section of the method. It can be seen that the order_no is already filled in, as is the placed_by attribute. The order_date has also been filled in, but is only visible with the text "Date" because we do not have an appropriate title method in place yet. The actual content of the order_date can be seen by clicking on its display method, which will show the creation date. Figures 7.17 and 7.18 show the display when we click on order_lines and create a new OrderLine. We then have the pop-up in which to enter the order line data. Each dialog is then completed by clicking on the pencil icon to write to the database.

```
/* place_order method */
method public place_order (order_no:string):SalesOrder in class
Customer
```

```
method body place_order (order_no:string)
       :SalesOrder in class Customer
{

       o2 SalesOrder so = new SalesOrder;
       so->order_no = order_no;
       so->order_date = new Date(0,0,0);
       so->placed_by = self;
       so->edit;
       salesorders +=set(so);
       return so;
}
```

Figure 7.14 Method signature and body for place_order

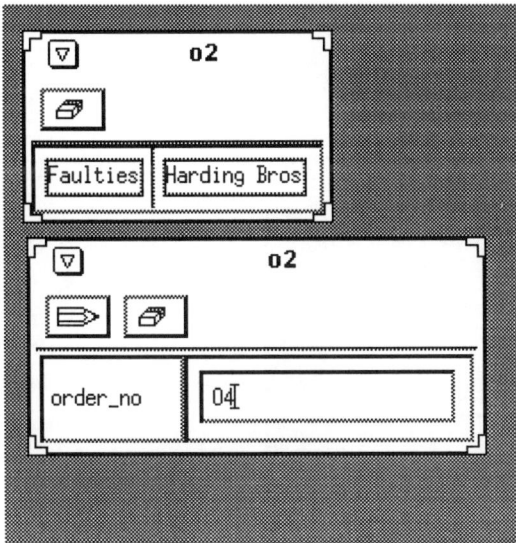

Figure 7.15 place_order method (entering order_no)

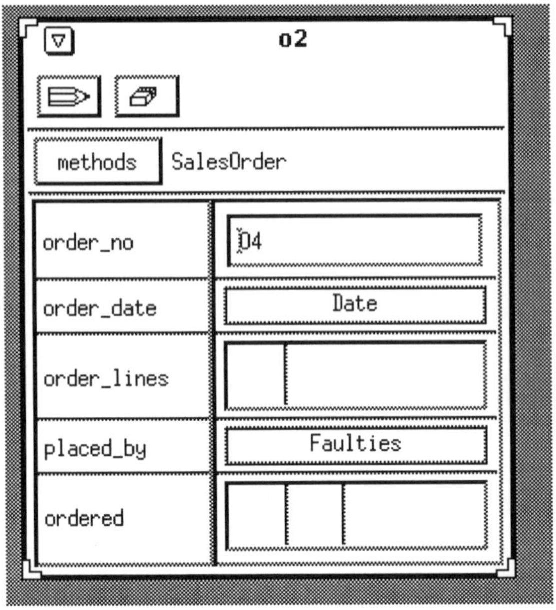

Figure 7.16 place_order method (SalesOrder edit)

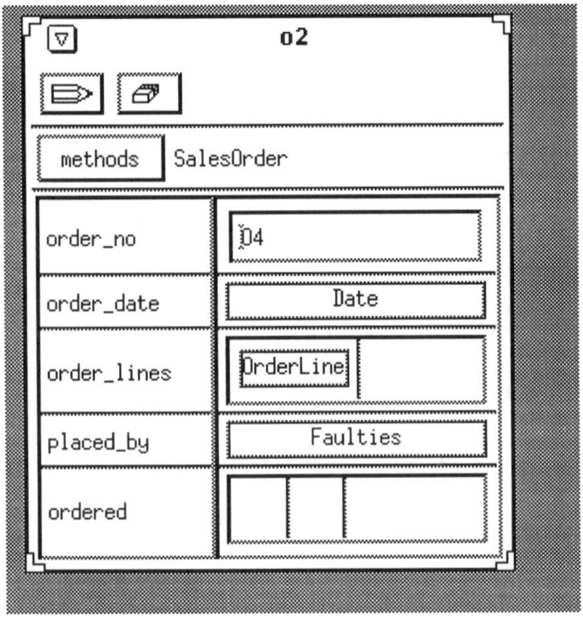

Figure 7.17  place_order method (creating an OrderLine)

Figure 7.18 place_order method (entering order line data)

## FILLING IN THE GAPS

To build a complete application a larger number of methods would have to be created to represent the activities required for the system. For instance, we would require:

- an alternative_product method for SalesOrders, to offer different products when one chosen is not available;
- a quantity on order method for Products;
- methods to improve the appearance of the application and provide validation and other checks;
- etc.

All these methods can then be built into an application on the lines of the skeleton one shown in Figure 7.19.

## GENERAL POINTS

The above application illustrates the general appearance of an actual ODBMS, and shows ways in which it supports the development of object database systems. Specifically:

```
application bruddsSOP
program
          public show_customers,
          public show_products
end;

transaction body show_customers in application bruddsSOP
{
  display(customers);
};

transaction body show_products in application bruddsSOP
{
  display(products);
};
```

Figure 7.19 bruddsSOP application

1) The system supports standard (but often complicated) requirements, e.g., concerning the displaying of objects on a screen, through class libraries. These classes represent ready-made solutions to general problems, and can be included in new systems, possibly specialised to meet the special needs of the application.

2) The environment supports incremental development. This is appropriate when a system is first created, since it enables the implementor to use a prototyping approach, but is also important throughout the life of the system, since it allows new information to be added to the object database to meet changing requirements.

3) Finally, note that the above system does not fully conform to any of the standards previously described—at the time of writing ODBMSs provide only partial implementations of the ODMG standards, which in turn are still evolving. Also, the general look and feel of an ODBMS tends to be unique to that particular system. However, the functionality and the underlying object model do correspond closely to that of the Object Data Model.

## 7.4 SUMMARY

The Object Query Language (OQL) and the Object Definition Language (ODL) must be used in conjunction with other programming languages to build object database systems. Programming languages are needed to program methods and application program computations.

**Programming language ODL/OML bindings** extend programming languages to provide object database definition and manipulation capabilities. ODMG has defined a binding for C++ called C++ ODL/OML. They have also defined bindings for Smalltalk and Java. Bindings can be tightly or loosely coupled, and their aim to create a seamless environment. The binding principles are: a single type system; retaining the characteristics of the programming language; few extensions; and free combination of database and programming language elements.

The loosest form of binding is **system interfacing** via an Application Program Interface (API), and the tightest is that of a **persistent programming language**.

The C++ ODL includes only one extension to the C++ programming language—an inverse clause to declare inverse relationships. Apart from that extension, additional built–in classes are defined for persistent objects and references to them.

C++ OML uses the additional built–in classes to create, delete, and manipulate persistent objects. In addition, OQL queries can be executed via a loose binding, using query or oql operations.

This chapter has also described how object database systems are created using the $O_2$ ODBMS. This example illustrates the way in which built–in classes and class libraries provide ready-made solutions to standard problems, and provide support for incremental development; and the current lack of standardisation of ODBMSs.

## EXERCISES:

(7.1)  ODL and OQL are not sufficient, on their own, to implement an object database system. Why is this, and what addition features are required?

(7.2)  OQL is not computationally complete. What does this mean?

(7.3)  How can OQL be used to perform object manipulations in which object states are altered?

(7.4)  An object database system can be constructed using ODL, OQL, and another programming language, such a C++. Explain the role of each of these languages within the implementation.

(7.5)   What are the three main approaches to combining object database functionality with computational facilities of programming languages ?

(7.6)   What does the term "binding" mean, within the context of computer languages?

(7.7)   One binding which enables C++ to be used to implement object database systems is called C++ ODL/OML. What do ODL and OML stand for?

(7.8)   What is the aim of providing a programming language OML/ODL binding?

(7.9)   A programming language ODL/OML binding may be tight or loose. Explain what this means, and the relative advantages.

(7.10)  List the ways in which a "seamless" programming language ODL/OML binding can be achieved.

(7.11)  Why is an extensible type system a useful feature when designing a programming language ODL/OML binding?

(7.12)  The creation of a seamless binding is difficult if there are differences between the Object Data Model and the object model of the programming language. Give examples of this problem in the C++ ODL/OML binding, and explain the compromises made.

(7.13)  Why is it useful to have bindings between object database systems and other non–object–oriented systems?

(7.14)  System interfacing is a very loose form of binding. Explain what this means.

(7.15)  Persistent programming languages are a very tight form of binding. Explain what this means.

(7.16)  Why is the Object Data Model ODL similar in syntax to C++?

(7.17)  What extensions to C++ are made for the C++ ODL/OML ?

(7.18)  The C++ ODL implements features of the structural part of the Object Data Model. Explain how each of the following are implemented:
   (i)     Object types and classes.
   (ii)    Persistent objects.
   (iii)   Mutable objects and literals.
   (iv)    Subtype/supertype relationships.
   (v)     Type extents.
   (vi)    Object keys.
   (vii)   Object names.

(viii)   Attributes.

(ix)    Relationships.

(x)     Operations.

(xi)    Collection object types.

(xii)   Structured object types.

(7.19)   Explain why the additional built–in class, d_Ref, is needed in C++ ODL/OML.

(7.20)   C++ ODL/OML includes an additional built–in class called d_Database. What is this used for?

(7.21)   In what ways can OQL queries be executed from C++ OML/ODL programs?

(7.22)   Explain the roles of the ODL preprocessor, the C++ compiler, and the linker in building an object database application.

The next sequence of exercises assume that you have O₂ or a comparable system on which to implement the Bruddersfield example in this chapter. Some exercises may require rewriting the class definitions.

(7.23)   Write a title method for the Part class that shows both the Part Number and Part Name.

(7.24)   Write a total_quantity_on_order method for the Products class.

(7.25)   Write a quantity_on_order_to method for the Products class.

(7.26)   Write an alternative product method for the Products class.

(7.27)   Write a change_quantity_ordered method for the Products class.

(7.28)   Develop part of the application to allow the interactive addition of a new product and specification of what the alternative products for it are.

(7.29)   Develop the application to ensure that an OrderLine is for an existing product and that the quantity ordered is a positive integer.

(7.30)   Modify the SalesOrder class so that the order_no is an integer and rewrite the place_order method so that it generates a new order number, one greater than any existing order number.

(7.31).   One of the advantages of using object–oriented technology is that classes can be reused. Explain how this feature is exploited in the O₂ database programming environment described in the chapter.

(7.32) Explain the ways in which prototyping is supported by the $O_2$ database programming environment described. Why is this important during the life of an object database system?

(7.33) Write a short and understandable report for the manager of a small company, explaining the benefits and problems of developing their business applications within an object database environment.

# 8

# OBJECT
# DATABASE DESIGN

This chapter discusses how object databases are designed. The area of object–oriented systems design is very large and a complete treatment would require a book on its own. The chapter therefore concentrates on the parts specific to database design. The methods described are illustrated using the Bruddersfield Bikes case study, introduced in previous chapters, and located in the broader context of object–oriented design. The chapter describes a top–down design method based upon entity analysis, and uses the Unified Modeling Language (UML) to represent the design.

Section 8.1 sets the scene by introducing object–oriented design methods, and comparing these with other database design methods. One specific method is then described in detail by working through some of the design stages for the Bruddersfield Bikes object database. The method is overviewed in Section 8.2. The individual stages are then described in greater detail. Section 8.3 discusses the first phase in which the problem area is analysed to identify candidate objects and classes. Sections 8.4 and 8.5 discuss refining objects and then revising attributes and classes. Finally, Section 8.6 gives a summary.

## 8.1 OBJECT–ORIENTED DESIGN METHODS
There are a number of different object–oriented methods for design, aimed at programming or software development in general, not specifically for databases (although this is not excluded and may be explicitly included in some cases). Important amongst them are the methods associated with Booch [Booch 94] (the Booch method), Rumbaugh [ Rumbaugh 91] (OMT), and Jacobson [Jacobson 92] (OOSE). These methods were developed independently and had different names

for similar concepts and different ways of representing comparable parts of the design process in diagrams. Starting in 1996 a process of unifying these methods is now underway to produce what was first known as the Unified Method (UM) and is now called the Unified Modeling Language (UML). It is planned that the UML will be submitted to the OMG as the basis for a standard in this area. UML does not prescribe the design process, but instead provides a diagrammatical language for representing the analysis and design of an object–oriented system.

## WHY IS UML IMPORTANT?

In the past, the object–oriented field has been plagued by terminological differences. The same, or very nearly the same, thing has been known by different names, and the same words have had different meanings in some methods. This is true of object–oriented programming languages as well as design methods—for instance, the implementation of operations on object instances are called methods and operations in different systems. (A guide to differences between object–oriented design notations can be found in the Unified Method Documentation Set [Booch 95, Notation Summary p 47].)

The confusion of terminology is a consequence of the manner in which object–oriented technology has evolved. Unlike second generation (relational) database technology, object–oriented technology does not have a single, widely accepted, underlying data model or system and language standards. The variety of conflicting terminologies therefore reflects the various routes by which the technology has emerged.

The lack of a consensus terminology for object–oriented systems can be confusing for the newcomer (or even those with plenty of experience). It also obscures the common features across different systems and makes it harder to transfer experiences. Hopefully with the emergence of the UML some of these problems will be overcome. If widely accepted as a standard, UML will provide a single terminology and diagrammatical language for expressing and communicating design ideas for object–oriented systems.

## TYPES AND CLASSES

In this chapter, and the book generally, we try to conform to the conventions of the UML, which is still under development. One important thing to note is that the UML, like many object–oriented design methods, does not make the distinction we have between types and classes. These terms are distinct in the Object Data Model:

1) **Type** refers to the interface specification for objects of a certain kind. Type therefore specifies how the external characteristics of objects of this type will appear to other objects, but says nothing about how that will be implemented. In fact a type may have many implementations, for example a Java implementation and a Smalltalk implementation. These would include sets of methods in those languages which give the object the same external appearance but via different pieces of code.

2) Types may be classes or interfaces. Instances can be defined on classes but not on interfaces.

3) **Implementation class** refers to a type and its implementation.

Object–oriented design normally refers only to classes, since the aim is a plan of how to implement a design in a real system—the term type is not often used in object–oriented design material. Generally, types and classes are regarded as synonymous e.g. [Booch 94, p 65]. Thus our discussions will be of determining the objects in a system and what classes are used to represent them.

## TWO–PHASE DATABASE DESIGN
Conventionally, database design proceeds in two stages (see Figure 8.1):

1) **Data analysis**—the purpose of this stage is to model the part of the world relevant to the database (its Universe of Discourse (UoD)) as a collection of abstractions. The result of data analysis is a **conceptual model** which represents the types of information to be represented within the database.

2) **Data design**—the purpose of this stage is to derive an implementation of the conceptual model using the data model supported by the DBMS that is to be used. The output from this phase is a logical model of the UoD that can be implemented directly by the database technology being used.

The second phase, data design, has been necessary because of the poor expressiveness of data models. Having determined the information that the designer would like to express within a database (the conceptual model), she then must express as much of this information as is possible within the limited set of abstractions supported by the DBMS. If for example, a relational DBMS is used, then the conceptual model must be transformed into a set of tables in the data design stage. The difference between what can be expressed in the logical model and what the designer wishes to express (in the conceptual model) is sometimes referred to as **the semantic gap**.

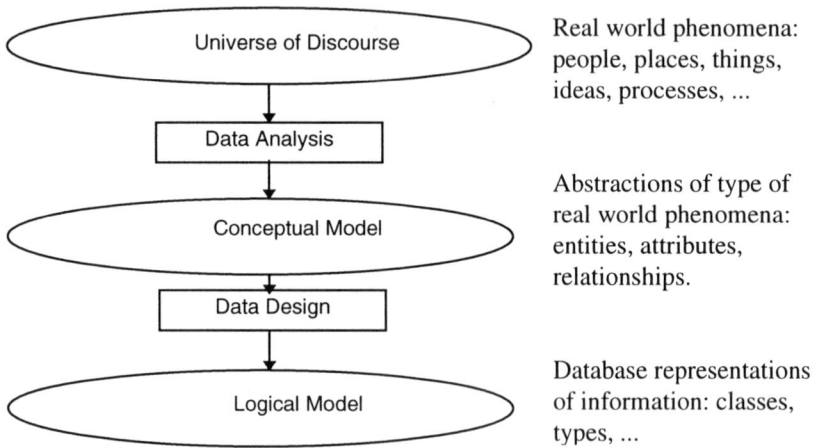

Real world phenomena:
people, places, things,
ideas, processes, ...

Abstractions of type of
real world phenomena:
entities, attributes,
relationships.

Database representations
of information: classes,
types, ...

Figure 8.1 Two–phase database design

When a relational DBMS is used, a further database design phase is **normalisation**, whereby the logical model is refined so as to remove any unnecessary duplication of data. Redundant data is undesirable partly because it may give rise to inconsistencies within the database when data is inserted, modified, or deleted (see [Eaglestone 91]). However, normalisation is necessary only to overcome problems caused by the restricted modelling capabilities of the relational data model.

The above process concerns only the logical structure of the database. **Physical database design** is a further process by which implementations of the database structures in the logical model are designed, such that the system has sufficient performance within the available hardware and software resources.

The data model used for representing the conceptual model is of a type called a **semantic data model**. Semantic data models represent the meaning of data using different abstractions for different types of real world phenomena. The most widely used has been the **entity relationship model** [Chen 76] which, as its name suggests, supports different abstractions for entities, their attributes, and relationships between them, including aggregation (i.e., where one entity is a part of another) and *is_a* relationships (i.e., where one entity is a specialisation of another).

## OBJECT DATABASE DESIGN

The Object Data Model has sufficient expressiveness to implement semantic data models directly. Specifically, the Object Data Model explicitly supports the three main types of abstractions also supported in the entity relationship model entities (as classes), relationships, and attributes. The data design stage therefore becomes redundant for object database design, since the Object Data Model can itself serve as the semantic data model for the conceptual model (see Figure 8.2).

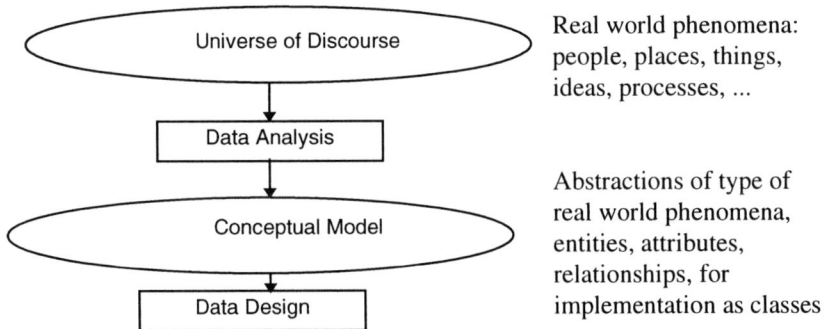

Figure 8.2 Object database design

However, there is an extra dimension in designing an object database that does not exist for previous generations of database technology. That is, the designing of object behaviour. Accordingly, many object database design methods also analyse the changes to the states of objects and the interchange of messages between objects that can occur during an object's lifetime, in order to determine appropriate object operations.

## ENTITY RELATIONSHIP ANALYSIS

Data analysis methods provide systematic processes by which conceptual models are derived. One such method, more commonly associated with relational database design, is entity–relationship analysis [Chen 76]. This is not inherently linked to relational databases and is in fact the sort of process we would wish to undertake to design an object database. From the previous chapters this sort of analysis will be familiar, since these discussed the entities that we were interested in modelling in object databases and the relationships between them.

A difference between the processes used in the design of a relational database, and those for designing an object database, is that in the latter case the conceptual model derived should be directly implementable as an object database. This is because the object model supports a richer model of the world which can represent the real world more naturally. In particular it is unnecessary to go through the design stages of normalisation that is required for a relational database design (as illustrated in the following example).

---

*EXAMPLE 8.1*

*If we identify a Sales Order as an object that we wish to represent, then we will also see that it can be for one or more items as well as having a single date and being for one customer. This suggests that the SalesOrder object will contain a list of SalesItems. This list can be implemented directly within the Object Data Model as an attribute with a structured type (see Figure 8.3 (a)).*

*The relational model does not support lists. These are repeating items that must be removed by normalisation (see Section 2.2, A brief history of data models, second generation database technology, Example 2.1). We must therefore split the representation of a Sales Order up into the parts or attributes that only occur once, such as the date and customer, and store these in one table. The repeating Sales Items must be stored in a separate table, the two tables being linked by common values (see Figure 8.3 (b)). These tables must be joined together to recreate all the information about the sales order as a single entity.*

---

The basic abstractions used in entity–relationship design are entity, attribute, and relationship. These can be defined, simply in terms of design, as:

- **entity**—a thing which we are interested in that exists independently in the real world. This thing may be a material object, a concept, an event, or process;

- **attribute**—a fact about an entity. Facts which characterise, identify, or describe an entity are its attributes;

- **relationship**—a fact about an entity which links it to another entity.

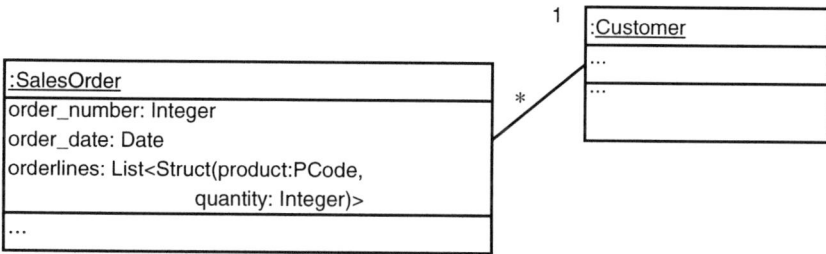

Figure 8.3 (a) The Example 8.1 SalesOrder class

SalesOrder

| Order_number | Order_date | Customer_number |
|---|---|---|
| O9 | 290896 | C1 |
| O4 | 250896 | C1 |
| O6 | 121287 | C3 |

OrderLine

| Order_number | Product_number | Quantity |
|---|---|---|
| O9 | P1 | 100 |
| O9 | P2 | 200 |
| O4 | P2 | 50 |
| ... | ... | ... |

Figure 8.3 (b) Relational database representation of SalesOrders in Example 8.1 (the underlined column names are the keys)

These definitions echo the way that these terms have been used before, in developing the Object Data Model. Objects within the Object Data

Model represent entities, and the state of those objects represents the facts about those entities; that is, their attributes and relationships.

What may be more difficult is the way knowledge of the real world is mapped to an implementation in a database system, to give an accurate and useful representation of the part of the real world that is of interest. Different designers may, in fact, come up with different but equally valid designs to model the same real world situation. This may also reflect different interests on the same situation. In general, the design is a consequence of the perspective and idiosyncrasies of the designer and the context within which the design takes place. The following example illustrates this point by showing how marriage might be treated in designing a number of different databases.

---

### EXAMPLE 8.2

1) **Marriage as an entity**—*if we were designing a database that would hold information to be used by a registry office then marriage would be an entity that we were interested in and it would have attributes such as time and date. These would be useful for timetabling. It would also have the people to be married as attributes.*

2) **Marriage as a attribute**—*the database for the payroll operations of a company would regard each person as an entity and whether they were married or not would be an attribute of the person entity. The identity of who they were married to or when the marriage took place would not be of interest here. Only their current marital status is a concern, for use in calculating tax deductions.*

3) **Marriage as a relationship**—*a tax office database would regard a person as an entity but would be interested in who they were married to, so we would have a design that showed marriage as a relationship. This might be important for ensuring, for example, that only one person out of a couple received an allowance. In this database, the date but not the time of the marriage would be of interest.*

---

## TOP DOWN AND BOTTOM UP METHODS

There are two main approaches to data analysis: **top down** and **bottom up**. Both have their advocates, and advantages and disadvantages. Neither is right or wrong, and many approaches mix these techniques.

Top down can be thought of as working from the general to the specific and bottom up from the specific to the more general.

In a bottom up analysis the designer starts with attributes and works towards aggregating them together and finding which entities they belong to.

In a top down approach the designer starts by attempting to identify the entities. This is often done by analysing a written description of the area of interest. The entities or things of interest usually occur as nouns or noun phrases in this text. In some cases it is not easy to distinguish between entities and attributes (see Example 8.2), although the independent nature of an entity should help the designer to make this distinction.

In practice design is often a more iterative or cyclic activity than a written outline suggests. What happens is that the designer makes an analysis and formally or informally tries it out with small amounts of data or typical examples to see if it works, i.e., whether it models the real world accurately.

In the following sections we will take an essentially top down approach. This seems to fit better for object–oriented design, since a central feature of an object–oriented system is the representation of entities as objects, and important features such as inheritance have a natural top down flavour. However, there is also inevitably a bottom up aspect to the design of an object–oriented system if the potential for reuse of earlier designs and code is to be exploited, as described below.

## OBJECT DATABASE DESIGN REUSE

Reuse of existing database structures is not a new feature of database design. Database systems often evolve over a long period, during which frequent changes occur to the database schema, so as to represent altered or additional information. These changes will often utilise or adapt existing structures within the database.

The subtype/supertype relationships of the Object Data Model provide particularly powerful support for reuse of parts of designs and code.

These relationships allow new classes to either specialise or generalise existing ones.

---

**EXAMPLE 8.3**

*Consider the situation where Bruddersfield Bikes diversify and introduce a new type of product (high–energy foods for cyclists, for instance). This new type of product has different characteristics to those of previous products, including special storage requirements. However, there is sufficient similarity between the new and existing products to make it beneficial to represent it as a subtype of the Product object type. In this way the existing implementations of the Product type will be reused within the new product type, since a class which implements a new subtype automatically inherits the characteristics of the supertype and reuses their implementation.*

---

There are clear benefits to be gained from reusing existing classes.

1) Design and development is reduced by reusing pre–developed classes.
2) Higher reliability can be achieved by building from tried and tested components.
3) There is closer integration of the representations of new information within the object database.
4) There is less disruption to existing programs—later binding enables programs to execute new implementation of operations, for instances of new subtypes, without the need for the program to be modified.

The potential disadvantage is that compromises may have to be made where existing classes are almost, but not quite, appropriate. If reuse of a class, through specialisation or generalisation, is attempted where there is little commonality between the entities represented, then the amount of the class that is reused will be very small. In that situation, the disadvantage of an unnatural representation of information as data will outweigh any advantage.

Exploiting the potential for reuse within an object database system increases in complexity over time, as the size of the classes libraries available for reuse increases. There has been much research, particularly in the area of software engineering (e.g., see Proceedings of the ACM–SIGSOFT Bi–annual Symposiums on Reusability (SSR)), towards exploiting the potential for reusing components of computer systems (designs, code, architectures, etc.). For instance, two areas of research have been on design methods which optimise the potential for reusing the components produced, and on tools and techniques for matching requirements with those met by existing components in order to select components that may be reused. However, effective support for component reuse in object database design remains an open problem.

The object database designer should be aware of the potential for reuse of existing classes by specialisation or generalisation of them using subtype/supertype relationships. The availability of existing classes should therefore influence the choice of classes within the design.

## 8.2 AN OVERVIEW OF AN OBJECT DATABASE DESIGN METHOD

The design method described in the following sections is a top down method, based upon entity–relationship analysis. The UML notation is used to express the design, at its various stages of development.

The design proceeds through the following stages:

1) **Identification of objects in the system**—in this phase, the UoD is analysed to identify those entities which are candidates to be represented as objects within the object database.
2) **Refining the objects**—the characteristics of the classes are determined. This stage therefore includes the following subtasks:
   - **Selection of classes to use;**
   - **Identification of relationships;**
   - **Determining the cardinality of relationships;**
   - **Classification of relationships;**
   - **Identifying attributes;**
   - **Identifying operations.**
3) **Revision of the attributes and classes**—the design is reviewed and refined.

Each of the above stages are described and illustrated in the following sections.

## 8.3 IDENTIFYING THE OBJECTS IN THE SYSTEM
### IDENTIFYING CANDIDATE OBJECTS

The first stage of this object database design method is to identify candidate objects. In subsequent stages, some of these will be selected for implementation as classes within the object database.

Note the above use of the term object rather than entity. This is to draw a distinction between the real world and the computer world. The term entity refers to a real world phenomenon with independent existence, object refers to the representation of an entity within the object database (i.e., in the computer world). In this stage we are concerned with what should be represented within the object database and ask the question, where do we find our potential objects?

Most object design methods suggest a list of the potential sources for classes and objects that include the following categories of entity that an object may represent.

- Things, or tangible things.
- People.
- Roles.
- Organizations.
- Concepts.
- Events or processes.
- Places or locations.

These are not clear-cut categories but rather the areas in which we might find entities to be represented as objects. One person's view of the world may mean that they regard places as tangible things or think that an organisation is a sufficiently tangible thing that they would put a potential class directly in that category. This does not really matter what we are looking for here are guidelines which help us find and start categorizing objects that we are interested in.

1) **Things**—these are perhaps the easiest objects to identify. By things or tangible things we mean the physical objects in our system. In the Bruddersfield example a bicycle is an obvious thing. There may be a range of how tangible such objects are. An invoice, when on paper, has an obvious physical presence but may be harder to identify when it exists only as e-mail.

2) **People**—people may be thought of directly as tangible objects but it may also be easier, and more useful in developing inheritance, to regard them as a separate category.

3) **Roles**—this means the roles that people play within the system. Although this may seem redundant since people encompasses that overall classification, it may be useful where one person plays more than one role in the system. In our Bruddersfield example some employees also play the role of customer through the direct sales scheme. Similarly some managers may also be on a board and have the role of director. Some roles may in fact not be relevant to the study in hand and others may be modelled by relationships rather than as objects in their own right. An example of this can be seen in the roles husband and wife, which may be irrelevant to a business database and modelled via a "married_to" relationship between people in other situations.

4) **Organizations**—these may be thought of as things that are not too tangible and form a useful subgroup. Although the factory buildings of a firm might seem tangible, it is not the buildings themselves that we are interested in, in terms of the interactions of our system. It may be that the organization plays a particular role e.g., that of customer or supplier. It may also be the case that an organization groups a number of people or activities together. For example, all the sales people belong to the sales department.

5) **Concepts**—this category may be useful for those things which are not tangible, i.e., do not have a physical presence. In the Bruddersfield example we might wish to model what is done with "complaints". Some concepts, such as the staff discount in the special direct sales scheme, may eventually be modelled as attributes of other objects. This may reflect the lack of an independent existence, one of our key features of an entity or object, of some things which we categorise as concepts. It is better to start by discovering their existence and later realising that they are attributes or relationships than to omit them.

6) **Events or processes**—another grouping for non-tangible things. Some of these may involve tangible objects. For example, the process of "raising an invoice" will involve a sales order and an invoice, two physical objects. A distinction might be made between an event which takes place at one time and a process which may have an extended time period. Whether this is an important distinction may

depend on what we are modelling. A football match may have a known time period but it might be appropriate to model it as an event. These are important categories of objects since they represent ways in which the data in the database may change. Some events or processes may be modelled as methods or operations of other objects, rather than objects in their own right. This distinction can usually be made by examining whether the event has an independent existence. This was one of our key criteria for determining what an object is. A football match would seem to satisfy this test. It has attributes that enable us to identify a particular game, such as location, date, and time and the teams taking part could be modelled by links to two football team objects. Alternative ways of modelling this event, such as making it an attribute of a football team, can be seen to cause problems. If it is an attribute of a football team, which one? If it is an attribute of both, the information will be unnecessarily duplicated and there might be problems of ensuring that both versions are the same. Raising an invoice, on the other hand, has no real existence apart from the invoice object. This would be better modelled as an operation that objects in the invoice class can perform.

7) **Places or locations**—place may be important if we are actually concerned with physical location, as in the ship's navigational system of Example 1.4. In a business situation it may also be important for describing where events take place and where people are situated.

Most design methods are informal in the way in which the task of identifying candidate objects is achieved, and provide only heuristics, i.e., rules of thumb, to guide the designer. A common approach is to analyse natural language descriptions of the organisation which the database is to serve and select candidate objects on the basis of grammatical clues. In general, an object is implied by a noun or noun phrase.

The descriptions of the organisation that are analysed are the output of a preliminary phase in which information about the organisation is gathered, typically, in the following ways:

1) observing the organisation working;

2) interviewing individuals concerned with the organisation and the future object database system;

3) inspecting existing procedures and documentation within the organisation;

4) surveying experts and existing solutions to the problems the object database is to address;

5) utilising other information already known by the designer/s.

Example 8.4 is a natural language description of Bruddersfield Bikes' sales order processing, which will be used as a case study in this chapter.

---

### EXAMPLE 8.4

*"Bruddersfield Bikes sells bicycles and bicycle parts. Bicycles are made up from a number of parts. Some of these parts are manufactured by Bruddersfield Bikes others are bought from suppliers. The bicycles and parts are manufactured and assembled by the factory workers. These products are sold by the salespeople to customers. There are retail and wholesale customers. The firm also operates a special scheme for direct sales to employees. Sales orders from the salespeople are passed to the office staff who create the factory schedules for manufacturing and assembling. The sales orders are also used to create the invoices which are then sent to customers."*

---

The Example 8.46 statement covers the activities of Bruddersfield Bikes that will be represented the case study object database. Note that this is a fairly general high level description, reflecting the top down approach. Even at this high level we examine some areas in detail and others only in outline. More detailed descriptions of particular areas will be analysed as the design proceeds.

Candidate objects are identified by analysing the organisation description to find all nouns or noun phrases—each noun or noun phrase may name or describe some phenomenon which we may wish to represent as an object within the object database.

---

### EXAMPLE 8.5

*The following list is of candidate objects, derived from the nouns and noun phrases found in the Example 8.4 description.*

| | |
|---|---|
| Bruddersfield Bikes | retail customers |
| bicycles | wholesale customers |
| bicycle parts | firm |
| number of parts | special scheme |
| parts | direct sales |
| suppliers | employees |
| factory workers | sales orders |
| products | office staff |
| sales people | factory schedules |
| customers | invoices |

*The above list potentially infers the set of objects to be represented.*

Care is necessary in selecting candidate objects. Specifically,

1) candidate objects should be at an appropriate level of abstraction— for example, "thing" is too general to be useful, and "Barry Eaglestone" is too specific;
2) candidate objects will usually represent general categories of entity, rather than individual ones—"person" is a better candidate than "Barry Eaglestone", who is an instance of a person.

### EXAMPLE 868

*One immediate result of the analysis in Example 8.5 is that all of the noun/noun phrases except Bruddersfield Bikes are general ones. That is, we talk about customers, not Faulties, Harding Bros. etc. This suggests that all these entities we are discussing are likely candidate classes rather than individual objects, instances of particular classes. We also already have a more general term for Bruddersfield Bikes, the firm. We will therefore drop Bruddersfield Bikes from our list of candidate classes.*

### GROUPING CANDIDATE OBJECTS

Next we attempt to group the candidates. Candidate objects which are similar in some way are grouped in order to determine a set of classes which characterise the candidates. These groupings may also suggest *is_a* and aggregation relationships between objects.

## EXAMPLE 8.7

*The candidate objects listed in Example 8.6 can be grouped into the following collections. Each collection gathers together a set of objects which represent entities which are similar in some way.*

---

**Objects to do with Bruddersfield Bikes products:**

bicycles
bicycle parts
number of parts
parts
products

---

**Objects to do with organisations:**

Bruddersfield Bikes
customers
wholesale customers
suppliers

---

**Objects to do with people:**

suppliers
customers
wholesale customers
firm
factory workers
sales people
customers
employees
office staff

---

**Objects to do with types of sale:**

special scheme
direct sales

---

**Objects to do with product production:**

factory schedules

---

**Objects to do with processing sales of products:**

sales orders
invoices

---

*Note that each of the candidate groups in this example is headed by a descriptive statement which identifies the common concept that relates objects in the group.*

---

## ANALYSIS OF CANDIDATE GROUPS

By analysing the membership of each group in greater detail, the designer can further refine the collections of candidate objects and determine possible *is_a* and aggregation relationships between them. In particular, the designer should attempt to:

1) remove or refine objects which are too general or too specific to be useful within the object database design;
2) remove redundant objects, i.e., those which represent concepts already covered by other objects;
3) identify *is_a* relationships (i.e., where an object is a specialisation of another) and aggregation relationships (i.e., where an object is a part of another) which exist between the objects;
4) refine the groups into subgroups, where appropriate.
5) identify inter–group relationships.

The result of this phase is a refined set of candidate object groups, and significant relationships, including those which will eventually form the *is_a* and aggregation hierarchies. This is represented at the end of this  ·
section as an outline class diagram. Example 8.8 provides an example of the type of analysis of a candidate object group.

---

*EXAMPLE 8.8*

*The first collection of objects in Example 8.7 can be analysed in the following way:*

1) *The objects group themselves together clearly as the objects that the firm produces, i.e., bicycles and bicycle parts.*
2) *The candidates, number of parts and parts are respectively redundant and too general.*
3) *There is a strong suggestion of an inheritance hierarchy since we have the general term products, covering the things Bruddersfield Bikes sells, bicycles and bicycle parts. A bicycle is a product and a bicycle part is a product.*

---

The analysis of candidate groups is complicated by the existence of many alternative and often complementary analyses for the objects, from different perspectives and within different contexts. The result may well be a set of alternative classifications and relationships. These provide different options for the designer.

For example, the analysis in Example 8.8 emphasises the selling/product side of the description. The objects to do with products also occur in the production/manufacturing side of the description and it is known that a bicycle is made of bicycle parts. This suggests another role for bicycle parts. The designer might consider that a bicycle part is an attribute of a bicycle. A bicycle has a colour, a model number, a model name, a saddle, a frame, etc. Initially this might suggest each of these are attributes of a bicycle class. However, if we return to our earlier definitions of entities, attributes and relationships it can be seen that one feature of an entity is its independent existence. This will lead the designer to classify colour, model number, and model name as attributes since they have no independent existence apart from the bicycle. Saddle and frame, on the other hand, do have independent existence and so the designer will want to model their relationship to the bicycle. This can be done by designing the bicycle class to include a list of parts that make up the bicycle which will be linked to bicycle parts.

The second set of candidates are grouped together as organisations that Bruddersfield Bikes deals with (as well as itself, the firm). This falls into two parts, suppliers and customers, with customers having a specialised form in wholesale customers.

Before continuing with this analysis we should also look at the third set, grouped together as types of people. Customers also occurs in this group. This group again falls into two parts, employees and customers, with a specialisation of employees into an inheritance hierarchy as factory workers, sales people, and office staff. Further detailed analysis would be needed to see if these should be three separate subclasses of employee at the same level or if they should be structured as factory workers and office staff at one level and sales people as a subclass of office staff.

How then should the designer deal with customers which occurs in the groups of organisations and people? When we look again at the problem description it can be seen that customers, whether wholesale or retail, place orders, which is a fundamental activity in the description. This suggests that categorisations are needed other than the ones first determined by gathering the candidates into groups, e.g., products, organisations, people. The designer can then develop a system that has a customer class which will have attributes, such as account number and credit limit, and relationships to express the links to its sales orders.

The above analysis has identified the need for classes for products, organisations, people, and customers. These may be virtual classes (i.e., classes with no instances), like the abstract types discussed in the Object Data Model. These classes will have attributes such as: family name, given name for people; name, address for organisation. Actual classes such as employee will inherit the general attributes from the superclass such as family name and given name and also have the attributes such as National Insurance Number that are specific to that class and its subclasses. This will allow the designer to successfully model the situation above where two different types of object are also customers. This can be done through multiple inheritance. A wholesale customer class will inherit its organization attributes and relationships from the organization class and its customer features from the customer class. Similarly a retail customer will get their personal details via inheritance from the people class and their customer details such as account number from the customer class. This also allows the creation of a specialised supplier subclass of organisation that can have supplier specific attributes without this class having to have any customer features that do not belong in it.

The next group of candidates was special scheme and direct sale. Looking at this reveals a further category of customers, those who are also employees. The structure outlined above will allow this to be modelled by creating a subclass of employee which also inherits the attributes of customer.

The final candidates were factory schedules and sales orders and invoices. These could be consider as two separate groups or one. Factory schedules might be interpreted as a process, a different sort of object from the others we have been examining, which all have a physical form. In this interpretation the designer might have a separate part of the database modelling factory automation. A simpler interpretation might be simply concerned with producing a printed work schedule, in which case factory schedule, sales order,s and invoice might all be subclasses of a document class. We will return to this example to look at the attributes and relationships between the objects in more detail. But it can be seen that there are a number of links to be modelled such as the fact that an invoice is for products to be supplied to a customer who placed a sales order with a salesperson.

We have already shown, in the way the representation of customers has been developed, that the design process is not straightforward but rather an iterative or cyclic process. Further detailed information about the real world may also lead to the re-evaluation of the design.

---

### EXAMPLE 8.91

*If the text in Example 846 had a sentence, "Invoices for big customers like Faulties get their bulk discounts calculated", this would have revealed a more complex situation.*

1) *The above refinement introduces another noun phrase, "big customers", which suggests another class, "big_customers", inheriting most of its attributes from the "customer" hierarchy. In this case "Faulties" would clearly be a single object, an instance of this "big_customers" class.*
2) *The other new noun phrase appearing here is "bulk discounts". From the context we should recognise that bulk discounts do not have any independent existence but are something that a certain type of customer gets, so will be an attribute of the big_customer class.*

*There is an alternative analysis that we could undertake when we add "Invoices for big customers like Faulties get their bulk discounts calculated".*

3) *Rather than creating a new class, "big_customers," with an extra attribute, "bulk_discount", it might suggest that all customers, or all wholesale customers need to have some sort of size attribute. This might be an allocated code or based on turnover, and from this a method could calculate what discount should be applied.*

---

Neither of the scenarios in Example 8.9 is right or wrong. What the alternatives show is that different designs are possible and that the design process itself may highlight the need to get more information on users' requirements.

The output from this stage of the design process is an outline class diagram in which are depicted the selected objects (as boxes) and important relationships between them (arrows indicate *is_a* relationships, other types of relationships are represented by lines). Figure 8.4 gives one such diagram derived from the above analysis of the Bruddersfield Bikes system. Note that this diagram is a sketch of the ideas discussed above, and represents only one of the alternative analyses.

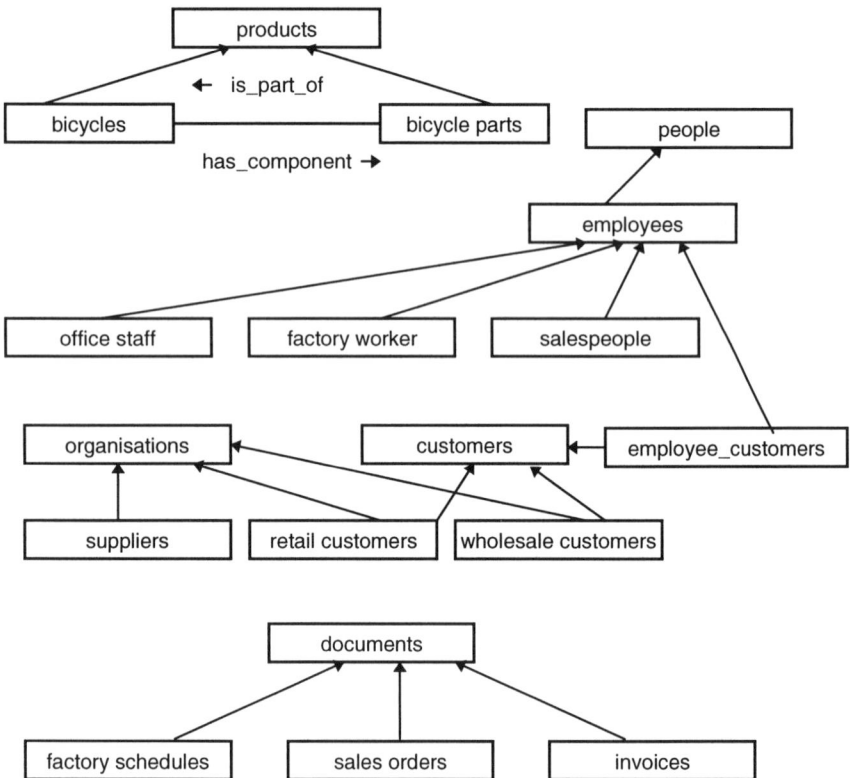

Figure 8.4 An outline class diagram produced by the first stage of the object database design

## 8.4 REFINING THE OBJECTS

The aim of this second stage in the design of an object database is to select the classes which will be implemented and determine their characteristics, i.e., attributes, relationships and operations.

### SELECTION OF CLASSES

One issue that the designer must tackle is how to move from the initial set of candidate classes (defined in stage one) to the ones that will finally be used. There cannot be a fixed set of rules for this sort of operation at best we can have guidelines. This section presents guidelines to assist the designer. Specifically, they address the issues of: which classes to omit; effective use of inheritance hierarchies; appropriate levels of abstraction; and the identification of abstract, as well as tangible, objects.

### *WHICH CLASSES TO OMIT?*

There are a number of categories of classes that should be eliminated from the list of candidate (derived in the first design stage). These are the classes that are

- **redundant;**
- **irrelevant;**
- **too vague.**

A **redundant class** denotes a concept that is already denoted by some other class. In such cases one or another of the synonyms is removed. It is usually preferable to retain the most specific of the class names.

---

### *EXAMPLE 8.10*

*In the Bruddersfield example it is not necessary to keep both "parts" and "bicycle parts" as classes, since they refer to the same thing. This is an example of a redundant class. Of the two terms, parts is the least specific, and so we name the class bicycle parts.*

---

In some cases the designer might need to go into greater detail to determine the status of an apparently redundant class. For instance, in Example 8.10, further research may be necessary to find out if there are part objects that are of interest but which are not bicycle parts.

An **irrelevant term** is one that does not represent useful information, from the perspective of the object database system.

---

### EXAMPLE 8.11
*"Number of parts" was irrelevant to the analysis of different classes of object, since it does not represent a new sort of object, although this term may be relevant later when we look at relationships.*

---

A term is too **vague** if the concept that it denotes is too general to be useful within the database.

---

### EXAMPLE 8.12
*The Bruddersfield example (Example 8.4) did not have a term that was too vague. However, if the description had been posed more in terms of a system requirement it might have contained a sentence such as "The user then inputs the sales order details into the system". Here the term "user" is too vague. Clarification is needed if the input is actually done by sales people or office staff. Also the term "system" is too vague.*

---

### EFFECTIVE USE OF INHERITANCE HIERARCHIES
**Inheritance** is often described as an *is_a* relationship. This term can be used to test which classes specialise others and should therefore be subclasses in an inheritance hierarchy (to implement subtype/supertype relationships). That is, to test if some class X is a subclass of Y, we pose the question, does the statement "X is a Y" make sense?

---

### EXAMPLE 8.13
*In the Bruddersfield cases study, above, some specialisations are clear. For instance, a wholesale customer is_a customer and should therefore be implemented as a subclass of the customer class.*

---

Many is_a relationships may not be as obvious as in Example 8.11. Some hierarchies will not become clear until the attributes of objects are analysed.

An *is_a* relationship between two classes, X and Y, is likely if the classes have many attributes in common. Further, if the characteristics of X are a subset of those of Y, then it is likely that Y *is_a* X.

---

## EXAMPLE 8.14

*In the Bruddersfield Bikes case study design we identified that:*

- *supplier is_a organisation;*
- *wholesale customer is_a organisation.*

*These relationships may have been initially omitted if the designer had focused her attention on what was different about suppliers and wholesale customers, rather than what they had in common. The is_a relationship would then have emerged only later in the design process, when the attributes for suppliers and customers were assembled, and it was realised that the two classes had a large number of attributes in common, e.g. company name, company address, phone number(s), bank details, ... The above is_a relationship is implied because both suppliers and wholesale customers have attributes of organisation, in addition to their own special attributes.*

---

## ARE THE CLASSES AT THE RIGHT LEVEL OF ABSTRACTION?

Abstraction is the representation of something, by focusing only on that which is important and ignoring irrelevant detail. Another issue, particularly related to inheritance, is getting the right **level of abstraction**. Designers are concerned with defining classes so that the level of detail they contain suits the problem they are trying to tackle.

---

## EXAMPLE 8.15

*It is not sensible (or necessary) in the Bruddersfield situation to produce classes above people, such as animal which people is then a subclass of. The animal class is at too high a level of abstraction. A zoological database, on the other hand might have a complex hierarchy of animals, mammals, human beings, etc.*

---

It should be clear when a class is unnecessary because it is at too high a level of abstraction, since the designer should find that they do not have new attributes, relevant to their problem area, to add at each new subclass.

Classes which are at too low (or specific) a level of abstraction are also undesirable. Such classes will result in too many subclasses.

---

### EXAMPLE 8.16

*It might be appropriate to have classes for "home_customers" and "overseas_customers", since these possibly represent groups of entities with significantly different characteristics. However, it does not make sense to have classes for "customers_in_Leeds" and "customers_in_Manchester", etc. since the only difference between these is the value of the address attribute.*

---

There are a number of factors that help in determining if a class is at too high or too low a level of abstraction.

1) **Are the extents under populated?** If the designer ends up with a large number of classes, many of which have only one or two instances, this is a sign that the designer may have overspecialised, i.e., the level of abstraction is too low for many of the classes.

2) **Are subclasses and superclasses different?** A way to test whether it is sensible to create subclasses is to consider whether there are really different attributes for each subclass or simply the same attributes but with different values.

3) **Are there superclasses without instances?** A long sequence of virtual classes before we reach any classes with instances should act as a warning sign that the level of abstraction is too high for many of the virtual classes.

4) **Does the addition of a subclass improve the object database querying capabilities?** This test should indicate whether it is beneficial, for example, to split customers into home and overseas customer classes, by asking "Is there different information that we hold for these two sorts of customer?". It may be that we do not need to make the distinction at all, or that an attribute indicating location is sufficient.

---

### EXAMPLE 8.17

*A further example of the problems of getting inheritance and higher level classes correct, can be seen by examining the ship's navigational system of Example 1.4. For this, we could have designed a system with the following classes:*

*1) A ship class represents other ships with a number of attributes, including some XY coordinate to represent the ship's current position. This would be a way of representing the fact that a ship has a position.*

2)  *Other static objects in the water, from oil rigs to navigational buoys, might be represented by a different class with another set of attributes including a location.*

3)  *A third class might represent geographical features such as the coastline and sandbanks again a location might be amongst the attributes, reflecting the fact that a sandbank has a location.*

*In this case the use of is_a to help us with creating an inheritance hierarchy is not so simple as the case of Bruddersfield Bikes where a retail customer is_a customer and a wholesale customer is_a customer. Here we cannot say a ship is_a location or a buoy is a location. The natural formulation appears to be that a buoy has a location and a ship has a location. Howeve,r an important question we might like our database to answer is "Is there anything at location XY?". Can we do this easily with the current structure? The answer would seem to be that we cannot, since we need to run this query over all the classes which might contain an object at XY and it is not clear how we know what **all** the classes are.*

*An alternative way of modelling this would be to recognise the importance of location as a high level construction or attribute that a number of different sorts of object might have. We could therefore start with a virtual class "object with a location" which all the classes mentioned above would inherit from, since a ship is_a object with a location, a buoy is_a object with a location, a sandbank is_a object with a location. It is not likely that this is the formulation a designer would come up with at a first attempt and it demonstrates the importance of an approach that allows for refinement.*

---

## ABSTRACT OBJECTS ARE IMPORTANT, BUT HARDER TO IDENTIFY

Another problem can be that tangible objects may seem more "real" and be easier to identify as objects than concepts.

---

### EXAMPLE 8.18

*For a library database, the book is a very tangible object. It is easy to identify a particular book e.g., Macbeth by Shakespeare. What may be harder to identify is that there is an underlying concept, the work, which represents Macbeth in a more general sense than the particular edition that we can see on the shelf.*

---

The value of representing abstract, as well as tangible, objects can be seen if we consider how an Example 8.18 system can answer the question

"Do we have Macbeth by Shakespeare?". If the system is designed with the book as a top level class, it is then necessary to search all this class for instances with the author Shakespeare and title Macbeth. On the other hand, if there is a higher level object, the work, the work class can be queried to produce not just a list of books with author "Shakespeare" and the title "Macbeth", but also videotapes, laserdiscs, sound recordings etc. that are versions of the work "Macbeth" and also books such as "Collected Works" that do not have the author/title combination we first searched for but contain the *work* within them. Such a design also makes it easier to model concepts such as translations which have a relationship to the concept of the work and not to a particular book.

## IDENTIFYING RELATIONSHIPS

Up to now, we have concentrated on entities and the objects which represent them within the system, although we have considered their attributes in the processes of determining features such as which classes are specialisations of others.

The next design task is to determine the relationships which can exist between the objects. In the same way that there are some general sources for objects, it is useful to have some guidelines for identifying relationships. Analysing the verbs that describe what the objects do is a starting point. There are a few common verbs, or verb phrases, that can be good indicators of relationships between objects, and of potential attributes.

1)  **is_a**—one phrase that has been used before is *is_a*, which we used with in identifying objects since this relationship is **specialisation** which we model with inheritance. For example, an employee *is_a* person. This may also be more explicit if we know that "a mountain bike *is_a* type of bike with special tyres for off–road use... ".

2)  **aggregation**—another important general category of relationship is that of aggregation. This is where one object is composed of a number of other objects. This may be described with phrases like *is made up, is a part of, is composed of* etc. In the Bruddersfield example a bike is made up of a frame, two wheels, a saddle etc. from the point of view of the composite object or a wheel is part of a bike, from the point of view of the component. In some cases this will be a

relationship between different classes and sometimes a relationship between members of the same class.

3) **has**—another important verb is has. In many cases this will indicate attributes of an object, e.g. an employee has a national insurance number, has a date of birth. Sometimes has may indicate a relationship, e.g., we could say an employee has a department. We would model this as a link from the employee class to the department class rather than as a simple attribute of employee. It should be possible to distinguish between these situations because the independent existence of departments, and hence their status as objects rather than attributes, should have been found through analysing the nouns in our problem description.

Some relationships may already have been identified as entities in their own right. An example of this is marriage as discussed above. So it is a good idea to compare the verbs in the problem statement with objects in the less tangible classifications for objects such as roles, concepts, and events.

The UML includes special representations for *is_a* relationships (an arrow) and aggregation (a diamond) (see Figure 8.5).

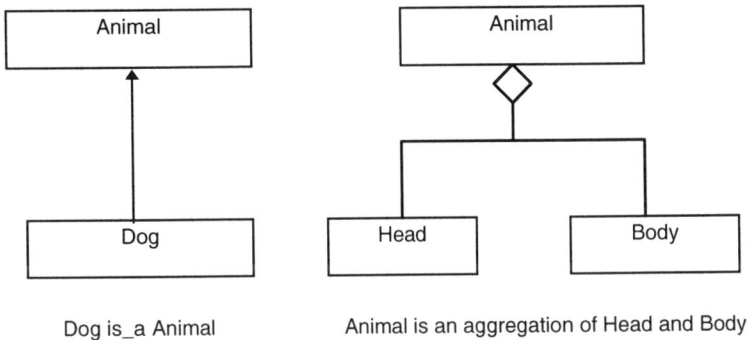

Dog is_a Animal          Animal is an aggregation of Head and Body

Figure 8.5 Representation of is_a and aggregation relationships

---

*EXAMPLE 8.19*

*A textual analysis, this time concentrating on the verbs and verb phrases, of the description of Bruddersfield's activities in Example 8.6 gives us the following*

*list. Note that some of the nouns are included to clarify the meaning of some of the verbs:*

| Candidate relationships between objects: |
|---|
| sells |
| are made up |
| bought |
| manufactured |
| assembled |
| sold |
| operates (special scheme) |
| passed (orders) |
| create (schedules) |
| create (invoices) |
| sent (invoices) |

Verbs can be analysed to see if they indicate links, or relationships between the classes of objects, as illustrated below for the Bruddersfield Bikes case study, using the list in Example 8.19.

**"sells " and " sold "**—The first verb "sells" represents the relationship between Bruddersfield Bikes and bicycles and bicycle parts. However, having removed the Bruddersfield Bikes class and reclassified bicycles and bicycle parts, the sells relationship no longer seems directly applicable. This does not mean that this is not the source of any relationship. Further down the list we have "sold" , in the past tense but describing the same activity. In this occurrence we can see that the "selling" activity does represent a relationship between objects that we have in the system. The relationship that products "are sold to" customers (see Figure 8.6).

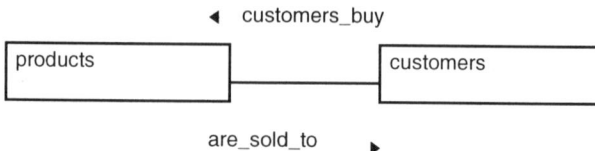

Figure 8.6

This relationship could have been described in its inverse form "customers 'buy' products". In this case we have therefore established a link and it also seems likely that this relationship will be of interest in both directions. This will enable our database to answer both "What products do we sell to Harding Bros.?" and "Who buys the Honley Flyer?".

"**bought**"—the verb "bought" also appears in our list, in what we can now see is a different context to buying/selling to customers. Parts were bought from suppliers. We therefore need a different relationship from products to suppliers covering the buying and selling of goods coming into the company (see Figure 8.7). This may also suggest that we need to look carefully at how we model all the physical objects that the company sells. Are there distinct features to items that come into the firm, "raw materials", that separate them from those that leave, "products"? Are there items that are bought in which are also sold on to customers?

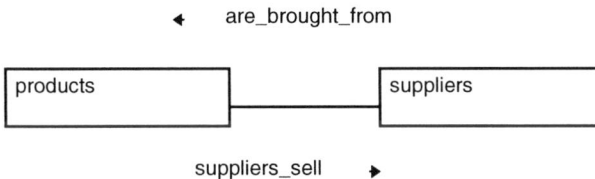

are_brought_from

| products | | suppliers |
|---|---|---|

suppliers_sell

Figure 8.7

"**are made up**"—the next item on the list is "are made up". This is a version of the aggregation relationship which is found in many situations where one object "*is part of*" another object. This is also referred to as the **bill of materials** or **parts explosion** problem and can present difficulties in some database systems. (This is because it is rare for a DBMS to support the LEAST_FIXED_POINT operator of the object algebra, which is needed to directly solve this problem.)

The situation here is that there is a relationship, not from one class to another, but from one class to itself (see Figure 8.8). The product bicycle is made up of a frame product, two wheel products, etc. Or to put it another way, a frame *is part of* a bicycle, etc. This relationship may occur repeatedly, e.g., those products that are part of a bicycle are themselves made up of other products. This relationship is represented by a structure where an object of the product class has a link to its components, which are also members of the product class.

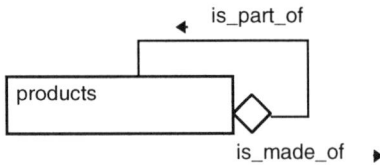

Figure 8.8

**"manufactured" and " assembled"**—the next verbs are " manufactured" and "assembled". These can be treated together since they occur in the same sentence. Both of these verbs cover the processes of converting the firm's raw material into products and who undertakes these processes, "the factory workers". The Example 8.4 description provides only a very brief outline of what may well be complex relationships between parts, products and workers. We have already seen that there are "selling" relationships between parts and products, and that some other aspects of these relationships are covered by the "are made up" relationship above. The extra factor that is introduced here is the agent, "the factory worker", who performs the process. This suggests a relationship between this subclass of employee and the parts and products they work with. This can be separated into two relationships. The factory worker *uses* a number of parts to *assemble* a product. If the designer decides that both the parts and finished products are the same type of object (in the same class) then there will be two separate relationships between the product and factory worker classes (see Figure 8.9).

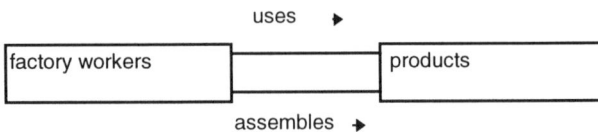

Figure 8.9

**"operates"**— The next verb in the list is "operates", which refers to the special scheme for purchases offered to employees. Analysis of the nouns led to the recognition of a special subclass of customers who were also employees. What we have here is the specialised form of the *sells* relationship between a customer and a product (see Figure 8.6) as it applies to employees rather than a new and different relationship. So although no new relationship has been discovered, it can be seen that specialised forms of operations relating to buying and selling will be needed for the employee-customer class.

"**passed**"— "passed" describes the movement of orders from sales people to office staff. This covers the actual movement of paper in a non-automated system. It can be assumed that this does not have a counterpart in an automated system and that the documents are available to the staff who need them. This does, however, highlight the ownership of, or responsibility for, the orders. If we want to record what orders have been taken by sales people, it will be necessary to create a link from each order to the salesperson who took it (see Figure 8.10). This sort of link can then be used to calculate commission, etc.

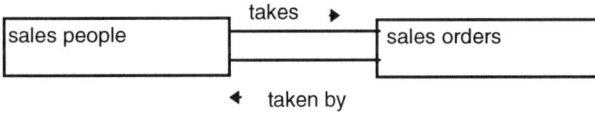

Figure 8.10

Whether a comparable link between office staff and the orders they process is needed or useful may take more detailed analysis. It may be that no link is required and that any member of the office staff can process any order. An alternative may be that office staff process the orders from particular customers, and hence there will be a relationship between them and hence an indirect connection can be established via the customer to link an order with a office worker.

"**create (schedule)** "—the creation of schedules is the next possible source of relationships. The printing out of a schedule may not seem to imply any relationships between objects. However, a more detailed analysis may suggest otherwise. The schedule creation may prove to be a part of processing an order, in which case it may involve checking the stock of parts that are needed to fulfil that order and allocating some of the stock to that order, or automatically raising an order if stocks are insufficient or fall below a certain level. Then there will then be a number of relationships between orders and parts that must be modelled.

"**create (invoices)** " **and** "**send (invoice)** "—The final verb phrases in the list were "create invoices" and "send invoices". These do not represent new relationships between invoices and any other object in the system.

We have already covered the relationships between invoices, parts, products, and customers. These are operations, or methods, that are applied to objects in the invoice class.

## DETERMINING THE NUMBERS INVOLVED IN RELATIONSHIPS

Having identified relationships between classes, the designer must then determine the characteristics of each relationship. This involves analysing the relationship cardinalities, i.e., the numbers and types of objects that may participate in occurrences of each relationship.

The cardinality of a relationship is determined by analysing the relationship paths in both directions, i.e., the relationship and also the inverse of the relationship. If a class X is related to Y, the designer must ask how many instances of Y can be related to a single instance of X via this relationship, and conversely, how many Xs can be related to a Y via the inverse relationship. The cardinality of a relationship also suggests the type of structure that will best represent the relationship, as illustrated in the next example.

---

### EXAMPLE 8.20

*Consider the factory worker assembling products (see Figure 8.9).*

1) *If we assume that, on the production line, workers take a number of parts and put them together into one type of product (each worker is responsible for just one type of bicycle) then there is a **one–to–many** relationship between the worker and the parts and a **one–to–one** relationship between the worker and the bicycle. Instances of the assembly relationship must therefore link one object of the factory worker class to one object of the bicycle product class, and instances of the inverse relationship must link one object of the product class to a collection of factory worker objects.*

2) *If each worker can assemble a number of different bicycles and each bicycle can be assembled by many workers, then the relationship between the workers and bicycles is **many–to–many**. In this case, instances of the assembly relationship and inverse relationship must respectively link a factory worker object to a collection of product objects, and a product object to a collection of factory worker objects.*

---

In some cases we may be able to specify the numbers involved in relationships in more detail this information may then be built into the system in the form of constraints. For example, a *dept_members* relationship may involve from **zero** to many employees, to allow for the situation when a new department is set up and not yet staffed. A relationship between a football match and teams will be constrained to associate exactly two teams with the match.

The cardinality of a relationship is denoted in a class diagram by annotating the ends of the lines that represent relationship. Numbers give counts of the number of participants in the relationship (an asterisk indicates many). Examples are given in Figure 8.11.

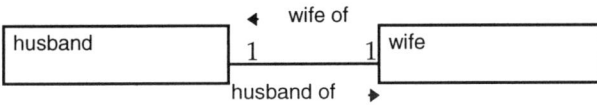

A one–to–one relationship between husband and wife

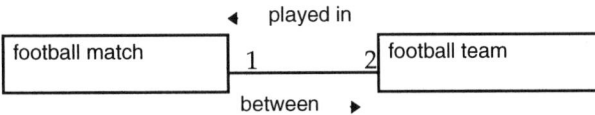

A one–to–two relationship between match and competing teams

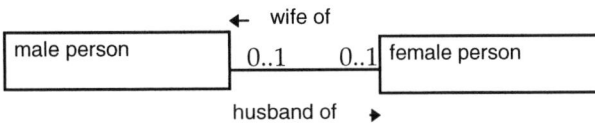

A zero or one–to–zero or one  marriage relationship between people

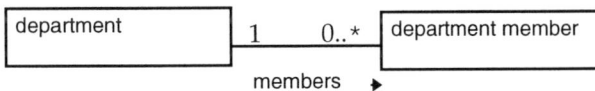

A one–to–zero or many relationship between departments and their members

Figure 8.11 Representation of cardinality of relationships

## IDENTIFYING ATTRIBUTES

The attributes of a class are all the facts or things that are known about an object that are not represented by relationships to other objects. Identification of attributes may require more detailed descriptions of individual object types.

In general, attributes will be the things that are totally dependent on the object, e.g., a date of birth is meaningless if we remove the person it does not have a useful existence on its own. On the other hand, if we remove a part supplied by Bloggs from the database because we use a different part instead, we do not want to lose the information about Bloggs who still supply other parts. Hence information about Bloggs will be in the form of a relationship from the part to a supplier rather than a simple attribute of the part.

---

*EXAMPLE 8.21*

*If the designer is considering attributes of a particular type of product, bicycle tyres, a more detailed description may be as follows:*

*"A bicycle tyre is made of rubber. It can come in a number of colours, widths, and diameters, and has different tread patterns. Tyres are supplied by one of three manufacturers and can be used on a number of different bikes."*

*Analysis of the above text suggests the following possible attributes:*

| Bicycle tyre attributes: |
|---|
| material |
| colour |
| width |
| diameter |
| tread |
| manufacturer |
| bike |

---

The candidate attributes in Example 8.21 can be analysed in the following way.

"**material**"—material is a possible attribute generated by generalising "made of rubber". If in fact tyres are made of a variety of materials, or grades of rubber, then it may be worth having a material attribute which will let us record facts about the material of a particular type of tyre. If, on the other hand, all tyres are of a standard type of rubber or any variations in material are not of interest, then we would not bother with a material attribute.

**"width"**, **"diameter"**, **"tread"** and **"colour"**—these are all physical features of a tyre that we will need to know. In practice further information is needed to decide if these are kept as separate attributes. If we have a tyre known as the "T1" we may then use T1s in a variety of diameters etc. in different bikes, in which case separate attributes for diameters etc. are needed. If, on the other hand, tyres are known by a scheme, on the lines of "T1/22/2", the diameter and width of 22 and 2 may be known from the tyre's name and therefore need not be stored separately. A similar situation could arise with colour and tread. However, if these features are encoded in a name, e.g., "T1/22/2/R/O" where R = Red and O = Off Road, then we would need a separate way of storing the information that mapped colour and tread codes to real colours and tread descriptions. The same might be true if the colour and tread were stored as separate attributes in coded form. In either case an operation to check the validity of a colour against a list of permissible colours would be needed to ensure database integrity.

**"manufacturer"** and **"bike"**—the other possible attributes are "manufacturer" and "bike". Clearly we want to store facts about who makes a particular tyre and which bikes the tyre is used in. Since we have already identified manufacturers and bikes as other objects that we are interested in, these are represented as classes in their own right in the database and hence these facts are represented by relationships between the tyre object and the bike and manufacturer object. From the point of view of the tyre manufacturers however, bikes would probably not be a class within their object database. The tyre company's database could have a bike attribute for objects in the tyre class which would be a list of the bikes (made by other firms) that they knew their tyres were supplied for.

Attributes are represented together with their names and any default values, within a class diagram in lists in the second part of a class box, e.g.,

```
┌─────────────────────────────────┐
│ Btype products                  │
├─────────────────────────────────┤
│ colour: string = "black"        │
│ width: long                     │
│ diameter: long                  │
│ trea : long                     │
├─────────────────────────────────┤
│ ...                             │
└─────────────────────────────────┘
```

Figure 8.12 Representation of attributes

## OPERATIONS

Operations on objects serve two purposes within an object database. They can be used to represent derived attributes, i.e., values computed from an object's state, rather than stored as part of the state. They can also represent the behaviour of the entity represented by an object, i.e., the behavioural semantics.

### OPERATIONS AS DERIVED ATTRIBUTES

There are some facts about the entities represented by objects that we may calculate rather than store as attributes. These will be represented as operations, or methods, on objects in a class. A classic example of this is a person's age. Instead of storing their age as a number, age will be calculated from their date of birth and the current (system) date whenever it is needed. Attempting to store age would present problems because it changes every year, unlike a date of birth, which remains constant. If we tried to maintain age in a database we would have to check all the employees every day to see if it was their birthday and if so raise their age. This is obviously wasteful in processing terms since we check all the employees every day and in storage terms since we would still need to keep the date of birth.

In the Bruddersfield example we can consider how we want to represent overdue invoices. If the system has a simple rule that invoices are overdue after 30 days, then we may use an operation to check the invoice's date in comparison with the current date and use this to trigger activities such as writing reminder letters. The conditions could be more complex and depend on the customer's credit rating, size of order, etc., but an operation would still work. If, however, the business system required more flexibility, so that extended payment terms could be put on individual invoices, then an operation alone may not be adequate to represent the firm's activities. We might need an operation that used the invoice date and current date to set an overdue attribute which could then be manually overridden.

The decision on whether a method or attribute is most suitable will depend on the situation we are modelling. Also, users may not know whether some facts about objects are in fact stored as attributes or calculated by operations. In many situations this may not matter but it may be a concern if they attempt to update the database. In general, "facts" which are derived via operations will be "read-only attributes", which can only actually be changed by updating the underlying fact.

## OPERATIONS WHICH REPRESENT BEHAVIOURAL SEMANTICS

The behavioural semantics of an entity type refers to the things that can happen to its instances during their lifetime. For example, the behavioural semantics for employees will include what happens when an employee is first appointed, is paid, promoted, or demoted, retires, or is dismissed. This information is represented as a set of object operations which provide the interface to the object. These are the means by which the state of an object is changed to reflect changes in the entity represented.

Analysis of behavioural semantics is done by analysing the changes that can occur to an object during its life, and the manner in which those changes take place. UML supports two analysis techniques which assist the designer with this aspect.

1) **State diagrams**—these represent all possible changes that can occur to the state of an object.
2) **Message trace diagrams** and **object message diagrams**—these represent the messages that pass between objects when specific transactions take place.

### STATE DIAGRAMS

An example state diagram for an Invoice object is given in Figure 8.13.
It diagram depicts what can happen to an Invoice object during its life. The oblongs represent different states and the arrows the transition from one state to another when some event occurs. For instance, the diagram

shows that an invoice's state changes from unpaid to paid when a payment is received. The black spot shows the start of the object's life, and the black spot in a white circle shows when it is eventually deleted.

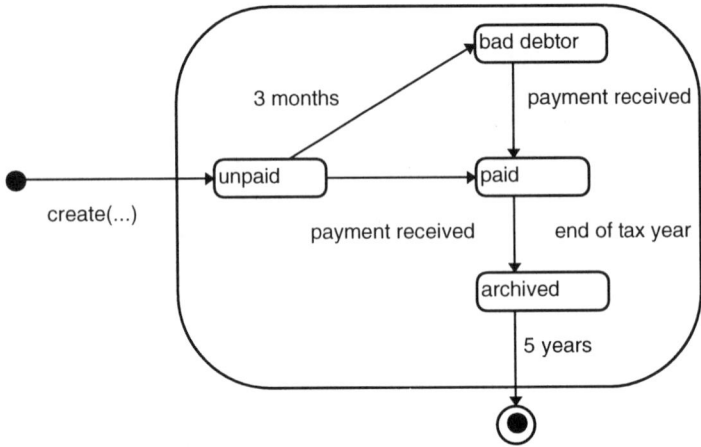

Figure 8.13 State diagram for Bruddersfield Bikes customer invoice

A state diagram can be produced for each class, but it is usual only for objects with an interesting dynamic behaviour. A state diagram is used to analyse which operations should be defined for an object. There must be an operation for each state transition, since the state of an object can be changed only by its operations.

In the Figure 8.13 example, the operations which are implied are: payment_recieved, become_a_bad_debt, and archive_invoice, in addition to the constructor and destructor operations.

*SCENARIOS*

The designer may arrive at, or test the correctness of, a state diagram by running through a number of scenarios. A scenario shows the use of the object database system within a particular situation, e.g., the placing of a sales order for a product which is out of stock. Describing scenarios is a way of testing the system design, in a manner similar to the way in which programs are tested using test data.

UML includes two types of diagram with which scenarios can be described—**message trace diagrams** and **object message diagrams**.

A message trace diagram represents objects in a transaction as vertical lines. Arrows between those lines then represent messages passed between those objects. The time sequence of the messages is represented, from top to bottom. An example is given in Figure 8.14.

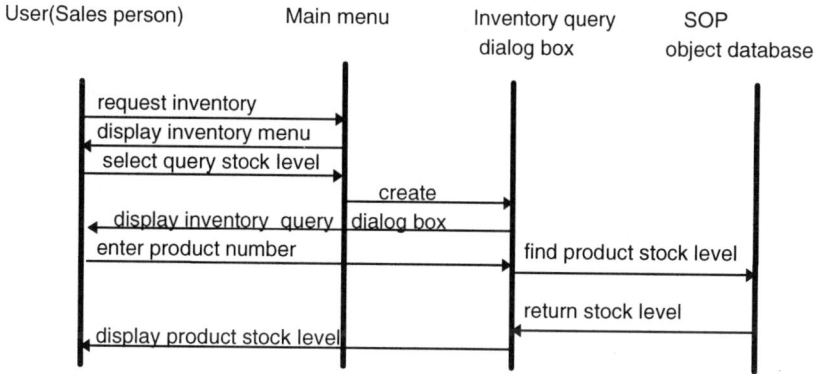

Figure 8.14 A message trace diagram for a transaction which queries the stock level for a specified product

Figure 8.14 represents the interaction between the database system and a sales staff user, who is querying how many of a particular product are in stock.

These diagrams enable the designer to think through and represent ways in which the system is likely to be used, in terms of the interactions that will take place. Object operations are implicit in those interactions. For instance, the Figure 8.14 sequence indicates that there must be an operation on Product objects which returns the current stock level of a specified product.

The scenario can then be followed through in greater detail, in terms of interactions within the object database system. This can be described using an object message diagram, in which the flow of messages and responses between objects is represented. An example is given in Figure 8.15.

The Figure 8.15 diagram representes interactions between Customer, Product, and SalesOrder objects, when a sales order is placed by a customer.

1)      The boxes represent objects (the underlined type name denotes an instance).

2)      The lines connecting the boxes correspond to relationships between objects.

3)      Connecting lines are labelled to denote a message being passed between objects.

- The arrow shows the direction in which the message is sent.
- The numbers (1, 1.1, 1.2) indicate the message sequence and which process (or thread) the message is part of.
- An asterisk in front of a message (e.g., *check_prod) shows that it is sent repeatedly to different instances of the receiving type.

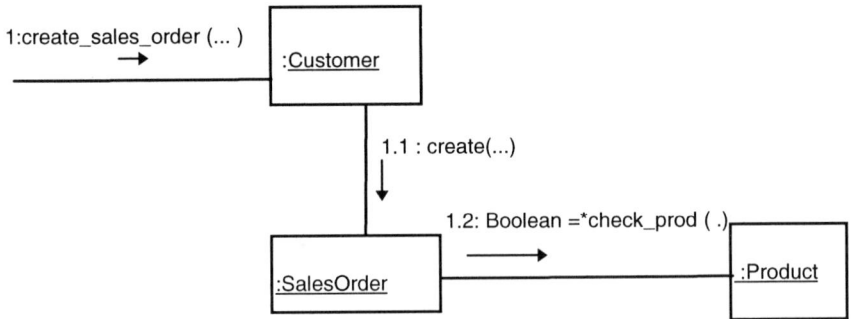

Figure 8.15 Object message diagram for placing a sales order

Figure 8.15 therefore shows that, when the customer receives a message to execute the create_sales_order operation, the Customer object then creates the SalesOrder object, which accesses Product objects to make sure that the ordered product exists. The diagram thus demonstrates the need for the create_sales_order, create, and check_prod operations.

Operations are depicted in class diagrams as a list in the third part of each object box, as in Figure 8.16.

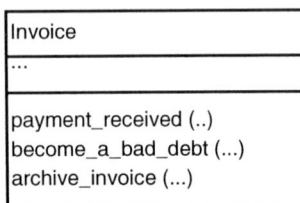

Figure 8.16 Representation of operations

In addition, the designer must specify each operation in detail, so that it can be programmed. The specifications will include:

1) **The operation name and signature**, i.e., the type of the value that it returns and of its parameters.
2) **A statement of what it does.**
3) **The input parameters**—the name and type of each.
4) **The output parameters**—the name and type of each.
5) **Modified object**—which objects have an altered state as a result of executing this operation.
6) **Preconditions**—that is, the conditions that must hold for the operation to be executed correctly.
7) **Postconditions**—the new conditions created by executing the operation.

An example is give in Figure 8.17.

---

**Operation:** promote(who: Person, new_position string) : Boolean

**Responsibilities:**  modifies an employee object so that the position attribute is replaced with a new value

**Inputs:** who - object of type Person
new_position - string

**Returns:** Boolean

**Modified objects:** who

**Preconditions:**  there must be an employee object in the database matching the who input parameter, if there is not the operation returns *false*

**Postconditions:** the employee object remains the same except for the position attribute being changed to the new (input) value)

---

Figure 8.17 Operation specification

# 8.5 REVISING ATTRIBUTES AND CLASSES

Identifying an object's attributes may also feedback into the designer's initial analysis of the objects themselves.

Consider, for instance, the employees and possible subclasses in the Bruddersfield Bikes example. It may be necessary to revise the classes after examining what attributes each potential subclass has. We have identified sales people as a potential subclass. This is because there are a number of attributes and relationships that are specific to sales people, e.g., a sales area (an attribute) and orders_taken (a relationship to a list of sales order objects), in addition to the general attributes of employees such as National Insurance Number and Department. There is a distinct identity to the salesperson class that distinguishes it from the employee class. A more detailed description of Bruddersfield's activities might have included information about the sales people along with information about other categories of staff.

---

### EXAMPLE 8.22

*"Sales people have responsibilities for a sales area and take the orders for the customers in that area. Personnel staff are responsible for hiring and firing other staff. Payroll staff process the wages for all the staff."*

*An analysis of these might have led us to give specific attributes to personnel staff and payroll staff in the same way that we did for sales people. For example, there might be a relationship between personnel staff and all the other workers they hired and a relationship between payroll staff and all the staff whose wages they prepare. We may, however, decide that these relationships are irrelevant or beyond the scope of what we want to model. If we decide that the payroll department is generally responsible for all the payroll and personnel is responsible as a department for employment, then these would no longer be relationships we wanted to maintain. In this case the distinctive features of payroll and personnel staff would disappear and we would collapse these subclasses back into office staff.*

---

Example 8.22 again shows that design is an iterative process and we may need to go round a design cycle a number of times, modifying our design in the light of more information or more detailed analysis.

## 8.6 SUMMARY

Object–database design methods provide a systematic way of designing an object database. The **UNIFIED MODELING LANGUAGE (UML)** provides a diagrammatic language for representing analyses and designs for object–oriented systems in general, and can be used in object database design.

Conventionally, **two-phase database design** takes place. The first phase is **data analysis**, which derives a **conceptual model**, and the second is **data design**, which produces a **logical model**. The conceptual model is a **semantic data model**, often the **entity relationship model**. The difference between what can be represented in the conceptual model and of what can be implemented (in the logical model) is called the **semantic gap**.

In object database design the Object Data Model can be used as the conceptual model. The process therefore becomes a single phase design process. **Entity relationship analysis** forms a basis for object database design, since objects represent entities. Entity relationship analysis describes the information to be represented in terms of **entities**, **relationships** and **attributes**. For object databases, it is necessary to analyse the **behavioural semantics** so as to determine the object operations. The analysis can produce many alternative designs.

Two approaches to database design are **top down** and **bottom up**. Top down fits naturally with many aspects of the Object Data Model, but there is a bottom up aspect if the designer is going to exploit the potential for **reuse** of existing classes.

The design method described uses the UML notation, and proceeds in the following stages—**identification of objects in the system, refining objects** and **revision of the attributes and classes**.

**Objects** are inferred from nouns and noun phrases, grouped, and refined. These are represented by the object database **classes**. **Relationships** are implied by verbs. For each relationship, its cardinality and type must be determined. **Attributes** must be defined for each class.

**Operations** are used to represent **derived attributes** and **behavioural semantics**. Analysis of behaviour is represented as **state diagrams**, and is analysed through scenarios, which are represented using **message trace diagrams** and **object message diagrams**.

The UML is still evolving, and includes support for the design of object–oriented systems in general. Many features and details of UML for its more general use are not included in the chapter. Interested readers should refer to the Rational Web site [http://www.rational.com].

## EXERCISES:

(8.1)    What are the origins of UML, what is it, and why is it important?

(8.2)    Why do object database design methods concentrate on classes, rather than types?

(8.3)    What are the two phases of two–phase database design methods, and why are they necessary if using a relational DBMS?

(8.4)    What is meant by a semantic data model?

(8.5)    What does the semantic gap refer to within the context of two–phase database design?

(8.6)    Explain why the data design and normalisation phase are unnecessary when designing object databases.

(8.7)    What is meant by the behavioural semantics of an object database?

(8.8)    Which abstractions is entity relationship analysis based upon, and why is it relevant to object database design?

(8.9)    Distinguish between top down and bottom up database design methods.

(8.10)   Explain why design reuse is important in object database design.

(8.10)   What are the stages of the object database design method?

(8.12)   Identify candidate objects by analysing the following statement:

"Students attending Honley University enrol on courses. There are prerequisites for enrolment—i.e., the student must have certain qualifications, or be accepted by Dr Brown the admissions tutor. The institute currently has 3,000 students enrolled. Once enrolled, the student will accumulate credits by taking various course modules, such as Programming and Object Databases. A grade is awarded for each completed module. The grade will be A, B, C, D, or E. A represents distinction, and E a fail. Students may be full time or part time. "

(8.13)   Group the candidate objects in (8.12) and select those to be implemented as classes in a student admissions object database for Honley University. Present the selected classes as an outline class diagram.

(8.14)   Draw a class diagram for a Person class showing the relationships *married_to, parent_of,* and *child_of.*

(8.15)   Draw a class diagram for part of a ship's navigational system showing how various classes for oil rigs, ships of different types, and buoys share attributes via inheritance.

(8.16)   The statement in (8.12) includes examples of objects at too high and too low a level of abstraction, and also redundant, irrelevant and vague terms. Identify and classify these.

(8.17)   Identify the *is_a* relationships implied by the statement in (8.12). Analyse each in terms of its usefulness within the admissions object database.

(8.18)   Explain how Honley University could be viewed as either an abstract or a physical entity.

(8.19)   Represent the aggregation and *is_a* relationships implied by the following statement using UML notation.

"The University of Honley is a technical university, with five faculties, each with departments. "

(8.20)   Show how the management structure within Honley University can be represented by a single employee class and appropriate relationships.

(8.21)   Define the type and cardinality of each relationship defined in the previous questions.

(8.22)   Identify the attributes implied by the text in (8.12).

(8.23)   The Honley University Student class includes an attribute which is a list of modules taken and grades awarded. Define operations for this class to implement derived attributes, number of modules taken, and average grade.

(8.24)   Draw a state diagram to represent the life of a Student object in the Honley University object database. Which operations are implied by the diagram?

(8.25)   Represent the following scenarios as message trace diagrams and object message diagrams:
   (i)      A student enrols for the Diploma in Database Design.
   (ii)     The student is awarded a D for the Normalisation module.

(8.26)   Write a short report on the difficulties of object database design for the manager of a company which is just switching from a relational to an object database system.

# 9

# MANAGING OBJECT DATABASES

There are a number of facilities that a database management system must provide to ensure the smooth operation of that system. These include making sure that the database remains consistent, that users operations do not interfere with one another, that the system can be recovered in case of computer failures, and that the system gives an acceptable performance. This chapter covers these aspects of object database systems.

Many of these features can be implemented in a number of ways and are not dependent on or determined by the Object Data Model. In fact the Object Data Model and the ODMG standard do cover transactions and locking and concurrency, but issues such as back-up and recovery, performance and tuning, and security are not addressed. In general, these features are covered at a high level, in terms of the services that are provided. Examples of how these areas can be tackled are illustrated by examples from the $O_2$ object database management system.

Section 9.1 discusses transaction management mechanisms. The use of integrity constraints to avoid implausible object databases is covered in Section 9.2. Back-up and recovery from system failure is discussed in Section 9.3. Section 9.4 discusses the ways in which the performance of an object database system can be improved. Mechanisms for ensuring the security of data are discussed in Section 9.5. Finally, a summary is given in Section 9.6.

## 9.1 TRANSACTIONS
The transaction is a concept for databases that is fundamental in enabling them to group changes together into logical units. This is

necessary so that all the changes, or none, are made and that the database moves from one consistent state to another consistent state.

The above consistency is ensured by following the procedure below for each logically related group of changes:

1) Start a transaction.
2) Make changes to the database which are only visible to the person performing the transaction.
3) When the changes are complete, finish or **commit** the transaction to make the changes permanent and visible to others.
4) If something goes wrong, the user can **abort** the transaction and the database will be in its initial state with none of the changes made.

How other users are affected by this is discussed below in locking and concurrency. Similarly, if the DBMS crashes or there is some other system failure, a part complete transaction will not have made any permanent changes to the database and the system should be returned to the consistent state prior to the transaction.

In summary, transactions are described as being ACID, an acronym for:

- **Atomicity**—all the transaction takes place or none of it happens. It is an all or nothing situation; the transaction cannot be divided into smaller parts.
- **Consistency**—the transaction takes the database from one consistent state to another consistent state. In the middle of the transaction the database might be inconsistent when only some of the changes have actually happened ,but this will be hidden from other users who will only see the before and after versions of the database and not any intermediate states.
- **Isolation**—also known as **serialisability**, this is the property that says a sequence of transactions or a set of concurrent transactions must have the same overall effect.
- **Durability**—once a transaction is complete, its changes have been made permanent within the database and will not be lost by something like a system failure.

The ODMG standard says that a database management system should provide a Transaction type, instances of which represent individual transactions. Transaction objects are created using the facilities of the built–in TransactionFactory interface. The Transaction type supports the operations listed below from its interface definition:

```
void begin();
void commit();
void abort();
void checkpoint();
void join();
void leave();
boolean isOpen();
```

The above operations have the following effects:

1) **begin** starts a transaction;
2) **commit** completes a transaction, making all persistent objects changed or created in the transaction permanent and accessible to other transactions;
3) **abort** returns the database to the state before the transaction started;
4) **checkpoint** writes modified objects to the database but allows the transaction to continue;
5) **join** and **leave** respectively associate and disassociate a **thread** with the current transaction object. The concept of a thread will be familiar to Java programmers. A thread is the name given to a single independent stream of execution within a program.
6) **isOpen** allows us to test whether a transaction is currently in progress. The associated exceptions, **TransactionInProgress** and **TransactionNotInProgress**, can be raised by transaction operations. For example, it is not possible to commit a transaction which is not in progress. An attempt to do this would therefore raise the latter exception.

There is an explicit begin operation in the above interface, but this is not the case for all systems. Some systems in fact start transactions automatically at the start of a session with the database and following any commit or abort. These transaction semantics only affect persistent objects in the database; any transient objects used by the system within a transaction are not governed by the rules of transaction management. It may thus be necessary to check or re–initialise any objects that are held as temporary variable values after a transaction, especially those that did not complete normally.

---

### EXAMPLE 9.1

*Bruddersfield Bikes wish to make a number of price changes to their products. In the middle of increasing the prices of all mountain bikes by 10% someone realszes that this will take the "Pennine Champion" to over £500, which had been seen as the maximum price for this model if it were to undercut the competition. This transaction is then aborted and advice sort on what to do about the "Pennine Champion". A new transaction is then undertaken to raise the prices by 10% except for the "Pennine Champion", which is increased to £499.*

---

### LOCKING AND CONCURRENCY

Locking is a means by which different users can change parts of the database without conflicting with one another. When a user starts a transaction she takes a **lock** on a part of the database. No other user can then access this part of the database until the first user has finished with it by completing their transaction with a commit or abort. Once the lock has been released, another user can then access this part of the database. Users will see the new versions of those objects if the transaction has changed them and committed. If the first transaction aborted or did not change the data, users will see the original data.

The purpose of locks of the above kind is to stop two (or more) users from trying to change the same data at the same time. It also stops one user from updating data while it is being read by another user or being read whilst being updated.

In general it is a good idea to lock as little of the database as possible so that users are less likely to be affected by one another's actions. In relational databases whole tables or large parts of tables have sometimes been the smallest unit that could be locked. Object databases should be lockable at the level of individual objects.

There are a number of different locking strategies that may be used by database management systems. These may allow locking at different levels (individual object, type extents, etc.). The Object Data Model supports one particular locking strategy by default, but others are possible.

The Object Data Model supports the following lock types:

1)  A **read lock** must be taken before an object can be read, and this will stop another user writing to (updating) that object, which would require a write lock. It may be possible for a number of read locks to be held on the same object.

2)  A **write lock** must be held before an object can be updated and will stop another user from reading or writing to an object.

3)  An **upgrade lock** is used when an application reads an object which it may later decide to update (upgrade locks are used specifically to avoid a condition known as deadlock, which is explained later).

The database management system will stop other processes while an object is locked and may communicate this status to a program so that the user can decide to wait for an object to become free, stop attempting to access the object, or wait for a fixed time period.

In some situations **deadlock** can occur when two or more users are attempting to lock parts of the database, and a cycle occurs. The database management system should be able to detect such situations and resolve them by choosing between the users in some way to break the deadlock, or stopping them all and forcing a restart of a number of transactions.

---

*EXAMPLE 9.2*

*In the middle of the price changes in Example 9.1 a salesperson tries to look at the on-line catalogue. Fortunately since the price changes are one transaction and that part of the database was locked until the transaction was complete she never saw the wrong prices. When she tried to look at all the prices she found that this was not possible since those products being repriced locked part of the database and stopped their query from running. A simpler query on "The Honley Flyer" which was not being repriced did run straightaway since that object was not affected by the transaction and was not locked.*

---

## MORE COMPLEX TRANSACTIONS

The Object Data Model covers only the behaviour discussed above. There are a number of areas for possible future revision that have been indicated by the ODMG [Cattell 96, pp 33–35]. Some object systems may already implement some of these additional features or other transaction operations.

1) **Nested transactions**—this allows a new transaction to be started within an existing transaction and consequently a sequence of operations may be completed and saved within a larger ongoing set of operations.
2) **Long-lived transactions**—current transactions are assumed to be reasonably short lived. If they are not, large parts of the database may be locked for most users. Transactions are implemented by transaction objects; currently these are transient objects and cannot themselves be stored in a database.
3) **Multiprocess transactions**—this would allow more than one process to take part in a transaction. The actions of two users, for example, engaged in some dialogue, might then be regarded as one atomic change to the database.
4) **Multi-database transactions**—If a number of databases can be connected some operations might need to access objects in more than one database, and changes to more than one database would need to be done together, in one single transaction, to maintain all the databases in a consistent state.
5) **Transaction consistency over transient objects**—currently only persistent objects are included in transactions.

## 9.2 CONSTRAINTS AND INCONSISTENCIES

Relational database management systems usually have a distinct form of rule, the **integrity constraint**, for limiting what may be done to the data in the databases. An integrity constraint is a condition that must be true for all instances of the database in order to ensure that it is self-consistent and therefore plausible.

Integrity constraints may be implemented in a number of ways:

1) Built–in integrity constraints—some integrity constraints are built into the data model itself. For example, the relational model has two

such rules. Entity integrity ensures that every table has a key, which cannot have null values. In other words every object must have a name. Referential integrity ensures that there are no cross references to non–existing rows of tables. You can only refer to objects that exist.

2) Implicit integrity constraints—some rules, such as type enforcement, may not be explicitly labelled as integrity constraints but just be enforced by the system. For example, by defining a variable on the literal type char we are constraining its values to be single characters.

3) Other rules may be put into the database, typically in SQL (or other query languages), specifying a permissible range of values for some data item (e.g., employee.age > 17 and employee.age < 66) or the relationship between objects.

This distinct notion of integrity constraints does not exist in an object database. Instead the behaviour and values of an object will be constrained by its methods. If we wish to enforce a range check, disallow null values, or insert default values for attributes, this can be coded into the object's constructor method.

Some constraints that are needed in relational systems are not necessary in object databases. In particular, referential integrity which ensures the consistency of links between tables is not needed. For instance, in a relational system information on a product might be spread over several tables and all the data would be assembled by joining the tables on a common product identifier. To keep such a system consistent a rule would be needed to enforce a cascading change through all the tables if the product identifier were changed. In an object system the data need not be split up like this and any references or links between objects are made by system allocated object ids which cannot be changed by users.

Object systems will often provide the Database Administrator (DBA) with special software tools for checking the consistency of an object database. For instance, $O_2$ provides a number of utilities that can be used to check for and eliminate erroneous references and other possible problems in a database. These include:

1) **o2check**—this tool can either generate information about problems with objects and complex values or replace erroneous references to objects with nil pointers and complex values to uninitialized values.
2) **garbage base** —this tool cleans up any unreachable objects in a given database.
3) **o2reformat**—this program (discussed below) also fulfills a similar function.

## 9.3 BACK-UP AND RECOVERY

Database management systems must provide mechanisms to safeguard against system failures. This is done by saving the data such that it can be retrieved into the system to allow a recovery from problems such as a failure due to a disk crash. It may also be necessary to restore a database to an earlier coherent state if a user has, for example, deleted data by mistake (and committed that transaction).

In most cases operating system level facilities for back-up and recovery will not be adequate. This is because they will not offer any guarantee of synchronization between the different files where the database's data is stored. Consequently, an incoherent snapshot of the database may be all that is saved on system back-ups. Database systems therefore include a number of utilities that should provide back-up and recovery to ensure a coherent system.

A database system may provide the above facility in a number of ways, e.g., waiting to save the database until no transactions are in progress and then locking the entire system while the data is saved, or saving the current files in one place and saving a record of current process so that these can be redone to the saved files. These utilities may also be required for activities such as saving the state of the database while a new version of the  operating system, or database management system is installed, or transferring the database from one machine to another.

As an example, $O_2$ includes a number of programs that provide this sort of functionality:

1) **o2base_dump** and **o2base_load** dump and load  databases into ordinary UNIX files. A directory per database is produced and

performance relevant factors such as indexing and clustering information can be included or not.

2) **o2reformat** dumps or loads a logical dump of a database to or from a file. In addition to providing a normal back-up facility, this can also be used when a new version of the database is going to be introduced, when the storage requirements of a database need changing, or as a garbage collector since only reachable objects in the database are saved in the dump process.

3) **o2tar** backs up or restores a database into a file in the tar format, which may be useful for creating a back-up to tape. This program only runs when the normal o2server program is not running and hence there are no transactions in process and a stable database state is ensured.

## 9.4 TUNING AND PERFORMANCE

A database must be capable of operating fast enough to be usable. (The aspects relating to interaction between users and operations which may slow the database down have been covered in the section above on transactions.) It is important that the response time of the database system does not deteriorate unacceptably as the amount of data in the database increases—we should expect a quick response whether there are a few objects in a class that we are querying or a few thousand.

The DBA will have a number of tools at her disposal to get the system to perform satisfactorily. Some of these will be used in setting up a database, others will be used during the life of the database as a result of observing the loads on the database and how well it responds.

There may well be environment variables that can be set for the size and location of buffers and swap space. These will affect the resources available and are likely to be used in query processing. Here a balance may be needed between the resources required by the machine generally and those allocated to the DBMS.

Most systems will support some form of indexing of objects, although this is not part of the Object Data Model itself. As an example, in the $O_2$ odl, it is possible to create an index on a class. This establishes a key to an element of the class that is frequently used for accessing particular members of that class. In this case the system need not scan through all the members of the class in search of objects that match a query. Instead the index, which is smaller, will be searched and used to reference the matching objects. The general syntax is:

```
index classname on key
```

where the key may be a simple attribute of the class or an attribute of a more complex object.

---

*EXAMPLE 9.3*

*The Bruddersfield DBA notices that queries on parts are either by its name or by its part number, so she creates two indexes:*

```
index part on name
index part on part_id
```

*She also notices that in addition to queries on Customers by the name there are a number of queries by town. Since the address on a Customer is an structured object it is possible to index on its town attribute:*

```
index Customers on address.town
```

---

There may be an overhead to maintaining an index on classes whose contents change very frequently, so DBAs must balance the performance issues of fast access and fast updates in some cases.

In many systems it may also be possible to affect performance by modifying the behaviour at a lower level. An example of this is the $O_2$ **cluster** command that allows you to make modifications to the physical location of objects on the computer's disk. With object clustering if you know that one object is frequently accessed by another it is possible to instruct the system to locate them as close as possible to one another. This can decrease the number of disk accesses the DBMS has to make.

The cluster command has a number of forms that include clustering all of a class, sorted clusters that organise a set of objects in a sequence based on an index on that class, and specifications of physical factors relating to disks such as fill factors on pages.

All of these tuning and performance operations will be undertaken by a DBA and should not affect the user's view of the database or the operation of any programs or queries except to make them run faster. In general, users will be unaware of what indexes etc. exist within a database.

## 9.5 SECURITY

The data in a database system may be of a confidential nature, such as medical records or financial details. In these cases it is desirable to be able to restrict access to the data.

Security restrictions may take a number of forms.

1) It may be that some users can access only data for their own department, although the database might contain the equivalent information for all the departments in an organisation.
2) There may also be some items of data that we would like some users to be able to see but not update, such as price lists.
3) There may also be cases where data could be updated by a user but we would not permit the deletion of the data by that user.

Any database system must provide facilities to allow these activities. This is normally done by mechanisms to grant different levels of access to different groups of users. Precisely how the groups are set up and administered is specific to each system.

In general there will be a notion of a **super-user** or **database administrator (DBA)** who can set up permissions for other users and control what permissions other users can give to one another. It is also usual for the DBA to have facilities for establishing other safeguards, such as access by password and encryption of data. In $O_2$ there are a number of mechanisms that can be used.

At the top level, access to an $O_2$ system itself can be controlled through an entry in the **systems** file which can include a list of permitted users. It is then possible to vary the permissions available to users of a system using the **create rights, modify rights**, and **delete rights** programs that will set up the allowable permissions for methods or programs. Similar rights can also be created on named objects and values. These rights can be allocated to individual users or to groups established with a **create group** or **modify group** command, these rights and groups being set up by an $O_2$ super-user.

The rights are applied during interactive use, such as an OQL session, and an object's methods may always be invoked by other programs or methods, so further control at the operating system level may also be needed for some levels of security.

The notions of public and private within methods and classes do not provide security at the level we are considering here, but only control the visibility of the methods and classes from one another.

The restrictions above apply at the level of data but it may also be necessary to control users' ability to alter the structure of the database. In $O_2$ it is possible to allow or disallow changes at the database schema level by setting the status to FREE or CONTROLLED. **modify rights** will then control what different groups of users can do to the schema or meta-data of a database. The $O_2$ super-user may also modify ownership of database objects, which may also affect what can be done.

## 9.6 SUMMARY

An object database system must ensure that the object database is consistent, plausible, and secure from system failure or inappropriate use. **Transactions** are the mechanism by which groups of logical changes take place as a single change. Changes are made permanent and visible when a transaction is **committed**. They are removed if the transaction is **aborted**. Transactions ensure that the object database passes the **ACID** test (**atomicity, consistency, isolation**, and **durability**). Transactions are supported in the Object Data Model by a special transaction type.

Concurrent transactions are supported by using a **locking protocol** that ensures that data being accessed by one transaction is not altered (or read, if it is being altered) by another. **Read** and **write locks** respectively ensure that a data item is not **altered**, or **read** and **altered** until the lock is released. Systems must also avoid or resolve **deadlock** (where an impasse is reached).

**Integrity constraints** are used to ensure that databases are plausible. Object databases are constrained by the type definitions and encapsulation.

**Back-up** and **recovery** mechanisms copy the contents of a database, so that the database can be recreated after a system failure.

A database system must also enable the DBA to monitor the performance of the system and make adjustments, e.g., to improve response times. Two techniques used in object database systems are creating **indexes** for fast access to object in collections and **clustering** objects, so that objects accessed together are stored close to each other.

**Security** is necessary to safeguard data from inappropriate access. The DBA will restrict access by granting different levels of access to different groups. Other techniques, such as **passwords** and **encryption** of data, may also be used.

## EXERCISES:

(9.1)    What is a transaction? Why are transactions necessary?

(9.2)    What does it mean to commit or abort a transaction?

(9.3)    What is the ACID test for transactions?

(9.4)    How are transactions supported in the Object Data Model?

(9.5)    How does locking stop one transaction from interfering with another:
       (i)   where one is reading and the other writing a data item?
       (ii)  where both are writing to the same data item?

(9.6)    What is deadlock?

(9.7)    Give five examples of complex types of transaction.

(9.8)    What facilities would you expect an object database system to provide for back-up and recovery?

(9.9)    What is meant by indexing and clustering in an object database? How do these techniques speed up database response times?

(9.10)   Describe the security features of a database system with which you are familiar.

# 10

# CONCLUSIONS AND THE FUTURE

Database technology is at an interesting stage in its development. A new generation is emerging which will supersede the previous generation of (relational) database technology. This new generation extends the capabilities of databases, mainly by adding features of object–oriented technology. Two mainstream third generation database technologies are those of object databases (the subject of this book) and object–relational databases. Object database and object–relational products are now becoming increasingly available and are already in use. Standards, such as those of the ODMG and the next version of SQL (SQL3—the proposed International Standard for relational database languages which includes object support), are gaining acceptance. However, the exact nature of the third generation database technology has yet to become firmly established, as it is still evolving.

This chapter provides a speculative appraisal of current and future developments. The requirements for a third generation database technology are identified, in Section 10.1, by taking a backwards look at the weaknesses of relational databases. A number of complementary third generation technologies are then overviewed. Section 10.2 discusses in greater detail two of the most important parts of the third generation—these are object–relational databases and the next version of SQL. Sections 10.3, 10.4, and 10.5 discuss semantic, deductive and temporal databases respectively. Section 10.6 addresses multidatabase technology, which enables integrated access to many database systems connected by computer networks. Finally, Section 10.7 concludes the book with a few personal speculations.

## 10.1 LIMITATIONS OF THE SECOND GENERATION DATABASES

Object database technology is one of a number of responses to the shortcomings of second generation database technology. Second generation databases are based upon the Relational Data Model, published in 1970 [Codd 70] as a theoretical data model for large databases. A relational database represents all information explicitly as values in tables (see Section 2.2: A brief history of data models, second generation database technology). Database manipulations are described using an algebra, with operators analogous to "cut and paste" operations upon tables. Throughout the 1970s and 1980s, the Relational Data Model was the dominant focus for both researchers and software providers, resulting in a sophisticated theory and technology. After an initial experimental period, relational databases have served as the mainstream state–of–the–art database technology since the 1980s. The adoption of International Standards for relational database languages has been a key factor in the technology's widespread adoption—the SQL relational database language and its counterpart for remote access to databases, RDA (Remote Database Access) are defined by ANSI and ISO.

The main strengths of the Relational Data Model are:

1) **Simplicity**—all information is visible as values in tables. There are no implementation–type features visible, such as file structures and access methods. The relational algebra and query languages, such as SQL, which implement it support simple "cut and paste" operations on tables.

2) **Rigour**—the Relational Data Model has been defined with theoretical rigour and provides a mathematical basis for researching issues such as database design, database languages, and query optimisations.

3) **Practicality and generality**—RDBMSs have provided efficient implementations of the Relational Data Model, and have been successfully used for a wide range of areas of applications (in business, industry, scientific research, engineering, etc.).

In spite of these strengths, relational technology has limitations and has proved inappropriate for certain demanding classes of application. The gap between relational theory and actual implementations of RDBMSs has been cited as an explanation of these shortcomings [Codd 90]. In 1985, Edgar Codd, the inventor of the Relational Data Model, published twelve rules [Codd 85] in an attempt to establish the requirements for a true implementation of the Relational Data Model and to rectify misunderstandings which were giving rise to this underperformance of relational technology. In summary, the rules are:

1) All information must be represented as values in tables.
2) Each data item must be accessible by the combination of table name, key value, and column name.
3) The RDBMS must support null values for representing missing or inapplicable information in a systematic way.
4) The database description (the schemas) must be represented at the logical level as values in tables.
5) At least one relational database language should be expressible as strings of characters and have a well–defined syntax. It should be usable interactively or within applications programs, and should support data definition, view definition, data manipulation, integrity constraints, authorisations, and transactions.
6) Where possible, views should be updatable (a view is a derived table, and is defined by storing the query which returns it within the database).
7) Insertion/update/deletion operations should operate on tables and should handle a set of rows at a time.
8) Database users and applications should be unaffected by changes to the ways in which tables are stored.
9) Applications should be unaffected by changes to tables which do not destroy the information they access.
10) Integrity constraints should be specifiable in the relational database language and be stored in the database, not in the programs.
11) Applications and users should be unaffected if the database is distributed over a number of computers networked together.
12) A low–level database language should still be constrained by the integrity constraints.

These rules are all based upon the underlying principle (rule 0) that all database management should be possible entirely through features of the Relational Data Model.

Codd's twelve rules expand the scope of the Relational Data Model to embrace practical data management issues. This broadening of scope was later consolidated by Codd, when he published version two of the relational model (RM/2) [Codd 90]. RM/2 comprised the original structural, manipulativ,e and integrity parts, but also additional parts concerning aspects of database management, such as authorisations, the data dictionary, views, attribute naming, and data types.

The above rules and Codd's extended definition of relational database technology prescribe improved data management features for RDBMSs. However, they do not address the major weakness inherent in the Relational Data Model. That is, its limited capacity to represent the structure, behaviour, and meaning of data. This weakness can be explained in terms of the **semantic gap** between the conceptual model of the Universe of Discourse (UoD) produced during the data analysis phase of designing a database and the logical model produced by the data design phase, which is actually implemented using the DBMS (see Figure 10.1).

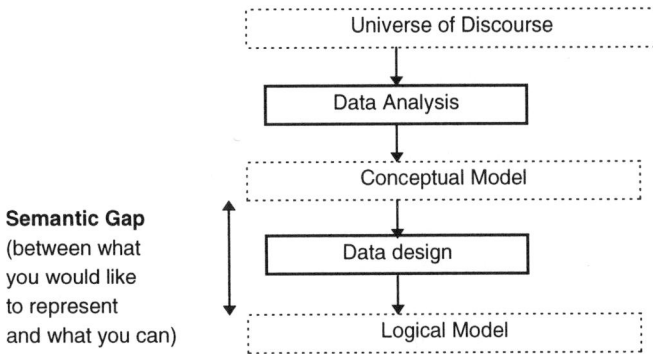

Figure 10.1 The semantic gap in the database design process

Data analysis produces a conceptual model of the information that the designer wishes to represent within the database, but very little of that information can be represented in the logical model when using an RDBMS to implement that conceptual model. Relational tables say very little about the meaning of the data they contain.

There are two classes of application for which relational databases are particularly inappropriate, because of this representational weakness:

1) **Object intensive applications**, e.g., design applications, multimedia, and office systems, in which entities have complex structures and behaviour.

2) **Rule intensive applications**, e.g., expert systems, which require access to both facts and also the logical rules which apply.

The representational weaknesses of the Relational Data Model stem from the following limitations:

1) **Inability to represent structurally complex and behaviourally complex entities**—in a relational database a complex entity must be represented as values in many tables associated by common values. Operations upon those tables are programmed within applications or can be stored within the database as database procedures, but are separate from the objects upon which they operate. (Also, although more strictly an implementation issue, the set of column types supported by RDBMSs typically include only textual and numeric data, but not the other types required, for example, in multimedia information systems, such as sounds, images, and video.)

2) **Lack of semantic features**—In the database context, data semantics refers to the real world meaning of the data, i.e., the real world phenomenon that a data item denotes. The relational model provides a language with which to structure and manipulate data, but does not represent any interpretation for the structures or manipulations in terms of their real world meaning. For example, a relational table called X could represent anything!

3) **Inability to represent knowledge, other than simple facts**—there is no natural way to store general rules in the database. Only limited forms of rule such as integrity constraints can be stored in the database itself other rules have to be embedded in the code of applications programs rather than in the database.

4) **Inability to remember the past**—in a relational database, if an entity is updated its previous value has gone forever. If, for example, we update John Smith's salary, the old value will be removed from the database and we would not be able to query the database to find out last week's salary bill. Some extended relational systems, such as Postgres, have tackled these issues by methods such as timestamping changes and storing old data in "hidden" tables however, for frequently changing data this may have a considerable overhead.

It is primarily the above four limitations that have provided motivation for the third generation of database technology, in preference to a relational database technology with enhanced data management.

The following sections overview new database technologies that have emerged in response to the above limitations of the Relational Data Model.

## 10.2 OBJECT–RELATIONAL DATABASES

Object–relational databases extend the Relational Data Model to address its weaknesses, identified in the previous section. In particular, object–relational databases have been developed to represent entities with complex structures and behaviours, such as exist in many scientific and engineering applications, office applications, and multimedia and graphical information systems. The Relational Data Model has proved to be inadequate for such applications.

Two approaches have been taken to overcome this limitations, within the context of the Relational Data Model. The first is to extend formally the theoretical data model so as to extend its expressiveness. The Nested–Relational Data Model, described below, illustrates this theoretical approach. The second approach is to provide informal extensions to the Relational Data Model and languages by "grafting on" additional facilities. The description of SQL3 illustrates this pragmatic approach.

### THE NESTED–RELATIONAL DATA MODEL

There have been many attempts to extend the Relational Data Model in such a way that it can directly represent complex entities, while retaining its strengths, such as simplicity and theoretical rigour. An example of this type of extension is the **Nested-Relational Data Model** (or **Non–First–Normal–Form (NF2) Relational Model**) [Roth 88, Scheck 91].

The Nested–Relational Data Model removes the constraint that tables are "flat" (this constraint is called **first normal form**, and requires each column of a table to take only atomic values). In the Nested–Relational Data Model, the values stored in tables can also be tables, and so on (see Figure 10.2). The Nested–Relational Data Model can be viewed as a step towards an Object–Relational Data Model, in that it removes one of the important limitations of the Relational Data Model concerning the representation of complex entities.

| Employee_number | Projects | |
|---|---|---|
| | Project_number | hours |
| E1 | P1 | 10 |
| | P4 | 5 |
| E2 | P1 | 20 |

Figure 10.2   An example Nested Relational Data Model table

Nested tables can be used to represent hierarchically structured entities. This was also possible using the first generation Hierarchical Data Model (see Section 2.2: A brief history of data models,first generation database technology), but the Nested–Relational Data Model also provides the strength of a theoretical basis with its algebra. The only major extension to the algebra of the Relational Data Model is the addition of nest and unnest operators, similar to those of the object algebra (see Section 5.5 :Type conversion, nest and unnest).

The Nested–Relational Data Model has the virtue of providing a simple but formally defined extension to the Relational Data Model. However, this theoretical work has been largely ignored by the mainstream developments in database technology. Instead, these model structurally and behaviourally complex entities by utilising features of object–oriented systems.

## OBJECT–RELATIONAL DATA MODELS

There are two general approaches towards third generation database technologies with integrate object–oriented features:

1) **Object databases** (as described in this book)—these extend object models to include database capabilities, typically associated with relational technology, such as persistence, query languages, and data management facilities.
2) **Object–relational databases**—these extend the relational data model to include data modelling features typically associated with object–

oriented systems, such as encapsulation, object identifiers, and inheritance.

The object–oriented features of both object and object–relational databases provide them with extensible type systems which can be used to represent structurally and behaviourally complex entities. One particular use for these features is the definition of new types for non–textual and non–numeric data. This has become an important feature, given that low–cost computer hardware now has the capabilities for handling **media objects** such as images, graphics, sounds, and video. For example, an ISO/IEC project, SQL/MM, is currently developing an abstract data type library for **multimedia applications**.

In the late 1980s, object and object–relational databases were seen as rivals, rather than as complementary technologies. The respective visions of what the third generation of database technology should be like were published by groups of leading researchers, as "manifesto" documents— "The Object–Oriented Database Manifesto" [Atkinson 90] and "The Third Generation Database Manifesto" [Stonebraker 90]. (see Table 10.1).

There is considerable overlap between the sets of requirements set out in the two manifestos. Both attempt to establish requirements for a new database technology with the data modeling power of an object–oriented system. However, whereas the Object–Oriented Database Manifesto sees object–oriented features as core requirements about which the third generation must be built, the Third Generation Database Manifesto sees them as a means of extending a core Relational Data Model. The first approach has resulted in the Object Data Model. The second evolutionary approach has produced object–relational database technology, epitomised by the next version of the International Standard relational database language, SQL, usually referred to as **SQL3**.

## SQL3

SQL3 is still evolving (the current completion date is estimated to be 1999). Work is also underway between the ANSI standards committee ANSI X3H2 and the ODMG on the possible convergence of SQL3 and OQL [Wade 96]. The following details are based on the working draft specifications and proposals of SQL3, produced by ANSI X3H2 [ANSI 95].

Table 10.1  Features of the two manifestos

| The Object–Oriented Database Manifesto | The Third Generation Database Manifesto |
|---|---|
| **Essential features**:<br>Support for complex objects<br>Support for object identity<br>All objects should be encapsulated<br>Support for types and classes<br>Support for class or type hierarchies<br>Support for overriding, overloading and late binding<br>Computational completeness<br>An extensible type system<br>Support for persistent objects<br>Support for very large databases<br>Support for concurrent users<br>Recovery from hardware and software failures<br>Simple ad hoc query languages<br><br>**Features the manifesto is unsure about**:<br>View definition and derived data<br>Database administration utilities<br>Integrity constraints<br>Schema evolution facilities<br><br>**Desirable but optional features**:<br>Multiple inheritance<br>Type checking and type inferencing<br>Distributed databases<br>Data transactions<br>Versions<br>Open choices<br>Programming paradigm<br>Representation system<br>Types<br>Uniformity | **Object and Rule Management**:<br>A rich type system (including user–defined abstract data types, structured type generators, function as a type).<br>Subtype/supertype relationships and multiple inheritance.<br>Functions, including database procedures, methods, and encapsulations are a good idea.<br>Object identifiers should be assigned by the DBMS only if a user–defined primary key is not available.<br>Rules (triggers and constraints) will become a major feature.<br><br>**Increasing DBMS functions**:<br>Programs should access a database through a non–procedural high–level access language.<br>It should be possible to specify a collection either using enumeration (i.e., listing its contents) or using a query which retrieves its contents.<br>Updatable views are essential.<br>Performance indicators should not appear in the data model.<br><br>**Open system requirements**:<br>A database should be accessible from many high–level languages.<br>Persistent programming languages are a good idea.<br>SQL is here to stay as the universal language of databases. |

The SQL3 specification extends SQL to provide object–oriented features but remains upwardly compatible with previous SQL standards. These features include:

1) **Abstract Data Types (ADTs)**—ADTs are user–defined data types (these are similar to object types (see Chapter 3), but the operations are not restricted to operating on a single instance). Earlier SQL standards provide a single abstraction for modelling entities, the table, and include built–in types (Integer, Character, etc.) which can be used as column types. The first major revision, called SQL2, extended the set of built–in types to include, for example, times and dates. However, relational database designers were still restricted to using only the types which were built–in. This new extension is to allow relational database designers to define new data types for non–standard and application specific data.

2) **Generalisation and specialisation hierarchies**—these hierarchies are similar to subtype/supertype hierarchies in the Object Data Model (see Chapter 3). In SQL3 there are separate hierarchies for tables and ADTs. This facility allows a table or an ADT to be redefined into a specialised form, reusing the original definition.

3) **Assertions and triggers**—assertions and triggers are used to allow the database to react to new situations.

The general approach evident in the SQL3 working draft is to provide the additional features as optional extras for the database designer. For instance, SQL3 supports object identifiers, but it is up to the designer to decide if they are to be used or not—in the Object Data Model all objects have object identifiers. A consequence is that SQL3 is becoming a very large language, compared with the original SQL standard or the ODMG standards (ODL and OQL). On the basis of a page count, the syntax definition of SQL3 is approximately five times longer that the combined specifications of ODL and OQL in the ODMG standard! In this respect, SQL3 has lost one of the main qualities of the original Relational Data Model its simplicity. It has also lost its theoretical rigour—only a very small part of SQL3 is concerned with implementing the original Relational Data Model. The additional features are not formally defined.

In the following sections some of the object-oriented features of. SQL3, such as support for encapsulation, supertypes/subtypes, are outlined so that they can be contrasted with the way these features are supported in the Object Data Model.

SQL3 provides two way to model entities—as rows in tables and as ADTs. There is also considerable overlap between the features of these two abstractions—for example, they both support inheritance hierarchies and object/row identifiers.

## ABSTRACT DATA TYPES (ADT)

An ADT is a user–defined data type. Its definition includes structures and the operations on those structures. An SQL3 ADT is similar to an object type definition in the Object Data Model and has a similar use. When an ADT is defined, an implementation is also provided (in that respect it is analogous to a class). The implementation is the stored data together with the data structures and code that implement the behaviour of the ADT. The object–relational database designer must define ADTs (and tables) for each type of value and entity that they wish to represent and which cannot be represented using the built–in data types. As in the Object Data Model, new types (ADTs) can be recursively constructed from others.

---

### EXAMPLE 10.1

*Many of the features of the SQL3 ADT facility are illustrated in the following example ADT declaration.*

```
1       CREATE OBJECT TYPE person_type
2       (       name VARCHAR NOT NULL,
3               sex CONSTANT CHAR (1),
4               age UPDATABLE VIRTUAL GET WITH age
5                   SET WITH set_age,
6       PRIVATE
7               birthdate DATE
8               CHECK (birthdate < DATE '1992-01-01'),
9       PUBLIC
10              EQUAL DEFAULT,
11              LESS THAN NONE,
12              ACTOR FUNCTION age (:P person_type)
13                  RETURN REAL
14                  RETURN <code to calculate the age>
15              END FUNCTION
16              ACTOR FUNCTION set_age
17                  (:P person_type, ...)
```

```
18                    RETURNS person_type
19                    <code to update the birthdate>
20                    RETURN :P
21          END FUNCTION,
22          DESTRUCTOR FUNCTION remove_person
23                (:P person_type)
24                    RETURNS person_type
25                    <various clean_up actions>
26                    DESTROY :P;
27                    RETURN :P;
28          END FUNCTION;
29    );
```

The Example 10.1 declaration is for an ADT, instances of which represent persons. As in the Object Data Model, the type declaration specifies type properties (lines 2–4) and operations (lines 10–28). The implementations of the operations are also included in the specification (lines 14, 19, and 25). In this respect the ADT is more like a class than an object type.

ADT instances can exists only within a table—SQL3 currently retains the basic idea of the Relational Data Model, that all data is presented as values within tables. The SQL3 equivalent of the extent of a class in the Object Data Model is therefore a table envelope for an ADT—the rows contain the ADT instances. This is created by:

```
CREATE TABLE PEOPLE OF person;
```

Attributes of the ADT become columns of the table and instances are the rows, as shown below.

PEOPLE

| Name | Sex | Age |
|------|-----|-----|
| Barry Eaglestone | male | 38 |
| Mick Ridley | male | 37 |
| Carole Stainton | female | 39 |

ADT instances can then be managed using the usual SQL select, update, and delete statements.

## OBJECT IDENTIFIERS

Object identifiers (OIDs) are an optional extra for an ADT. SQL3 supports three options:

1) WITH OID VISIBLE
2) WITH OID NOT VISIBLE
3) WITHOUT OID

As in the Object Data Model, OIDs are unique and immutable identifiers used for referencing instances. An ADT declared **WITHOUT OID** is called a **VALUE ADT**, and must be referenced by its value. Value ADTs are like literals in the Object Data Model. An ADT declared **WITH OID** is called an **OBJECT ADT** and is like a mutable object. Alternatively, an ADT may be explicitly declared as a VALUE or OBJECT ADT, as in the Example 10.1 OBJECT ADT declaration (line 1). If the OID is visible, then it may by passed as a parameter.

If a column is defined on an OBJECT ADT, then it can either contain the ADT instances (this is specified using the INSTANCE keyword in the ADT definition) or the OIDs to reference the instances. The SQL3 INSERT statement illustrates the approach taken by which OIDs can be retrieved. INSERT is extended to return the OID of the new row (instance) as an "alias",

```
INSERT INTO PEOPLE <insert spec>
ALIAS new_person
```

## SUBTYPE/SUPERTYPE RELATIONSHIPS

SQL3 supports subtype/supertype relationships between ADTs. Supertypes are declared using the UNDER keyword in an ADT definition. For example, we can declare an ADT called employee as a specialisation of person as follows:

```
CREATE OBJECT TYPE employee
UNDER person
( ... );
```

This mechanism is the same as the subtype/supertype relationship in the Object Data Model. Multiple supertypes are allowed. A subtype inherits the definitions of its supertypes, and also provides its own definitions. In this way a subtype can define a more specialised data definition without losing the properties and operations of its supertype. As in the Object Data Model, this mechanism also supports the reuse of type definitions—new types are built under older, less specialised ones, rather than having to rewrite properties from scratch. An instance of a subtype is also an instance of all of its supertypes, but is associated with the "most specific type" (the lowest type in the type hierarchy of which it is an instance).

All operations on a type can be invoked on its subtypes, but there may be different implementations of the operation for each type. There is therefore potential for name conflicts. These ambiguities are avoided by the following rules:

1)  When creating a subtype from two supertypes, if the two supertypes inherit an attribute from a common supertype, then only the one from the common supertype is inherited by the subtype. For instance, consider the situation where Employee_Customer is an SQL3 ADT, which is a subtype of Employee and Customer, which in turn are both subtypes of Person. Employee and Customer will both inherit Name and Address attributes from Person, thus causing a name conflict for Employee_Person. To resolve this, Employee_Customer inherits the Name and Address attributes from Person, rather than either Employee or Customer.
2)  Otherwise it is invalid to have the same attribute in two supertypes—one of them must be renamed.

## ADT ENCAPSULATION
Encapsulation is the hiding of implementation details behind an interface, and is a major feature of the Object Data Model—instance characteristics (attributes, relationships, and operations) provide an interface to objects of a particular type, but encapsulation means that the way in which those characteristics are implemented is invisible to the user. In SQL3, encapsulation is an optional extra which can be applied on a "sliding scale". Attributes and operations declared in an ADT

definition can be either encapsulated (i.e., invisible to the user) or not. The three options are:

1) PUBLIC—this means that attributes and operations are visible to all authorised users.
2) PRIVATE—the attributes and operations are visible only within the ADT for implementation purposes.
3) PROTECTED—the attributes and operations are visible within the ADT and within all of its subtypes.

The Example 10.1 ADT declaration includes both private (line 6) and public parts (line 9). The one private attribute is called birthdate, and is private because it is used only to compute the public (visible) age attribute. Private components of an ADT definition are there as parts of the implementation rather than the interface.

## ADT OPERATIONS

As in the Object Data Model, SQL3 ADT operations can be defined to provide an interface by which its value can be access and manipulated. These operations can be for the following purposes.

1) To compare instances of the type (EQUALS, LESS THAN, etc.). These determine the ordering and equality of instances, and can be used in standard SQL statement predicates.
2) To retrieve useful information from the instance. This type of operation is called a FUNCTION. An SQL3 FUNCTION operates on one or more ADT instances and returns a single value. Note that this contrasts with an operation on an object in object data models, which must operate upon a single instance.
3) CONSTRUCTORS/DESTRUCTORS—these create and delete instances and are automatically invoked by the SQL3 INSERT and DELETE instructions. It is only this type of operation that can create or destroy ADT instances.
4) To convert (CAST) instances into other types.
5) To change the value of an instance.

The Example 10.1 declaration illustrates a number of operator definitions. The definition of instance equality is the default one, i.e., instances are equal if the attribute values are equal:

```
10              EQUAL DEFAULT,
```

The less than operator is undefined:

```
11              LESS THAN NONE,
```

Operations which return useful values or update the ADT attribute values are called **actor functions**. The Example 10.1 definition declares two of these. The first retrieves useful information, i.e., the person's age:

```
12              ACTOR FUNCTION age (:P person_type)
13                  RETURN REAL
14                  RETURN <code to calculate the age>
15              END FUNCTION
```

The second example actor function alters the state of an instance, by setting the age attribute to a new value:

```
16              ACTOR FUNCTION set_age
17                  (:P person_type, ...)
18                   RETURNS person_type
19                  <code to update the birthdate>
20                  RETURN :P
21              END FUNCTION,
```

Finally, the Example 10.1 ADT definition includes a destructor function, which deletes an ADT instance of type person:

```
22              DESTRUCTOR FUNCTION remove_person
23                  (:P person_type)
24                  RETURNS person_type
25                  <various clean_up actions>
26                  DESTROY :P;
27                  RETURN :P;
28              END FUNCTION;
```

Operations can be implemented either by a single SQL3 instruction or as (external) functions coded in some other programming language.

A single SQL statement that implements an operation may be a compound statement, i.e., a block of statements together with local variables and exception handling. A compound statement can be thought of as an SQL3 program or procedure. Its syntax is:

```
<compound statement> ::=
        [ <beginning label>: ]
        [ <variable declarations ]
        BEGIN
                [SQL statements> ]
                [ <exception handler> ]
        END [   <ending label> ]
```

where the exception handlers have the form,

```
EXCEPTION [ {WHEN <condition>
    THEN <SQL statements>)} ...]
```

The syntax for an external function definition is:

```
<external function declaration> ::=
        DECLARE EXTERNAL <external function name>
        <formal parameters>
        RETURNS <result data type>
                [ CAST AS <cast data type> ]
        LANGUAGE <language name>
```

SQL3 also includes new statements which can be used to program operations on ADTs. These include:

1) NEW/DESTROY—used in a CONSTRUCTOR/DESTRUCTOR to create/destroy an ADT instance;
2) ASSIGNMENT—assigns the result of an SQL expression to a variable, column or attribute of an ADT;
3) CALL—to invoke an SQL procedure;
4) RETURN—to return the value of an operation on an ADT.

There are also control structures to support sequences of SQL statements, looping (LOOP, LEAVE), branching (CASE, IF), and exception handling.

The net effect of including these additional features it to move SQL3 nearer to a programming language, rather than simply a query language.

## *ADT POLYMORPHISM*

SQL3 gives support to polymorphism, as does the Object Data Model. Polymorphism is the ability to invoke an operation on any of a number of different objects and to have that object determine what to do at run time. A polymorphic function is one that can be applied in the same way to a variety of objects. The techniques used are:

1) **Overloading**—multiple definitions of the same operation. Name resolution is determined by a set of rules which allow a processor to distinguish between them by examining the type of the input data.
2) **Coercion**—the ability to omit certain type conversions;
3) **Inclusion**—the ability to manipulate objects of a subtype as if they were of a supertype.
4) **Generalisation**—the ability to specify that a parameter should take on the type of some supertype while processing a specific function call.

Resolution rules determine which implementation of a named function should be executed. They choose the "best match" from candidates within the scope, as follows:

1) Begin with all functions in scope.
2) For each argument, determine the functions that are a best match, and take the intersection (one function).
3) "Best match"—exact match is better than matches based on type coercion (CASTING); an implicit conversion to the closest supertype is better than SQL or user-defined type coercion; implicit SQL-defined CAST is better than implicit user-defined CAST.

## *ADT SUMMARY*

The general syntax for an SQL3 definition of an ADT is:

```
<ADT_definition>::=
        CREATE [OBJECT | VALUE] TYPE
        <ADT name>
        [ <Object identifier options> ]
        [ <supertypes> ]
        [ <attributes and operations> ]
```

Note that the definition specifies whether the ADT instances are objects or values (which correspond to mutable objects and literals in the Object Data Model). Object ADT instances have OIDs which may or may not be visible. An ADT may have supertypes from which it inherits characteristics. The ADT instance characteristics are attributes and operations, which may be encapsulated (PRIVATE) or not (PUBLIC). Alternatively, they may be accessible only to the type and its subtypes (PROTECTED).

## PARAMETERISED TYPES

A parameterised type defines a family of ADTs, e.g., SET(N). These correspond to type generators in the Object Data Model, and can be defined using templates (which will be familiar to C++ programmers):

```
CREATE TYPE TEMPLATE <name>
        ( { <template parameters> } ... )
        <ADT body>
```

There are a number of built–in parameterised types, called generators, for generating standard structured types, e.g., LIST, SET, and ARRAY:

```
ARRAY {[ <lower> ... <upper>] } ...
        OF <base type>
LIST OF <base type>
SET OF <base type>
CHOICE ({<identifier>:base type>} ...)
RECORD ({<identifier:<base type>}...)
```

## SQL3 TABLES

SQL3 also extends the table abstraction to make rows more like objects. For example, row identifiers (which are analogous to object identifiers) can be maintained as unique and immutable identifiers for the rows in a table. They can be used as a column value or foreign key. Any table can have a row identifier defined by specifying WITH IDENTITY in the table definition. The row identifiers are in an implicit column called IDENTITY which is ignored unless explicitly referenced.

There is also a subtable facility (analogous to subtyping). A table declaration can specify supertables, using:

```
UNDER <table name>
```

In this case all columns are inherited from the supertable.

```
CREATE TABLE person
(name CHAR(20),sex CHAR(1),
 spouse person IDENTITY);

CREATE TABLE employee UNDER person
(salary FLOAT)

CREATE TABLE customer UNDER person
(account INTEGER);
```

Operations on table rows can be associated with tables to implement object–like operations. These can be specialised for subtables to support polymorphism for those operations:

```
CREATE TABLE polygon
        (xvalue LIST(FLOAT), yvalue LIST(FLOAT));

CREATE TABLE rectangle UNDER polygon;

CREATE FUNCTION area (P polygon IDENTITY,
        xs LIST(FLOAT), ys LIST(FLOAT))
                RETURNS FLOAT
BEGIN ... END;

CREATE FUNCTION area (R rectangle IDENTITY,
        xs LIST(FLOAT), ys LIST(FLOAT))
                RETURNS FLOAT
```

```
BEGIN  ...  END;
```

There is also a row type facility by which a row is a new kind of data type. The components of row types are called fields. The aim is to provide a single data type that represents an entire row in a table, so that complete rows can be treated as values, stored in variables, passed as parameters, etc. These row types can also be used as types for columns, thus supporting a degree of relation nesting:

```
CREATE DOMAIN uk_address ROW
(      street CHAR(30),
       city CHAR(20),
       postcode ROW
             (original CHAR(5) plus4 CHAR(4))
);

CREATE TABLE employee
(      last_name CHAR(20),
       first_name CHAR(20),
       age   INTEGER,
       address uk_address
);
```

SQL3 explicitly breaks with the original definition of a table as a relation, by allowing tables to be SETs, BAGs, or LISTs.

The sections above detail only the object–oriented features of SQL3. SQL3 is an extensive and large language and includes many other data representation and data management features. Those interested should refer to the SQL3 draft proposals and papers in [ANSI 95] and the X3H7 features matrix in [Manola 95].

## 10.3 SEMANTIC DATABASES

In the database context, data semantics refers to the real world meaning of the data, i.e., the real world phenomenon that a data item denotes. In general, this meaning can be represented by having different types of database element to represent different types of real world phenomena. In this respect, the Relational Data Model was a step backwards. The first generation network data model (see Chapter 1) represents more of the semantics of the data than does a relational database because it has different types of structure to represent entities and associations between entities. Increasing the amount of meaning represented within a database is considered a good thing because the DBMS can then use the semantic information to ensure better data integrity, and more meaningful responses to queries and manipulations.

The relational model provides a poor representation of information as data, and can be thought of as a syntactic model rather than a semantic model. By this, we mean that the relational model provides a language with which to structure and manipulate data, but does not represent any interpretation for the structures or manipulations in terms of their real world meaning. As we have said earlier, a relational table called X could represent anything. Even joining two tables which both have a column called "name" may or may not be sensible. There are a few Relational Data Model features which are a consequence of the meaning of data rather than the whims of the designer. These include column types (called domains), keys, and the dependencies between columns, but in general, a relational database does not represent the semantics of the data it contains.

**Semantic data models** are a response to this limitation. A semantic data model is one in which more of the meaning of the data can be represented by using different types of data model element to represent different types of real world phenomena. The most influential semantic data model has been the Entity Relationship Model [Chen 76] in which entities, their attributes, and the relationships between entities are represented by different abstractions. The Entity Relationship Model is not a true data model since it does not include a manipulative part (e.g., an algebra or query language) with which to describe applications. However, it does have a structural part which can be represented both textually and graphically. One variant of the graphical representation is illustrated in Figure 10.3. Note the different abstractions included— rectangles, diamonds, and circles respectively represent entities, relationships, and attributes. In addition, arrows represent *is_a* relationships. The numbers give the cardinalities of the relationships, and the black circles are the keys.

There have also been a number of attempts to extend the Relational Data Model to capture more of the meaning of data. For example, Codd defined a semantically enriched version of the relational model, called **RM/T** (the T stands for Tasmania) [Codd 79], in which different types of table represent different types of information. RM/T has three types of table, E–Relations, P–Relations, and Graph–Relations, which are used, respectively, to represent entities, their properties, and the associations between entities, such as *is_a* and aggregation relationships. The RM/T relational algebra and integrity constraints extend those of the Relational Data Model to manipulate these special types of table and to ensure that they are plausible.

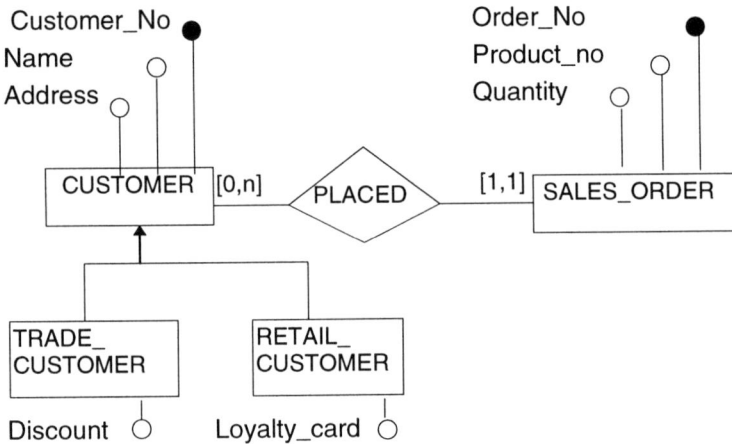

Figure 10.2 Example entity relationship diagram

Semantic data models have had little direct influence on third generation database technology. Their main impact has been on design methods— semantic models (the Entity Relationship Model in particular) are typically used in database design methods to represent a conceptual model of the information to be represented in a database, prior to implementing it within the constraints of the data model of the DBMS. The semantic model approach has been largely superseded by that of object–oriented technology. The strength of the latter is that, instead of having a fixed number of different types of abstraction for different types of real world phenomena built into the model, an extensible type system allows designers to define new types to model different types of real world information.

## 10.4 DEDUCTIVE DATABASES

The rows of the tables in a relational database represent facts about the world within which the database system operates, its UoD. Other knowledge relating to those facts is implicit in the table structures, or can be stored as integrity constrains, but must mainly be programmed into the application programs and database procedures.

---

### EXAMPLE 10.2

*A medical diagnosis system could use a relational database to represent facts about patients as rows within tables, and integrity constraints can be defined to ensure that these facts are self–consistent and plausible, but the relational technology is not capable of representing and applying the rules by which a consultant diagnoses an illness. These must be programmed as applications.*

---

The Example 10.2 medical diagnosis system is an example of a rule–intensive application—it requires inferences on the basis of **facts** and the **rules** that apply to them.

* Facts are assertions about the part of the world within which the system operates.
* Rules are sentences which allow us to deduce facts from other facts.

The area of artificial intelligence provides a number of programming languages which have been designed for this type of problem. In particular, there are logic programming languages, such a Prolog, which enable the programmer to encode facts and rules using logic, and provide an inference mechanism by which those facts and rules can be applied to solve problems posed by the user.

**Deductive databases** can address the issues above by merging artificial intelligence and database technology. Deductive databases typically extend the Relational Data Model, which can only store facts, to include **rules** which apply to the entities described by the data. In such systems, the logic based inference system can apply the knowledge represented in the deductive database (the rules and facts) to answer questions posed by the user. There are a number of areas where this can be useful, one example being the implemention of default rules.

---

*EXAMPLE 10.3*

*In a database of birds we want to be able to store a number of facts about birds in general, or default, rules. These should enable us to avoid storing the same facts for every bird. For example we can store a rule that says that "birds can fly" and then overule that in a few specific cases such as "penguins cannot fly" and" ostriches cannot fly" rather than having to store "... can fly" for all the "normal" birds. The inference mechanism can then anwer queries about which birds can fly using both the rules and the facts.*

---

Early deductive systems provided a "loose coupling" between relational DBMSs and Prolog systems. These couplings allowed Prolog facts to be stored as rows in the tables of the relational database. Prolog and the RDBMS communicated via an SQL interface. Generally there would be a larger number of facts managed by the RDBMS and a smaller number of rules held in the Prolog system.

A major problem for deductive systems can be the excessive time taken to execute queries, particularly those which involve the recursive evaluation of rules. Accordingly deductive database query optimisation has been a focus for research and development [Banchilon 86, Chakravarthy 88]. More recently, work towards a stronger integration of database and logic programming has resulted in deductive database systems with direct access to data.

The general approach taken in deductive databases is illustrated by examining the de facto standard deductive database language, Datalog. Datalog is a restricted subset of Prolog and has a purely declarative semantics; that is, some of the procedural features of Prolog are absent. Knowledge is represented in a Datalog deductive database as collections of facts and rules, as in Prolog. Both facts and rules are represented by logical formulae, known as **Horn clauses.**

A Horn clause is constructed from:
- **Constants**—these are literals, and are used to represent the property values, as in the Object Data Model. (The convention is to start constants with lower–case letters.)

- **Variables**—these take constants as their values, and are used to assert general rules about the UoD. (The convention is for variables to start with an upper–case letter.)
- **Predicates**—these are the conditions concerning property values, which are either true are false within the UoD for given sets of constants or variables.

Examples of predicates are:

```
parent_of (barry,david).
parent_of (X,Y).
customer (X,Y,huddersfield).
```

1) The first predicate represents the fact that Barry is the parent of David (parent_of is the predicate symbol, and barry and david are constants). If Barry is the parent of David, then the value of this predicate is true; otherwise false.
2) The second predicate represents the fact that X is the parent of Y, where X and Y are both variables. The truth or otherwise of this predicate depends on the constants assigned to X and Y.
3) The third predicate represents the fact that there is a customer with customer number X, name Y, and address huddersfield.

A Horn clause is used within a Datalog deductive database to represent both facts and rules. A Horn clause is constructed from predicates and has the form

L0 :—L1 . . . ,Ln

where each Li is a predicate. The left–hand side of the clause is called the head and the right, the body. A clause which does not have a body, e.g.,

```
customer (X,Y,huddersfield).
```

represents a fact. A clause with a body represents a rule. An example of a rule is:

```
grandparent_of (nora,david) :—
      parent_of (nora,X), parent_of (X,david).
```

The above Horn clause represents the rule that nora is the grandparent of david if nora if the parent of X and X is the parent of david. We can further generalise this rule by replacing the constants with variables;

```
grandparent_of (X,Z)  :-
        parent_of (X,Y), parent_of (Y,Z).
```

This Horn clause represents the rule that some person, X, is the grandparent of some person, Z, if X is the parent of some person, Y, who is the parent of Z.

A Datalog program is a set of facts and rules. There are two conditions that constrain a Datalog program to ensure that the set of facts that can be derived by applying the rules to the facts in the program is not infinite. These are:

1) Facts can contain only constants (not variables)—a fact which satisfies this condition is said to be **ground**.
2) Variables which occur in the head of a rule must also occur in the body of the same rule.

Datalog has been developed for logic programs (deductive database applications) which include a large number of facts stored in the same format as in a relational database, and possibly actually stored in a RDBMS. Datalog exploits the obvious similarity between the Horn clause representation of facts and the rows of tables in a relational database— the predicate symbols correspond to the table names, and the constants to which the predicates apply are the data values within a row of the table. In this way, a deductive database stores a set of (ground) facts as a relational database, called the **extensional database** (see Figure 10.4).

In addition, other facts and rules are stored in a Datalog program, called the **intensional database**. The intensional database may be thought of as the application. The following is an example intensional database for the Extensional Database in Figure 10.3 (This example is taken from [Ceri 89], which gives an excellent tutorial on Datalog).

```
rule1:      same_generation (X,X):−
                person (X).
rule2:      same_generation (X,Y):−
                parent_of (X,X1),
                same_generation(X1,Y1),
                parent_of (Y,Y1).
```

The above two rules represent knowledge about how we determine whether two people are of the same generation. Rule one states the obvious—a person is of the same generation as him or herself. This rule derives a table, with one row for each person, where each row contains the person's name twice, e.g., <barry,barry>. The second rule states that two people are of the same generation if their parents are of the same generation. This second rule is recursive (it is defined in terms of itself)— the head predicate also occurs in part of the body. The table derived by this rule comprises rows, each of which contains a pair of person names, where those people are of the same generation, e.g., <barry,jenny>, <david,michael>.

Facts

parent_of (barry,david)
parent_of(jenny,david)
parent_of(nora,jenny)
parent_of(jenny,michael)
parent_of(barry,michael)

person(barry,huddersfield)
person(jenny,huddersfield)
person(david,cardiff)
person(michael,huddersfield)
person(nora,leicester)

Relational Table
Parent_of

| Parent | Child |
|--------|---------|
| barry | david |
| barry | michael |
| jenny | david |
| jenny | michael |
| nora | jenny |

Person

| Name | Address |
|---------|-------------|
| barry | huddersfield |
| jenny | huddersfield |
| david | cardiff |
| michael | huddersfield |
| nora | leicester |

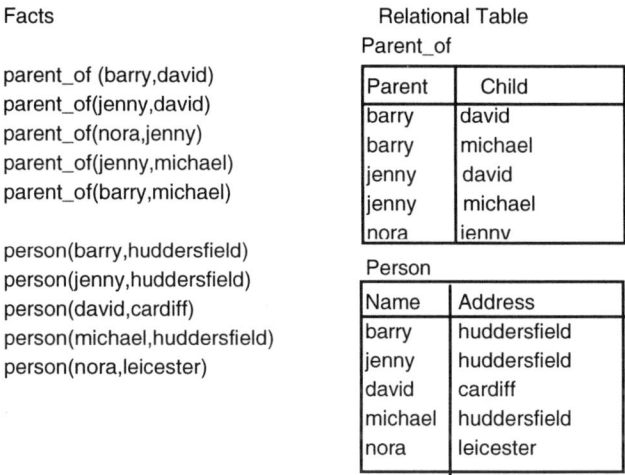

Figure 10.3 An example extensional database

As can be seen from the above example, the intensional database can be viewed as a query on the extensional database. The result of the query is the set of derived tables. Sometime the user is interested only in a subset of the knowledge in the derived tables. In this case the user can specify a

**goal**. A goal is a single predicate, preceded by a question mark and a dash, e.g.,

```
?-parent_of (jenny,X)
```

The above goal expresses the query, "who are the children of jenny". The derived table contains the rows <jenny, david> and <jenny, michael>.

```
?-same_generation (jenny, X)
```

This second goal expresses the query, "who is of the same generation as jenny". The resulting table will comprise the rows, <jenny,jenny> and <jenny,barry>.

Goals are used to formulate ad hoc queries on the facts in the extensional database.

Deductive databases are direct applications of mathematical logic and are therefore based upon a sound theoretical basis. The query facilities supported are more powerful than those of other databases because of the ability to query both rules and facts. The price paid for this additional expressiveness is that of efficiency. In particular, queries which apply recursive rules can be computationally very expensive. Also, the use of the Relational Data Model for storage of facts means that Datalog deductive databases inherit the limitations of the Relational Data Model for representing information as data.

More recently, deductive database research and development has addressed the latter problem by following a course analogous to that of databases. For example, Datalog has been extended to represent complexly structured objects by including functions and set constructors to build objects which are collections of other objects. The way is also open to link object databases with logic systems in the same way that relational databases have been; that is, letting the database store the objects and allowing the logic system to reason about them.

Deductive databases have considerable potential as reasoning databases, but to date this technology has made little impact. Few applications have been identified which can fully exploit the expressive power of deductive database technology. In addition to the issues of efficient query evaluation mentioned earlier there are a number of other features that are needed to build Deductive Database Management Systems. These include transaction processing and other multi-user issues, as well as typing. Datalog, like Prolog, is an untyped language, in contrast to the languages we have been discussing, in which types are very important. The large majority of database systems in use are currently relational, and seem likely to be superseded by object or object–relational databases, not deductive databases.

## 10.5 TEMPORAL DATABASES

Databases represent, as data, information about the part of the world in which they operate, their UoD. Data is updated to reflect changes in the world, such as a customer placing a sales order. However, when an update occurs, the value of the updated object prior to the update is lost. In this way, a database represents a "snapshot" of the UoD, but does not remember its history. This latter limitation can cause problems for certain types of application in which historical data remains relevant. Examples can be found in medicine, geology, and archeology. For example, medical applications are concerned not just with the current state of patients, but with their medical histories.

Temporal database technology attempts to overcome this limitation by making updates non–destructive—by this, we mean that when the value of an object is updated, the state of the object before the update is retained. This is usually done by time–stamping data. Time–stamped data has special attributes which record time values relevant to the data, e.g., the time when the data was first stored.

Temporal databases can be visualised in terms of time cubes. A conventional database may be thought of as creating a two–dimensional space, where the dimensions are entity and characteristics—each data object represents a characteristic of an entity. This space provides a snapshot of the world. Temporal databases add a third dimension, time, thus forming a cube—each data object in a temporal database represents a characteristic of an entity at a particular time (see Figure 10.5).

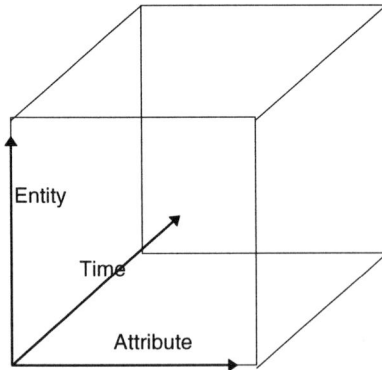

Figure 10.5  A Time–cube representation of a temporal database

Temporal database languages extend conventional database languages, such as SQL, to range queries over the time dimension as well as the entities and their characteristics. This allows us to ask information about the histories of entities represented, as well as their current state.

Temporal databases distinguish between three types of time. **Valid time** represents when the information represented by data objects is valid within the world. **Transaction time** concerns the computer world, and represents when data objects were created and when they were superseded by new data. The meaning of **user–defined time** is defined by the user, and is application specific. Conventional databases typically support time and time intervals as built–in types, and thus support user–defined time. Systems which also support valid time are called **historic databases**, and those which support transaction time are called **rollback databases**. **Bitemporal databases** support both.

Temporal databases have attracted an enormous volume of research throughout the 1980s and 1990s [Tsotras 96]. Those interested should refer to [Bohlen 95], in which a review of temporal database products is provided, and also [Jensen 92], which provides the consensus glossary of terms and concepts used in temporal databases.

Most temporal databases are relational, but recent research has focused on object and object–relational temporal databases [Snodgrass 95].

A related area to temporal databases is that of **versioning**. Here the problems of alternative versions of entities are considered. A typical application area for this is the storage of designs, where different design options might be stored, and compared and possibly merged. Versions can be considered as alternative time lines. Some extended relational systems, such as Postgres, support versioning.

## 10.6 MULTIDATABASES

The distribution of computer systems is a major preoccupation with many researchers, technology providers, and users. The reason is that the infrastructure is now in place which will support connection and interoperability between computer systems on a global scale. The internet provides infrastructure for worldwide transaction processing systems. The most obvious candidate application area, the World Wide Web (WWW), presents an immediate problem since its protocol (HTTP) is stateless and therefore not suitable for transaction processing without the addition of a mechanism to simulate state.

Multidatabase management systems (MDBMSs) facilitate distribution of database systems by providing a layer of management on top of the DBMSs for individual databases. This multidatabase layer provides integrated access to data stored in the individual databases.

There are two motivations for distributing databases systems:
* to provide wider access to data via communications networks;
* to place data where it is used when it is economical to do so.

Wider access through computer networks can be enhanced by software which allows information from multiple databases to be integrated. Also, distribution of an organisation's data within the organisation may fit in with its politics and structure. For example, databases may be stored within divisions, departments, and offices, giving groups within the organisation responsibility for their own data, while the MDBMS provides global access to all of the databases as if they were one corporate database, e.g., to provide organisation–wide management information.

There may also be financial advantages:

1) Putting data where it is used reduces communications costs.
2) The system may expand and upgrade incrementally, with less disruption, by adding or replacing the networked computers.
3) Computers can be selected to meet the diverse requirements of the different groups within the organisation.
4) By supporting wider access, the markets for information services are broadened.

Greater reliability may also result from database distribution. When a computer or part of the network becomes unusable, it does not necessarily disable the whole system, and alternative copies of the data and network links can allow applications affected by the faults to continue to operate. The ability to continue a service, possibly with reduced facilities, after faults have occurred is called **graceful degradation**.

## TYPES OF MULTIDATABASE SYSTEM
There are two general classifications of multidatabase database system:

1) Distributed(or non–federated) databases—one database is physically stored as many component databases, on different computers, connected by a computer network.
2) Federated databases—integrated access is provided to many separately administered database systems, on different computers, connected by a computer network.

### DISTRIBUTED DATABASES
A distributed database comprises a collection of data distributed over a number of different computers, linked by a computer network. Each computer can perform both local applications (which access the database on that computer) and global applications (which access data stored on a number of computers).

The integrated access to many databases is supported by a global schema which describes the component databases as though they are a single database, together with other schemas which describe how the database is split into parts (the fragmentation schema) and where those parts are physically stored (the allocation schema).

In this type of architecture, there is only limited local autonomy, and no distinction is made between multidatabase and local users—all users access the databases as if they were a single database.

Distributed (relational) DBMSs appeared on the market in the mid–1980s (e.g., INGRES/STAR (distributed Ingres), SQL*STAR (Distributed Oracle)) but have not achieved widepread use.

## FEDERATED DATABASE SYSTEMS

A federated database system provides integrated access to a number of independently administered database systems, possibly of different types (e.g., relational and object). This contrasts with a distributed database in which the component databases are in effect parts of a single database distributed by virtue of their lack of autonomy.

Federated databases can be further classified according to where the integration of the component databases takes place. Loosely coupled federated systems rely on the user to establish the connections between component databases, whereas tightly coupled ones present users with views of the multidatabase in which this integration has already taken place. The schemas which describe the integrated multidatabase system to users are called federated schemas. The system may support one or more federated schemas, each of which integrates a part of the multidatabase.

## SCHEMA INTEGRATION

The problem of defining a federated schema in which parts of the component database are integrated poses two problems:

1) The syntactical problem—how do we integrate different schemas which represent the same information in different ways?
2) The semantic problem—how do we determining which schema elements mean the same thing?

The first of these problems is made straightforward by using a single data model at the multidatabase level, even where the component databases use different data models. The single multidatabase model is called the system's **canonical data model (CDM)**. Many current research projects use an object data model as the CDM, because it has the expressive power to also represent the tabular structures of a relational database.

The semantic problem is less straightforward. The integrator must understand the meaning of the component database schemas that they integrate, but this means "getting inside the head" of the original component schema designer to identify what they had in mind. As multidatabases get larger, this becomes a more complex task, because of the number of comparisons that must be made and the breadth of knowledge needed. Computer support for the schema integration task is the focus of research, but remains an open problem.

In loosely coupled federated databases the problem of schema integration is devolved to the multidatabase user, on the assumption that she will know approximately what information she requires and where it can be found.

## MULTIDATABASE TRANSACTION MANAGEMENT

Transaction management for multidatabase systems remains an open problem. It is much more complex than for a single object database (see Chapter 9) because a single multidatabase request becomes many requests to the component databases, each of which must commit successfully or leave no trace—i.e., it must be atomic.

A distributed database will manage transactions using conventional locking protocols, such as two phase locks and a two phase commit. Two phase commit operates as follows:

1) The request coordinator polls each of the component databases that must participate in executing the transaction to determine whether or not they can definitely execute their part of the transaction successfully.
2) Each participating database returns a "yes" vote if they can ensure successful execution and enters a "prepared" state. Otherwise, the participating database aborts its part of the transaction. If all participants vote "yes", the coordinator sends a commit request to each participant; otherwise an abort.

The above protocol cannot be used in a federated database system, because the component databases are stand–alone, autonomously administered systems. This means that the multidatabase cannot assume that they will support and communicate a "prepared" state to a coordinator process. Instead, protocols have been devised using compensating transactions. A compensating transaction is one that undoes the effect of another transaction. For example, if one transaction creates an instance of a Customer object, the corresponding compensating transaction will delete it.

For further reading, an excellent overview of object–oriented multidatabase systems, including discussion on the above issues, is given in [Bukhres 96].

## 10.7 EPILOGUE

This book has provided a snapshot of an emerging object database technology. This is one of a number of new database technologies that have emerged to address the weaknesses of relational technology. At present, it appears that the two dominant third generation database technologies will be: the technology based upon the ODMG standards, described here; and that based upon the next version of SQL, SQL3.

Object database technology addresses the problem of how structurally and behaviourally complex entities can be modelled, by providing a solution based upon an extensible type system. This, together with low cost high–performance hardware, widens the range of database applications, for example, to encompass multimedia applications.

The potential range of applications is also widened by the recent explosive growth of use of the internet and in particular of the World Wide Web. This offers a challenge for distributed computing. Beyond the simple presentation of small static amounts of text it is clear that there is a need for systems that can handle large amounts of data, be it text, audio, video... and manage change within this data.

Object databases seem ideally positioned for such tasks, particularly in conjunction with Java, which is rapidly establishing itself as the object programming language of choice, not just the de facto standard for Web applications. Current methods of linking Java and databases, such as

JDBC (Java Database Connectivity), do not have a clear underlying model but rely on flattening objects into a relational framework because of JDBC's roots in ODBC (Open Database Connection) which is an essentially relational standard.

The Object Management Group's CORBA (Common Object Request Broker Architecture) provides a coherent framework for Distributed Object Computing. It does this by specifying an architecture through which the objects in different applications, at different locations, can communicate. An important feature of this is IDL, the Interface Definition Language, which, as its name suggests, provides a way of specifying the interfaces between objects. It does this independently from any particular programming language (although it has its roots in C++) so that object implementations may be in any language it only specifies data types.

The ODMG's ODL, as a super set of IDL, can then be seen as an important part of building distributed object systems where an object database can act as a persistent store of (possibly large) amounts of data that can be used by a number of applications. These applications may then be built in different programming languages and work across networks using a variety of protocols.

Finally, we note that the third generation of database technology is currently "built upon sand", from an academic point of view. The technology has raced ahead of the science. We hope that the future will bring a widely accepted formal foundation for object databases which can then be used to provide a better understanding of the technology, and the means by which the technology can be developed to address the many open questions identified in the text of this book.

# BIBLIOGRAPHY

[Abiteboul 95] Abiteboul, S., Hull, R. and Vianu, V., Foundations of Databases, Addison Wesley, Reading, MA, 1995

[ANSI 86a] ANSI X3H2, Database Language NDL, ANSI X3.133-1986, American National Standards Institute, New York, 1986

[ANSI 86b] ANSI X3H2, Database Language SQL, ANSI X3.135-1986, American National Standards Institute, New York, 1986

[ANSI 89] ANSI X3H2, Database Language SQL, ANSI X3.135-1989, American National Standards Institute, New York, 1989

[ANSI 92] ANSI X3H2, Database Language SQL, ANSI X3.135-1992, American National Standards Institute, New York, 1992

[ANSI 95] SQL3 drafts and discussion documents can be found at ftp://speckle.ncsl.nist.gov/isowg3/dbl/

[Atkinson 90] Atkinson, M. et al., The Object-Oriented Database System Manifesto, in Kim, W., Nicolas, J-M., and Nishio, S. eds., Deductive and Object-Oriented Databases, pp 223-239, Elsevier, 1990

[Atkinson 96] Atkinson, M.P., Jordan, M.J., Daynes, L. and Spence, S. Design Issues for Persistent Java: a type–safe, object–oriented, orthogonally persistent system, Proceedings of the 7th International Workshop on Persistent Object Systems (POS7), 1996

[Banchilon 86] Banchilon, F., Maier, D., Sagiv, Y. and Ullman, J.D., Magic sets and other strange ways to implement logic programs, in Proceedings of the 5th ACM SIGMOD-SIGACT Symposium on Principles of Database Systems, pp 1-15, 1986

[Bohlen 95] Bohlen, M.H., Temporal Database Implementations, SIGMOD RECORD, 24(4), December 1995

[Booch 94] Booch, G., Object-Oriented Analysis and Design with Applications, Second edition, Benjamin/Cummings, Redwood City, 1994

[Booch 95] Booch, G. and Rumbaugh, J., Unified Method for Object-Oriented Development Documentation Set Version 0.8, Rational Software Corporation, 1995

[Booch 96] Booch, G. et al., UML Resource Center, http://www.rational.com/uml/index.html

[Brodie 92] Brodie, M.L., The Promise of Distributed Computing and the Challenge of Legacy Systems Procs BNCOD 10, Gray, P.M.D., and Lucas, R.S. eds. Springer Verlag LNCS 618, 1992

[Bukhres 96] Bukhres, O.A. and Elmagarmid, A.K., Object–Oriented Multidatabase Systems: A Solution for Advanced Applications, Prentice–Hall, Englewood Cliffs, 1996

[Cattell 96] Cattell, R.G.C. ed., The Object Database Standard: ODMG-93 Release 1.2, Morgan Kaufman, San Francisco, 1996

[Cattell 97] Cattel, R.G.C. and Barry, D.K. eds., The Object Database Standard: ODMG 2.0, Morgan Kaufman, San Francisco, 1997

[Ceri 89] Ceri, S., Gottlob, G. and Tanca, L., What You Wanted to Know About Datalog (And Never Dared to Ask), IEEE Transactions on Knowledge and Data Engineering, 1(1), March 1989

[Chakravarthy 88] Chakravarthy, U.S., Grant, J. and Minker, J., Foundations of Semantic Query Optimization for Deductive Databases in Foundations of Deductive Databases and Logic Programming,Minker J., Morgan Kaufmann, 1988.

[Chen 76] Chen, P., The Entity-Relationship Model—Towards a Unified View of Data, ACM Transactions on Database Systems, 1(1), 1976

[Codd 70] Codd, E.F., A Relational Model for Large Shared Data Banks Communications of the ACM, 13(6), pp 377-387, 1970

[Codd 79] Codd, E.F., Extending the Database Relational Model to Capture More Meaning, ACM Transactions on Databases, 4(4), Dec 1979

[Codd 85] Codd, E.F., Is Your DBMS really relational?, Computerworld Oct. 14 1985

[Codd 90] Codd, E.F., The Relational Model for Database Management Version 2, Addison–Wesley, Reading, 1990

[DBTG 71] DBTG (Data Base Task Group) CODASYL Programming Language Committee Report ANSI Data Base Task Group 1971

[Date 86] Date, C.J., Relational Database Selected Writings, .Addison-Wesley, Reading, 1986

[Eaglestone 91] Eaglestone, B., Relational Databases, Stanley Thornes, Leckhampton, 1991

[Jacobson 92] Jacobson, I.M., Object-Oriented Software Engineering, Addison-Wesley, Reading, 1992

[Jensen 92] Jensen, C.S., Clifford, J., Gadia, S.K., Segev, A. and Snodgrass, R., A Glossary of Temporal Database Management Systems, SIGMOD RECORD 21( 3), September 1992

[Leung 93] Leung, T.W., Mitchell, B., Subramanian, B., Vance, S.L.,Vandenberg, S.L. and Zdonik, S.B., The AQUA Data Model and Algebra, Proceedings DBPL (1993) , pp 157-175, 1993

[Manola 95] Manola, F., ed., X3H7 Object Model Features Matrix, http://info.gte.com/ftp/doc/activities/x3h7/front.html

[Nelson 91] Nelson, M.L., "An Object-Oriented Tower of Babel", OOPS Messenger 2(3) July 1991

[OMG 91] Object Management Group, The Common Object Request Broker: Architecture and Specification, Revision 1.1, OMG Document No 91.12.1

[Roth 88] Roth, M.A., Korth, H.F. and Silberschatz, A., Extended Algebra and Calculus for Nested Relational Databases, ACM Transactions on Database Systems, 13, (4), pp 389-417, 1988

[Rumbaugh 91] Rumbaugh, J., Premerlani, W., Eddy, F. and Lorenson, W., Object-Oriented Modeling and Design, Prentice–Hall, Englewood Cliffs, 1991

[Scheck 91] Scheck,H.J. and Scholl,M.H., From Relations and Nested Relations to Object Models, Proceedings BNCOD 9, Springer Verlag, LNCS, pp 202-225, 1991

[Snodgrass 95] Snodgrass, R., Temporal Object–Oriented Databases, A Critical Comparison, Modern Database Systems, Won Kim ed., ACM Press, Addison–Wesley, New York, 1995

[Spence 97] Spence, S., The Pjava Project, http://www.dcs.gla.ac.uk/pjava

[Stonebraker 90] The Committee for Advanced DBMS Function Third-Generation Database System Manifesto, SIGMOD Record, 19(3), 1990

[Stroustrup 92] Stroustrup, B., The C++ Programming Language, Addison–Wesley, Reading, 1992

[Subramanian 95] Subramanian, B., Leung, T.W., Vandenberg, S.L. and Zdonik, S.B., The AQUA Approach to Querying Lists and Trees in Object–Oriented Databases, Proceedings of the 11th International Conference on Data Engineering, 1995

[Tsichritzis 76] Tsichritzis, D.C. and Lochovsky, F.H., Hierarchical Data Base Management: A Survey, ACM Computing Surveys 8 (1) , 1976

[Tsotras 96] Tsotras, V.J. and Kumar, A., Temporal Databases Bibliography Update, SIGMOD RECORD, 25 (1), March 1996

[Wade 96] Wade, D., SQL/OQL Merger, http://www.jcc.com/sql_odmg_convergence

# INDEX